"Decisively, this is the most realistic and powerful portrayal of Chinese and Indian consumers. Together, as the world's largest, most influential and discerning consumers, no company can shape its future without them. A brilliant guide to unlocking spectacular growth."

—Deepak Parekh, Chairman, HDFC

"A tour de force of insight into Chinese and Indian consumers, told via many compelling stories. All business is local, and a firsthand understanding of these consumer markets is essential for any business leader in future. This book delivers it."

—John A. Quelch CBE, Distinguished Professor of International Management, Vice President and Dean, CEIBS

"A must-read for consumer companies seeking to capitalize on the explosive growth in India and China, but also a how-to manual for jump-starting growth in more mature, developed markets."

—Irene Rosenfeld, Chairman and CEO, Kraft Foods

"Great insights into the aspirations and driving forces behind the all-important consumers of China and India. A thought-provoking and entertaining glimpse into how these consumers will redefine the future."

—Jerry Stritzke, President and COO, Coach

"A vivid view of the lives of consumers in China and India, combining solid research and strategic business insights. All leaders of large organizations in Asia, local or expat, should read this book to gain a new perspective of customer, market, and strategy."

—Xudong Yin, Chairman, Beijing Novartis Pharma Co Ltd.

"By the end of the decade, there will be more than one billion middle-class consumers in China and India. This is a historical opportunity for multinational companies, but also quite a challenge for many of them. Thanks to their solid experience within The Boston Consulting Group, the authors of *The $10 Trillion Prize* offer a unique consumer insight that is both quantitative and qualitative, economic and sociologic, global and intimate. They also draw very concrete directions to answer the needs, aspirations, ambitions, and demands of this new generation of consumers. By doing so, they play their consulting role in a generous and innovative way that should be very precious to many leaders worldwide."

—Jochen Zaumseil, Executive Vice President, Asia Pacific, L'Oréal

THE $10 TRILLION PRIZE

THE
$10
TRILLION
PRIZE

Captivating
the Newly Affluent
in China and India

MICHAEL J. SILVERSTEIN | ABHEEK SINGHI

CAROL LIAO | DAVID MICHAEL

with Simon Targett

HARVARD BUSINESS REVIEW PRESS

BOSTON, MASSACHUSETTS

No part of this publication may be reproduced, stored in or introduced into a retrieval system, or transmitted, in any form, or by any means (electronic, mechanical, photocopying, recording, or otherwise), without the prior permission of the publisher. Requests for permission should be directed to permissions@hbsp.harvard.edu, or mailed to Permissions, Harvard Business School Publishing, 60 Harvard Way, Boston, Massachusetts 02163.

Library of Congress Cataloging-in-Publication Data

The $10 trillion prize : captivating the newly affluent in China and India / Michael Silverstein ... [et al.].
    p. cm.
  Includes bibliographical references.
  ISBN 978-1-4221-8705-0 (alk. paper)
  1. Consumers—China. 2. Consumers—India. 3. Affluent consumers—China. 4. Affluent consumers—India. 5. Consumers—China—Attitudes. 6. Consumers—India—Attitudes. I. Silverstein, Michael J. II. Title: Ten trillion dollar prize.
  HC430.C6.A13 2012
  658.8′40951—dc23

                                                          2012015049

The paper used in this publication meets the requirements of the American National Standard for Permanence of Paper for Publications and Documents in Libraries and Archives Z39.48-1992.

To the many kind, generous, passionate,

driven Chinese and Indians who honored us by sharing their beliefs

about their future and the place of China and India

in the world of 2020

CONTENTS

PREFACE

The rise of China and India, and the growing impact of these countries on the global economy, is a story that has been written about extensively. Historians, economists, and business professors, among others, have all sought to explain the extraordinary emergence of the world's most populous nations in a library of books that have tumbled out of publishing houses over the past ten years.

So why publish yet another book on China and India?

The answer is this: no book has truly focused on the vital force that will transform these countries and their economies in the decade ahead—namely, the new consumers—or shown how companies can capitalize on the new opportunities. No one has written clearly about these consumers' hopes, dreams, and ambitions. No one has closed the loop on income growth, education, jobs, and the net expansion of markets for food, apparel, housing, transportation, health care, education, and financial services. The complete picture—with all the detail of the rural and urban communities, the rich and the poor, and the burgeoning middle class—has yet to be drawn.

This book aims to fill the gap.

New Consumers, New Opportunities

Consumers in India and China are the new kings and queens of the global economy. They have fast-changing tastes and appetites, and they are transforming the world with their consumption. Consider the following facts, which provide a snapshot of what the opportunity is for the rest of this decade:

- There will be nearly one billion middle-class consumers—some 320 million households—in China and India by 2020. They are demanding "more, better, now" for themselves and their children.

- The number of billionaires is rising: in 2001, China had 1 billionaire and India had 4; today, there are 115 billionaires in China and 55 in India.

- The two markets will give rise to some of the world's most powerful companies. China already has three of the world's top ten companies, ranked by market value: PetroChina, China's ICBC bank, and China Mobile.

- Some eighty-three million Chinese and fifty-four million Indians will become college graduates over the next ten years. Over the same period, the United States will see just thirty million new college graduates.

- The rapid growth in both China and India has led to enormous growth in the consumption of the building blocks of households—from copper to corn to chicken to coal—plus almost every other ingredient important to better lives, particularly a diet higher in protein but also vertical dwellings with modern conveniences and vehicles of transportation of all kinds.

We estimate that the consumer markets of China and India will triple over the current decade and amount to $10 trillion annually by the year 2020. It is a once-in-a-lifetime prize. But how can it be won? That is the purpose of this book. *The $10 Trillion Prize* presents a *manual for growth*: the inside track to achieving success in China and India—and, as a consequence, the rest of the world—by *captivating*, and therefore winning, the hearts and minds of the new consumers.

After reading this book, leaders at companies with global ambitions will know how to *segment, listen to,* and *engage* the increasingly affluent consumers in China and India. It is easy to be swayed by the sheer number of consumers in the two countries and to think that success is just a matter of selling to a small fraction of them. But averages can be deceptive, and off-the-shelf statistics and generalized data can lead companies into making bad decisions and expensive mistakes.

We want readers to take the following steps in engaging the new markets in China and India:

- Meet consumers "up close and personal": understand how they make decisions about goods and how their hopes for the future translate into astounding market growth in food, health care, education, and transport.

- Understand the size, shape, and timing of the opportunity. Segment the market according to income and geography—especially the urban and rural divide. See how the application of special "consumption curves" can predict the future.

- Build the *paisa vasool* approach—the perfect mix of affordability, design, and features—into your global tool kit. Engineer every product and service with this approach. Make value for money the standard in Chinese, Indian, *and* Western markets.

- Hear how market leaders are shaping their future with a *ten-by-ten strategy*: ten times as big in ten years.

- Systematically understand risk and risk reduction in the world's most challenging markets.

- Use the book to create what we call the *triple crown*: a win in China, a win in India, and a win at home.

- See how Chinese and Indian consumers will shape a new future for the world—and how they will do so with drama, emotion, conflict, and hard choices.

- Understand the differences and similarities between China and India: one child versus five children; autocracy versus democracy; speed and authority versus choice; massive investment with few market safeguards versus returns guarded by capital markets; state capitalists versus private entrepreneurs.

- Ask questions that will unlock spectacular growth and organizational resolve in China and India.

The Research: Client Work, Interviews, and Data

The $10 Trillion Prize is based on extensive on-the-ground experience, one-on-one interviews with hundreds of consumers, and access to business leaders and entrepreneurs in China and India.

Our company, The Boston Consulting Group (BCG), has a long history of advising clients and governments in these countries. In China, we began work in the 1980s, opened an office in Hong Kong in 1991, and were the first multinational consulting company to be authorized to conduct business in mainland China, establishing an office in Shanghai in 1993. Our office in Beijing opened in 2001. In India, we opened our Mumbai office in 1996, after nearly a decade of work in the country. The New Delhi office opened its doors in 2000. This year, we opened our third Indian office, in Chennai.

As an author team, we are veterans of these markets. Together, we have more than fifty years of on-the-ground experience in China and India, stretching back to the 1980s. We have advised major Chinese and Indian companies as well as multinationals seeking to enter these countries and build their businesses there. Our clients—some of the world's largest consumer companies—have turned to us for advice on innovation, market access, distribution, and consumer understanding. Throughout *The $10 Trillion Prize*, we draw on a valuable resource: the proprietary consumer-tracking studies produced by BCG's Center for Consumer and Customer Insight. Across Asia, the center has conducted some five hundred consumer insight projects over the past ten years. The flagship is an annual global consumer sentiment survey of twenty-four thousand people in twenty-one countries.

We also build on the insights drawn from our prior work on consumer needs, including research that we published in the books *Trading Up: The New American Luxury* (2003); *Treasure Hunt: Inside the Mind of the New Consumer* (2006); and *Women Want More: How to Capture Your Share of the World's Largest, Fastest-Growing Market* (2010).

In *Trading Up*, for example, we identified the trend among middle-class Americans to buy more expensive goods in a handful of product categories and to become expert in the art of consumption—looking for technical, functional, and emotional benefits in products and services. Over the past two years, we have traveled throughout China and India and seen many parallels. Chinese and Indian consumers are also hungry for product information— they want to understand the back stories of products and their creators. They are allocating their budgets to achieve a visible level of affluence in many categories of goods and cutting corners in others to achieve necessary savings. The Chinese and Indian consumers are ambitious and dream big. They understand technical and functional differences and love to "ladder up" emotionally. They love to tell their friends about their shopping adventures and to celebrate their purchases.

The $10 Trillion Prize is based on both qualitative and quantitative consumer research. We studied Chinese and Indian consumers in their homes, meeting their families and discussing their current and anticipated lifestyles. We probed them about their diets, their purchases, their histories, and their hopes and dreams. Readers will get to know the new generation of consumers, including the brilliant student we call "Mr. Number 19" because of his ranking on the highly competitive entrance exam to the Indian Institutes of Technology; the determined thirty-three-year-old woman from Shanghai who already makes more than fifty times as much as her parents did and still wants more; and the fifty-nine-year-old rural Chinese woman with three years of formal education who has built her home brick-by-brick and constructed a garage for the car she would like to buy one day.

Readers will also get to know the new generation of corporate titans—Chinese and Indian entrepreneurs who are thriving by meeting the needs of the newly affluent consumers—including Frank Ning, who runs Cofco, one of the world's biggest food processing companies; Adi Godrej, chairman of the Godrej Group, one of India's biggest consumer goods conglomerates; and Anand Mahindra, vice chairman and managing director of Mahindra & Mahindra, India's major manufacturer of tractors and low-cost—and now global—sport utility vehicles.

The Promise of the Book

The $10 Trillion Prize is written for leaders who need a better understanding of the consumers in China and India. It carries ten key messages:

1. For the first time, we calculate *the size of the prize*: the $10 trillion that Chinese and Indian consumers will be spending on goods and services in 2020. Over their lifetimes, Chinese children born today will consume nearly thirty-eight times as much as their grandparents did, while Indian children will consume nearly thirteen times as much as their grandparents did.

2. We describe the *driving spirit* of the consumers: their ambition, their energy, their confidence, their optimism. As a young Chinese woman told us, "I want two houses—a house in the city and a house in the country. I want two children. And I want to send

them to school in America. I want beautiful clothes, a handsome, educated husband, and time to enjoy it all."

3. We stress the need to *segment and target* these consumers—not only by income but also by region, city, rural community, and gender. The great engine of change is the rising middle class: by 2020, an astonishing 320 million increasingly affluent households whose nearly one billion members will be following their dreams and, in so many ways, emulating Western consumers. In addition, there are the millions of poor, now moving beyond survival, as well as the superrich (more than 1 million households), now joining the global elite. But it is not enough to divide consumers by class. To survive in the big city, you need more income, more hustle, and a tolerance for long commutes. As we will see, middle-class consumers in a megacity such as Beijing or Mumbai can exhibit altogether different patterns of behavior than those in smaller cities. You need to understand these consumers, personify them, and cater to their individual needs.

4. We recommend the adoption of a *paisa vasool*—literally, "money's worth"—strategy. Chinese and Indian consumers will be hungry for material goods over the next decade. They will want more than they can afford. Their income growth will be substantial, even if they will still end the decade earning only 10 to 25 percent of Western incomes. They will want goods with full features, luxury elements, and reliability. To serve these consumers, you will need not only raw material and packaging innovations but also a comprehensive, low-cost business model. And these will be transferrable to other markets because consumers around the world will want products that do not compromise on features, ingredients, design, or value.

5. We urge the importance of *"local, local" customization*. These consumers need to have products and services that are tailored to them—and them alone. If they are rich or poor, if they are urban or rural, if they live in a big city or a little city, if they live in the north or the south, if they are educated or illiterate—all of these factors matter and require refinements to the product and the way it is designed, packaged, and sold. China and India are markets with heterogeneous populations demanding locally customized products.

6. We identify the *accelerator mind-set*. Speak to entrepreneurs in China or India, and they talk of their ten-by-ten strategy of growing tenfold in ten years. If this sounds extraordinary—even unattainable—in the West, it sounds perfectly rational in the East. Today, in China and India, there is a determined, can-do attitude, and the word *impossible* is not one commonly heard on the lips of business leaders. Strategy is as they see it: a big-picture vision, colossal dreams, and no limits on opportunity. They do not feel beholden to anyone or bound by textbook business rules and the constraints of commonly held business logic. They start with a clean slate, focus on a specific opportunity, scale up or refocus as needed, learn by doing, and drive relentlessly forward.

7. We introduce the notion of a *boomerang effect*. The impact of more than two billion consumers wanting more—more foodstuffs, water, housing, transport, luxury goods, education, and health care—will be inflation in supply-constrained commodities, price volatility, scarcity of some resources, and hypercompetition to meet consumers' needs. The boomerang effect will spread far beyond China and India.

8. We warn of the *hit-the-wall scenario*. What if China and India do not continue on the path of marvelous straight-line growth? Political instability, natural disasters, bursting asset bubbles, rotten and corrupt institutions, the failure of government entities to invest in the future—each of these could cause projections of growth to veer dangerously off course, with cataclysmic consequences for China, India, and the companies that are pinning their hopes on the new and dynamic generation of consumers. This is why we say that it is important to factor these risks and hazards into any scenario planning process. It is important to be alive to the possibility that the story of "Asia Rising" could change into the story of "Asia Uprising." The successful future development of China and India depends upon the ability of their leaders and citizens to solve many difficult challenges.

9. We portray the *left-behinds*—millions of people who, for all the success of the Chinese and Indian economies, remain disconnected and disgruntled with their lot. For now, they offer limited commercial opportunities, but they could offer the prospect of a second wave

of growth as the Chinese and Indians pursue policies to foster social harmony.

10. We maintain that there is *no inevitability about the decline of the West*. We are profoundly optimistic—yet, we think, measured and realistic—about the opportunities in China and India and the positive impact on the global economy, on companies, and on individuals. It was not so long ago that political commentators and historians were talking about the triumph of the West. Now they are talking about decline and the fall of the American empire. But we do not consider this likely. On average, American and European consumers are vastly richer than Chinese and Indian consumers—and this is not going to change anytime soon. If Americans and Europeans adopt the accelerator mind-set, opportunity and growth will rebound. We believe that the consumer revolution is *a winner for all*, a force for good that can benefit everyone. The new interactions between East and West are energizing, enlightening, and empowering—and ensure that companies and their leaders look far beyond the horizon to a world of infinite possibilities.

We hope you use this book to see the market opportunity in China and India through the eyes of consumers moving from *D* income to *C* income, from *C* income to *B* income, and from *B* income to *A* income. We offer a checklist of requirements for success along with our assessment of risks and how to mitigate them.

The Structure of the Book

The $10 Trillion Prize is arranged in three parts, which are preceded by an introduction (chapter 1).

In chapter 1, we tell the story of the dramatic growth in consumption and quantify the size of the commercial opportunity: the $10 trillion in annual spending that the consumer markets of China and India will generate by the year 2020. We explain how consumers' rising income—which takes them, in many cases, from subsistence to middle class—seems like the wheel of fortune: they truly feel as though they have won the jackpot.

We draw on BCG's proprietary studies of Chinese and Indian consumer attitudes and take a panoramic view of the new generation of spenders, exploring the underlying passions and preferences that influence their buying behavior. These consumers have high aspirations, are optimistic about the future, and are eager to enjoy their first taste of affluence.

In part I, "The Rise of the New Consumer in China and India," we identify the fortunes to be made at the top, middle, *and* bottom of the income pyramid. We contend that to really succeed in China and India, you must know everything there is to know about the new consumers, which means dissecting the markets into segments based on wealth, education, attitude, geography, age, and gender. The analysis is based on BCG's proprietary market segmentations of the two countries.

In chapters 2, 3, and 4, we examine the rising middle class, the superrich elite, and the vast hordes of "left-behinds." In chapter 5, we take the reader on a virtual tour around the countries, traveling to the cities and the rural districts. We describe two revolutions: one relating to infrastructure, the other to agriculture. In chapter 6, we examine the development of the female economy in the two countries.

Part II, "Preferences, Appetites, and Aspirations," digs deeper, providing detailed portraits of the new consumers as they go about their daily lives— as well as the companies that serve them with the right products at the right price and with the perfect mix of ingredients, design, and packaging. Chapter 7, "Food and Drink," focuses on the different tastes of the new consumers and profiles companies meeting the demand, including Kraft (Oreo cookies), Tingyi (noodles), Cofco (French wine), PepsiCo (Kurkure), and Pernod Ricard (green tea and Chivas Regal whiskey). We describe the key turning-point decisions made by these companies' top executives to change the formulation, distribution channel, or marketing of their products to reach new consumers.

Chapter 8, "House and Home," examines the rise of home ownership and the companies meeting the need for financing (HDFC), decoration (Asian Paints), and household appliances (LG Electronics). Chapter 9, "Luxury," looks at the new consumers' growing appetite for expensive goods and highlights companies such as LVMH and Gucci (leather goods, watches, and apparel) that are capturing market share. Chapter 10, "Digital Life," investigates the lives of the digital generation, examining how consumers are using the Internet and mobile devices, and how companies such as Bharti

Airtel, Taobao, and Nokia are prospering by meeting these consumers' needs. Chapter 11, "Education," focuses on the thirst for knowledge, with parents going above and beyond to pay for schooling that will give their children a head start in life, and students—including superachievers—who are prepared to dedicate their lives to fulfilling their parents' dreams as well as their own.

Part III, "The Lessons for Business Leaders," draws together the take-aways from the corporate stories in *The $10 Trillion Prize*. Chapter 12, "*Paisa Vasool*," examines one of the most powerful strategies for success in China and India, as well as in the rest of the world. Chapter 13, "The Boomerang Effect," looks at the global impact of the race for resources. With more money, consumers have started to spend as never before, and this has driven up the demand for food, water, copper, iron ore, cement—the building blocks of modern life. This increased demand is giving rise to the boomerang effect—price volatility, inflation, and the disruption of comfortable expecta-tions in the West. Chapter 14, "Fast Forward," introduces the accelerator mind-set and features profiles of business leaders and company founders whose approach to business and life explains their good fortune and provides a useful model to foreigners looking to replicate their success. Chapter 15, "The BCG Playbook," reflects on the size of the commercial prize and fea-tures BCG's guide to captivating the newly affluent consumer.

The $10 Trillion Prize concludes with an epilogue that sets out the opportu-nities for individuals in the West—the original consumer kings.

The Contest for the $10 Trillion Prize Has Begun

China and India are very different in many ways. So why put them together in a book? The answer is simple: the increasing size of their populations, the growing power of their economies, and—most important of all—the emerg-ing mass of ambitious, educated, middle-class consumers who want more now. The two countries combine to represent the number one and number two consumer opportunities of today. Both countries have enormous upside. The increase in annual consumption by 2020 will be $4.2 trillion in China and $2.6 trillion in India. Anyone with global aspirations will need to compete successfully in both China and India.

There are some who fear China's and India's growth, viewing it as a harbinger of doom for companies in developed economies. But we do not see it this way. We think it heralds a bright new future with abundant opportunities for those willing to seize the moment.

In the classic film *On the Waterfront*, Marlon Brando plays the role of Terry Malloy, a former heavyweight boxer who once had a shot at winning a big title but blew his chance. Far from being a champion, he works as a day laborer on the docks of New Jersey. "I could have had class," he says regretfully. "I could have been a *contender*." Today's leaders need not have any such regrets—as long as they act fast.

There is no time to lose. The contest has begun.

ONE

Consumption in China and India

The Dawn of a Golden Age

What and why the new consumers buy, how they think and shop,
how their needs and tastes are changing

W E KNOCKED ON THE DOOR. There was no sign, just a street number. "Is this the Li family restaurant?" we asked, after a tortuous walk through the alleyways of Beijing's Xicheng District. The older woman who had come to the door nodded and then called for her grandson, who hurried to the entrance and, speaking English, invited us inside the plain cinder block building.

We were shown to one of three Formica tables and sat down on rickety folding chairs. A fan whirred in the background. We could see the chef and his assistants toiling in the kitchen, seemingly oblivious to the bright flames leaping over the pots on the open cooktop. Tantalizing aromas drifted through the room as we were handed the Chinese-language menu with pictures of a few of the delights soon to be coming our way.

Across from us, four garrulous Texans were feasting on the restaurant's most expensive option—a set of dishes that the menu dubbed "the grand banquet." At the other table, five Chinese men wearing white shirts and plain blue suits were delighting in the menu's midpriced option, nudging each other and smiling when they found a dish particularly good.

We too selected the midpriced option, and soon the dishes started to arrive: an exotic mushroom soup, a small plate of prawns with snow peas, hand-carved carrots, and jasmine rice. After that, shark fin soup, then abalone and more mushrooms, and then scallops on a bed of leeks. We paid a slight premium for the restaurant's version of Peking duck—paper-thin crusted skin, succulent meat. Dessert was three courses—a pineapple sorbet with small fruits, hand-decorated cakes with a raspberry sauce, and a double-chocolate torte with a hot filled center. At the end of the meal, we had to pay cash, because the restaurant did not accept credit cards. But it did not matter—we had enough renminbi to cover the cost of the meal: $10 per person. It was a meal that we will remember for a lifetime—magnificent cuisine in a humble setting served with grace and style by the cook's extended family.

Even then, nearly two decades ago, this was a bargain. The food was visually stunning, perfectly plated, sensuous, and exotic. It was, in fact, fit for an emperor. Li Shanlin, the restaurateur, is the grandson of the supervisor of the last emperor's imperial kitchen. His grandfather, Li Shunqing, was lord secretary to the dowager empress and was responsible for the imperial menu inside the Forbidden City.

Born in 1920, Li grew up watching his grandfather prepare imperial-style meals. But after university, where he studied aeronautical engineering, he became a scholar, teaching mathematics at the Capital University of Economics and Business in Beijing. During the Cultural Revolution, when Chairman Mao waged an offensive against intellectuals and party elites, the university was closed. Purged from his university post, he turned to the study of imperial cuisine, refining the recipes that his grandfather had handed down.

Li eventually returned to teaching. But at the age of sixty-five, when he finally retired, he reawakened his lifelong passion for cooking—and he took his chance, opening a three-table restaurant in the family home (figure 1-1). In the beginning, there were no employees; family members served, cleaned, and helped cook. Food preparation was classical, with a sharp knife, perfect ingredients, and a focus on taste, texture, and visual presentation. In this sense, he was way ahead of his time, spurning modern cooking equipment, microwave ovens, and food processors.

Although it was hard to find, Li's restaurant soon garnered critical acclaim. As a result, it then became hard to book a table. According to the family, Bill Clinton, Jackie Chan, Bill Gates, and the Rolling Stones have eaten at the original restaurant. And, indeed, as we paid, we saw a framed note from Bill Clinton, which expressed his thanks for "a wonderful time."

Today, if you visit the newest branch of the Li family restaurant, it is equally hard to book a table—but the experience, not to mention the cost, is altogether different. For a start, the restaurant—called Family Li Imperial

FIGURE 1-1

The first Li family restaurant in Beijing

Source: From Regent Tour, "Food & Lodging: Li Family Restaurant,"
www.regenttour.com/chinaplanner/pek/bi-food-li.htm.

Cuisine—is hard to miss. It is located just off East Zhongshan Yi Road, Shanghai's grand riverfront boulevard. The building is magnificent, with a glass and marble interior, a lily garden with a fishpond, spacious private dining areas, gold-plated dinnerware, and a wine list to rival Paris's finest restaurants (figure 1-2).

The top-priced set menu is RMB 2,000 (around $300). It features, among other things, scallops, deep-fried prawns, stir-fried cabbage with pheasant meat, bird's-nest soup, duck with shrimp paste and sesame, and steamed snow frog. This can be washed down with a bottle of a 1990 Château Lafite Rothschild for RMB 16,800 (around $2,700).

Shanghai has become one of the world's capitals of cuisine, supported by talent, investors, and fresh-food supply chains that did not exist when Professor Li first launched his enterprise. Now, the Li family restaurant successfully competes with other prominent restaurants in the city once known as the Paris of the East, including Jean Georges (from France's Jean-Georges Vongerichten), Laris (from Australia's David Laris), and Issimo (from Italy's

FIGURE 1-2

A beautiful water garden at the new Li family restaurant in Shanghai

Source: BCG photo.

Salvatore Cuomo), as well as the restaurant of Ho Wing, the former chef at The Hong Kong Jockey Club.

The Li family restaurant in Shanghai is the story of newly affluent Chinese consumers living like emperors: choosing the best food and wine, enjoying haute cuisine in a magnificent setting. It is about pleasure, personal indulgence, and, to some degree, hedonism. The painful years of subsistence living are distant memories that can be put behind with today's purchases.

The Rise of the Newly Affluent Consumers and the $10 Trillion Prize

In 1992—a few years after Professor Li had opened his first restaurant—Deng Xiaoping, China's supreme leader, made his famous southern tour of China's small but booming special economic zones, pushing aside more conservative party cadres and opening China up to foreign investors and to the private sector. Two years later, Gordon Wu, a Hong Kong tycoon, opened a superhighway connecting Pearl River Delta farmland to Hong Kong's container ports. The farmland soon became factory towns, foreign investment poured in, and China truly began to join the global economy. Through the 1990s, Zhu Rongji, the prime minister, drove massive economic reform programs that prepared China for joining the World Trade Organization, after which investment flows ratcheted up even higher, and China's growth accelerated.

In the two decades since Deng's tour, several factors have combined to create China's economic miracle—the greatest rise in economic productivity that the world has ever seen—a productivity boom that is still under way and that underpins the dramatic rise of the consuming classes. The following are some of these factors:

- Welcoming market forces into the economy: letting markets set prices, allowing entrepreneurs to set up shop, and forcing state-owned enterprises to compete with each other. China also dismantled its "iron rice bowl" model of state enterprise (a system in which workers were given job security)—a painful but necessary reform that displaced more than seventy million people.

- Making infrastructure investments that expanded the economy's productive capacity, tapping into high domestic savings, leveraging the system of five-year plans, and intelligently using the state's ultimate ownership of all land. These investments, coupled with agricultural reforms, also unleashed a migration to the cities, bringing people into urban environments, where much more remunerative employment opportunities existed.

- Embracing trade and foreign investment, using membership in the World Trade Organization as a catalyst for driving domestic reforms, and creating an investment environment highly attractive to foreign investors. The ability to leverage Hong Kong's trading prowess and Taiwan's technology has been a huge advantage here.

- Educating a highly capable workforce of women as well as men, and mobilizing this workforce into the high-growth sectors of the economy (indeed, a physical mobilization of more than 150 million migrant workers within the country), while sending the best and brightest abroad for even more study.

- Developing private-property rights, which has led to large-scale home ownership.

India's economic miracle began with different starting conditions and followed its own pathway, but is no less impressive. Prior to the 1990s, India's version of state capitalism, the "License Raj," was arguably even more effective at stifling productivity than China's Communist system. The Licence Raj system consisted of India's elaborate requirements for starting businesses, including multiple permits for opening, operating, or expanding an enterprise. At their height, License Raj regulations, red tape, and bureaucracy constrained Indian growth and productivity—and effectively created oligopolies with very high prices in many sectors. Entrepreneurialism was crushed by the resulting government-erected barriers to entry and by corruption. The first wave of changes happened in the 1980s—including changes in the monopoly laws and some sporadic sectoral reforms. In 1991, soon after Rajiv Gandhi was assassinated, the newly elected prime minister, Narasimha Rao, and his finance minister, Manmohan Singh (the prime minister as of this writing), found the old economic system in total crisis, with its foreign exchange reserves having dropped to $1.2 billion. With foreign debt obligations looming, the country was literally only weeks from bankruptcy. The duo launched a wide-ranging set of reforms that would liberalize the Indian economy. The reforms embodied several key elements:

- Dismantling the License Raj—promoting competition in more than seven hundred industries previously protected and reserved for small and medium-sized enterprises. This helped many manufacturing companies achieve efficiencies and become competitive, because they were no longer subscale.

- Supporting international trade by reducing the costs of import licenses.

- Removing protectionist measures that stifled foreign direct investment and actively courting foreign multinational companies to invest in India. This has resulted in the opening up of most sectors for foreign direct investment.

- Launching a program of privatization, with full or partial sales of the government's stake in state-owned enterprises.

The economic miracles of China and India, spurred by fundamental reforms begun two decades ago, have now driven a boom of productivity gains that will remain strong and even strengthen in the future. By 2029, if not sooner, China will have surpassed the United States as the world's largest economy (figure 1-3). By 2028, India will likely have surged past Germany and Japan, establishing itself as the world's third-largest economy.

China's productivity growth rate is forecast to be particularly strong in the current decade as its workforce gains experience, and growth tapers only moderately after 2020. India's productivity growth has been more sluggish and starts from a lower base, but it is predicted to grow strongly in the next three decades, as education and infrastructure improve, urbanization accelerates, and an abundance of young and energetic citizens enters the workforce.

Productivity is important because it strongly correlates with the growth of personal incomes—which, in turn, will fuel the consumer revolution. The increased consumption that results is proportional—we have coined it *the $10 trillion prize.*

We calculate that between 2010 and 2020, the people of China and India will consume goods and services worth a total of $64 trillion. Chinese consumers will spend $41.5 trillion over this period, with annual expenditures rising from $2.0 trillion to $6.2 trillion, an increase of 203 percent. Indians will spend $22.5 trillion, with their annual expenditures rising from $991 billion to $3.6 trillion, an astonishing 261 percent increase (figure 1-4).

In other words, Chinese and Indian consumers will be spending nearly $10 trillion a year by 2020—more than three times the amount they are spending today. Their combined share of the global market will grow from 8.2 percent to 15.7 percent.[1] In appendix A, we describe the mosaic of cultures in these two vast and heterogeneous countries and explain how a local market understanding is required for success.

Of course, there is uncertainty in any forecast of the future—forecasts presume stability, and in the real world, they can be knocked off course by economic downturns, natural disaster, political instability, and corruption. In appendix B, we issue a word of warning, highlight what we call the hit-the-wall scenario, and explain why the road to the $10 trillion prize could potentially be a rocky one.

FIGURE 1-3

GDP levels for the five largest economies, 1960–2030

China will pass the United States by 2029; India will pass Germany and Japan by 2028.

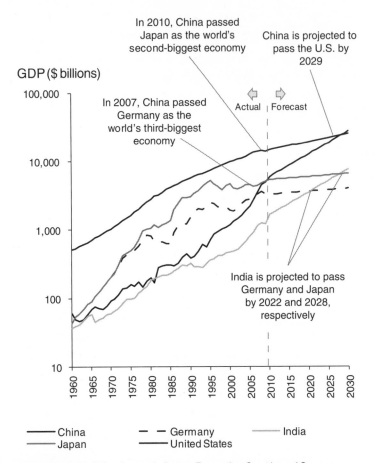

Sources: World Bank, World Development Indicators; Euromonitor, Countries and Consumers, Economy and Finance; International Monetary Fund, Data and Statistics, World Economic Outlook Database, October 2010; Timothy Moe, Caesar Maasry, and Richard Tang, "EM Equity in Two Decades: A Changing Landscape," Goldman Sachs Global Economics Paper 204, September 8, 2010; BCG analysis.
Note: All GDP figures are in 2010 U.S. dollars. Real annual GDP growth projections for 2010–2030 are 2.7 percent for the U.S., 8.0 percent for China, 8.0 percent for India, 1.0 percent for Japan, and 1.0 percent for Germany.

Nevertheless, for Chinese children born in 2009, continued economic progress will probably mean that over the course of their lives, they can expect to consume thirty-eight times more material goods than their grandparents (figure 1-5). Life expectancy has grown from forty-seven years for a Chinese baby

FIGURE 1-4

Consumer spending in China and India: the $10 trillion prize

We forecast consumption of $6.2 trillion in China and $3.6 trillion in India by 2020.

	China		India	
	2010	2020	2010	2020
Real annual GDP growth		8%		8%
Consumer spending at current prices ($ billions)	2,036	6,187	991	3,584
Population (millions)	1,334	1,383	1,200	1,333

Sources: Euromonitor, Countries and Consumers, Economy and Finance, Consumer Behavior, Population and Homes; BCG analysis.
Note: Consumer spending is projected to grow at the same rate as GDP.

born in 1960 to seventy-three years for one born in 2009. An Indian baby born in 2009 can expect to live to the age of sixty-four—twenty-two years longer than its grandparents—and consume thirteen times more material goods than its grandparents, too (figure 1-6). In comparison, a child born in the United States in 2009, although likely to enjoy the world's highest standard of living, might consume only twice as much as his or her grandparents and live only nine years longer.

The big reason for this growth in the standard of living in China and India, which will put enormous pressure on global supply, is rising incomes. From 2010 to 2020, annual per-capita incomes will increase, on average, from about $4,400 to $12,300 in China and from $1,500 to $4,400 in India (figure 1-7). As a result, China's upper class will grow from 24 million to 91 million households, the middle class will grow from 109 million to 202 million households, and the lower class will shrink from 260 million down to 138 million households (figure 1-8). The number of people living on less than $1.25 a day—the international poverty line—will fall from 208 million to 150 million. India's upper class will rise from 9 million to 32 million households, the middle class will jump from 63 million to 117 million households, and the lower class will decline from 152 million to 110 million households. The number of people below the poverty line will fall from 455 million to under 200 million.

FIGURE 1-5

Lifetime consumption patterns in China

Chinese born in 2009 will consume thirty-eight times as much as those born in 1960.

	Born in 1960	Born in 2009
Life expectancy (years)	47	73
Per capita consumption at birth	$102	$1,429
Per capita consumption at death	$1,129	$21,400
Lifetime consumption	$16,443	$632,024
	38x	

Sources: World Bank, World Development Indicators; United Nations, Department of Economic and Social Affairs, Population Division, Population Estimates and Projections (2010); Euromonitor, Countries and Consumers; Economist Intelligence Unit; BCG analysis.
Note: All figures are in constant 2010 U.S. dollars. Key assumptions: population growth flattens after 2050, and real annual GDP growth is 3 percent after 2020. These assumptions are conservative because of the lengthy forecast period. Detailed methodology and assumptions are available upon request.

Average incomes in the United States will grow more slowly, but they are still likely to be considerably higher than those in China and India—$68,800 per year in 2020. But it is the tripling of incomes in the world's most populous nations that will really drive global growth and patterns of consumer spending.[2] According to our research, one of the paradoxes of the modern world is that those who have little feel rich, while those who have much feel poor and threatened. And over the next forty years, those who have little will grow ever richer. In a recent report, the investment banking division of HSBC goes far beyond our forecast time frame, arguing that between 2010 and 2050, per-capita income will increase by 800 percent in China and 600 percent in India.[3]

FIGURE 1-6

Lifetime consumption patterns in India

Indians born in 2009 will consume thirteen times as much as those born in 1960.

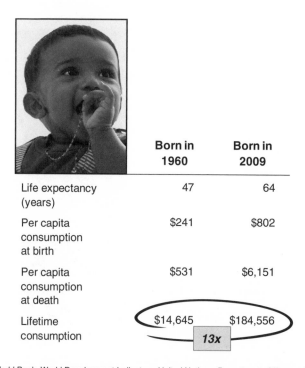

	Born in 1960	Born in 2009
Life expectancy (years)	47	64
Per capita consumption at birth	$241	$802
Per capita consumption at death	$531	$6,151
Lifetime consumption	$14,645	$184,556

13x

Sources: World Bank, World Development Indicators; United Nations, Department of Economic and Social Affairs, Population Division, World Population Estimates and Projections (2010); Euromonitor, Countries and Consumers; Economist Intelligence Unit; BCG analysis.
Note: All figures are in constant 2010 U.S. dollars. Key assumptions: population growth flattens after 2050, and real annual GDP growth is 3 percent after 2020. These assumptions are conservative because of the lengthy forecast period. Detailed methodology and assumptions are available upon request.

Another reason for the growth is that the newly affluent consumers will eventually dip into their extensive savings and tap into consumer credit. In China, consumers, companies, and the government save a staggering 53.6 percent of gross domestic product (GDP), while in India, the figure is 33.6 percent. In the United States, just 9.8 percent of GDP is saved for future use.[4] The savings from all sources fund a significant share of capital reinvestment. If even just a small proportion of these savings were diverted to pay for goods and services, it would amount to a massive, incremental "wall of money." This represents an upside case to the $10 trillion prize—taking the size of the prize to $13 trillion.

FIGURE 1-7

Per capita income in China and India, 1960–2020

Chinese growth exploded after 1992; the gap between China and India will continue to widen.

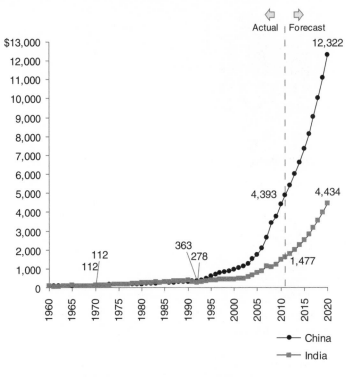

A billion newly created middle class

Sources: World Bank, World Development Indicators; BCG analysis.
Note: All figures are in nominal dollars.

Chinese consumers continue to save at a prodigious rate, particularly in the face of declining GDP growth. They remain concerned about the lack of a social security net, the rising cost of education for their children, and the need to provide funds to their male children to buy a first apartment. According to our 2012 surveys, attitudes among young consumers, especially those under the age of twenty-five, reflect a similarly conservative outlook and an interest in maintaining high savings rates—young people are now more willing to park their earnings for a while because of rising job insecurity. Nonetheless, we expect that their feelings of optimism for the long term will gradually translate into an increase in spending.

FIGURE 1-8

The distribution of income in China and India, 2010 and 2020

India and China will become large consumer markets because of their growing middle and upper classes.

		2010 income distribution		2020 income distribution		Gini coefficient (2007)
		Number of households (millions)	Share of households (%)	Number of households (millions)	Share of households (%)	
China	Upper	24	6	91	21	41.5 (40.0 in 2001)
	Middle	109	28	202	47	
	Lower	260	66	138	32	
India	Upper	9	4	32	12	36.8 (37.8 in 1997)
	Middle	63	28	117	45	
	Lower	152	68	110	43	

Sources: Euromonitor, Countries and Consumers, Annual Disposable Income; BCG analysis.
Note: The Gini coefficient is a measure of the equality of the income distribution, with 0 expressing total equality and 100 expressing total inequality. All income categories, when adjusted for purchasing power parity in 2005 constant dollars, translate to lower (<$15K), middle ($15K–$45K), and upper (>$45K). In nominal dollar terms, they are as follows: China 2010: lower (<$7.3K), middle ($7.3K–$23.2K), upper (>$23.2K); China 2020: lower (<$9.9K), middle ($9.9K–$31.3K), upper (>$31.3K); India 2010: lower (<$6.7K), middle ($6.7K–$20K), upper (>$20K); India 2020: lower (<$11.2K), middle ($11.2K–$33.5K), upper ($33.5K).

A third factor in the rise in the standard of living is that the Chinese and Indian governments are clearly focused on boosting domestic consumption. Both countries know that economic growth—and thereby social harmony—depends on driving demand at home. There is a tradeoff between current consumption and savings. Savings is one of the three drivers of national economic growth. The other two are labor force growth and labor force productivity. India has the potential to realize a triple, with strong performance in all three dimensions over the next decade.

The New Consumer Kings and Queens

The consumer is king, and China and India's newly affluent consumers will take a commanding position in the domestic and global economy. They have the ambition, energy, and resourcefulness required to make it in China and India today—and over the course of the decade, they will move to new homes, buy an array of appliances, pay for better food, invest in their children's education, and begin to travel in their own countries and beyond. It is a heady and uplifting time.

We interviewed hundreds of consumers in the course of our work, and we tell some of their stories throughout this book. The most important shared elements are these:

- Humble origins

- A drive to create a better life for themselves and their children

- An animated and specific dream of the elements of a better life, often filled with material goods—including a home and a car—as well as great experiences through travel and leisure activities, and access to modern health care and education

We introduce many of these consumers in the book (figure 1-9). Two of them are Rakesh Kumar Sahu and Zhou Zhanghong.

Rakesh is thirty-nine years old and lives in Lucknow, the capital city of Uttar Pradesh, India's most populous state, with more than two hundred million people. Rakesh started out as a snack seller with a handcart and earned only about 90,000 rupees (about $2,000) a year—barely enough to cover all of his necessities. Now, married and with a fourteen-year-old son, he owns and runs a small restaurant-cum-eating stall. Dark-skinned and quick to smile, he has a roundness that supports his belief that he is carrying an extra twenty pounds. It is a sign of his newfound wealth. His life over the past ten years has been, as he puts it, "a rocket." He currently earns 450,000 rupees a year (about $10,000), which puts him firmly in the middle class in India.

His clients are the local businesspeople and tradesmen who pass by his stall. Primarily, he serves a regular set of customers, people who enjoy his trademark *khasta puri*, *bada*, and *dahi bade* (popular Indian fried snacks). As you go into his restaurant, the smell of onion, garlic, cumin, turmeric, lemon, curry, coriander, and coconut—among other distinct aromas—rushes at you. He makes all of his food fresh from locally sourced ingredients. The only exception is his Pepsi cooler.

Rakesh has prospered as Lucknow and Uttar Pradesh have prospered. In recent years, the state and its capital have enjoyed a significant measure of government investment in roads, buildings, and infrastructure. They still lag

FIGURE 1-9

Major Chinese and Indian characters in the book

WX Liu

"Garage, but no car; plug, but no air conditioner"

KFC birthday girl: Li Duoduo

"Big sister at KFC is better than real sister"

"Harvard Girl"

"Ambition, drive, and giving back"

"Mr. Number 19"

"I can do anything"

Rakesh Kumar Sahu

"My life is filled with luck"

Harsh Mariwala

"We have continuously invented"

Source: BCG photos.

behind the rest of the country in education and health care, but things have improved over the last decade. The Mahatma Gandhi National Rural Employment Guarantee Act, enacted in 2005, has brought a minimum living standard to many people. The program guarantees jobs with a daily wage of about $2.60. In 2010, the government spent $8.1 billion on the program.[5] Some of that money goes to Rakesh in the form of snack purchases by the poor workers in Lucknow.

Confident and ambitious, Rakesh cuts the air with his hands to make a point, and his sentences come out rapid-fire. "Earlier, I had nothing. Today, because of my hard work, I have reached quite a height—now I have everything," he says proudly. "I used to live in a one-room rented flat. Now I own a flat with two rooms. I have also bought a plot of land and very soon I will build my dream house there."

Material goods have flowed into Chinese and Indian middle-class households. Rakesh has two televisions, two mobile phones, a washing machine, a small refrigerator, a Suzuki Versa van, and a motorcycle. Ten years ago, he ate cheap rice, avoided fruit because of the cost, and could never afford the medicine prescribed by his doctor. Now, he buys branded refined oil and basmati rice and eats all the fruit and vegetables he wants. His son is at a top Lucknow private academy—the City Montessori School—and he has money for an occasional movie and gifts for his wife. He can even save a full quarter of his income for a rainy day.

But he does not forecast many gloomy days ahead. He expects to see continued prosperity. Where Lucknow goes, he goes. "My life is good—more than I could ever have expected," he says. "My life will not go backward, only forward. Progress will be everywhere."

You can see the excitement on Rakesh's face as you listen to his story of success. It is the same with Zhou Zhanghong, a thirty-three-year-old woman in Shanghai.

A successful entrepreneur, she was born in a small farming village in Shandong, a province on China's northern coast. She has three sisters and two brothers. Her parents raised wheat and vegetables and had an income of just $1,500 a year to feed, clothe, and house their family of eight. She never had a chance to go to college.

"I had to drop out of school to allow my younger brother to attend school," she says. "He is the first son and was the better student. For me, it was a very tough life. I still remember wanting to buy a new pair of pants for RMB 13 (about $2), but we could not afford them. I just hoped that I would someday make money and be able to live on my own efforts."

Today, Zhanghong is a picture of upper-middle-class affluence. She is pregnant with her second child. If you can pay roughly $20,000, most provincial governments allow couples to have two children, in spite of the one-child rule introduced in 1978. As we talked in her office, she was wearing a gray cashmere cardigan and beautifully tailored black dress pants. She smiles and carries a lilt of optimism and excitement in her voice.

She is proud of her life story. At the age of eighteen, she left home and found employment at a printing factory in Nanjing. She learned how to set type and the basics of design. At that time, her annual income matched her family's income. "But it was not enough to generate much in the way of savings because of rent, clothing, and food needs. My boss appreciated my hard work, and I began to think I could make it big."

She was drawn to Shanghai, where she worked for another printing company. At that point, she married one of her work colleagues, and they decided to open their own business. Together they founded Shanghai Jingma Gift Company. This company is similar to Red Envelope in the United States—inexpensive items for birthdays, anniversaries, company celebrations, and personal use. It sells diaries, notebooks, calendars, leather goods, pens, watches, and other gift items. Consumers place orders either in-store or online. Her husband runs sales and marketing while Zhanghong is in charge of finance and internal management. After a grueling eight years, the company is now operating with twenty employees and is still growing fast: it is projected to have revenues of $3 million for 2012. The couple have an income of roughly $7,000 a month, which places them in the top 1 percent of households in China.

"I believe that as long as I work hard enough, I will achieve my goal. Life is full of opportunities and will only become better," Zhanghong says. She is grateful for her progress. "I remember our village first got electricity when I was twelve, and our aunt in the city gave us a used TV. That was the very first TV in the village. The entire village would come to our house to watch TV together at night."

Zhanghong is the chief financial officer both at work and at home. She is the key purchase decision-maker, managing the entire household budget. She and her husband earn more than fifty times what her parents were making in the village. She has reached a level of affluence where, she says, "It's not about how to *survive* but how to *live*."

They own two apartments (one is their home, one is an investment), two cars (one BMW, one minivan), and many branded modern home appliances, including a thirty-two-inch flat-screen color TV (a local brand called Changhong), a side-by-side refrigerator (Electrolux), a microwave oven (Galanz), two mobile phones (Oppo), two air conditioners (Midea), a washing machine (Rongshida), and a branded toilet (Kohler). They travel domestically twice a year and are thinking of visiting Paris or New York in the future. They have a very active social life and go to the movies at least once a week, dine out at better restaurants frequently, and play mah-jongg with friends on the weekends. Her favorite brands include Estée Lauder, Esprit, and Louis Vuitton. Her husband recently joined a golf club.

Zhanghong is very happy with her life and feels grateful for her experiences. "I learned how to treat every job with 100 percent dedication and not just focus on short-term return." As she is about to deliver her second baby and her elder son is going to enroll in elementary school next year, she plans temporarily to "slow down" at work so that she can spend more time with the family. But that does not mean that she is going to terminate her career. She sees her career as a lifetime journey and plans to rejoin the company soon after giving birth. "I feel it is my duty to further develop the business, to create better lives and futures for the employees."

In the next decade, Zhanghong expects to be the beneficiary of China's growth and development. "I am calm and very optimistic," she says. "I always believe in a bright future. I am confident that my hard work will pay off."

Consumer Sentiment: The Hopes and Dreams of the Newly Affluent

If Rakesh and Zhanghong are exceptional, there are many others, across China and India, who have great dynamism and determination to succeed, to spend money, and to be happy as never before. We know this from BCG's annual consumer attitude survey, which helps us to understand consumer passions and preferences. Our Center for Consumer and Customer Insight has now tracked the hopes and dreams of the Chinese for a decade and of Indians for five years. Consumers in China and India have high aspirations, are optimistic about their future, and are eager to enjoy their first taste of affluence. Their attitudes are in sharp contrast to those of the recession-humbled consumers in the Western world.

According to our survey of twenty-four thousand consumers around the world, 36 percent of Chinese and 19 percent of Indians expect to increase their discretionary spending over the next 12 months (figure 1-10). By comparison, only 11 percent of Americans, 8 percent of Europeans, and 5 percent of Japanese expect to do so.

FIGURE 1-10

Appetite to spend and willingness to trade up, by country

China leads the world in appetite to spend and willingness to trade up.

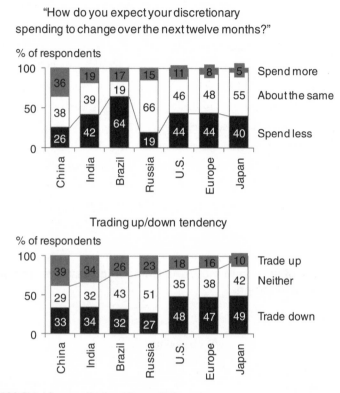

"How do you expect your discretionary
spending to change over the next twelve months?"

% of respondents

Trading up/down tendency

% of respondents

Source: BCG Global Consumer Sentiment Survey, 2011.
Note: Trading up indicates a willingness to spend more in a particular product category; trading down indicates a preference for saving or spending the bare minimum. The bottom income quartile is cut and the sample reweighted to represent the real income distribution in each country. Europe consists of Germany, the United Kingdom, Spain, Italy, and France. Because of rounding, percentages may not add up to 100.

Also, many consumers in the two countries expect to trade up to higher-quality goods: 39 percent in China and 34 percent in India, compared with 18 percent in the United States and 16 percent in Europe. The driving impulse is the desire for greater technical and health benefits. Electronics, apparel, and home decor are the top trading-up categories. Also, spending on health care is rising in both countries, although China's per-capita spending in this category has increased at double the rate of India's and now stands at $309 per capita, compared with $132 in India.[6]

One of the biggest budget expenses of the newly affluent consumers is food at home and in restaurants (including sit-down, stand-up, and to-go outlets)—and they are buying a wider variety of foods than ever before. We expect an individual's average daily calorie consumption to rise by roughly 10 percent in both India and China by 2020. But if the preference for fresh vegetables is rising, it is not likely to lead to a healthier population. In China, the new diet also has more meat, and this, together with the consumption of prodigious amounts of cigarettes and alcohol, is likely to lead to an epidemic of obesity, cardiovascular disease, and diabetes.

We have identified a virtuous circle that is driving the new optimism of the Chinese and Indian consumers (figure 1-11). Besides higher incomes, the newly affluent are opting for smaller families. In China, of course, the one-child policy has created a nation where four grandparents and two parents devote their love and resources to one family heir. This permits massive investment in that child's social welfare, health, and education. But

FIGURE 1-11

Virtuous circle of growth in India and China: high savings, smaller families, more investment

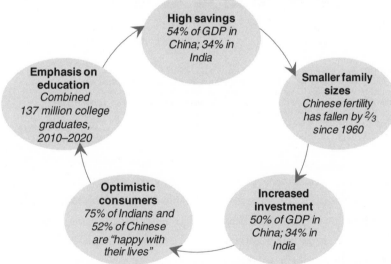

Sources: World Bank, World Development Indicators; Euromonitor, Countries and Consumers; BCG Global Consumer Sentiment Survey, March 2011; BCG analysis.

even in India, where efforts by Indira Gandhi to sterilize mothers had to be abandoned in the 1970s, there is a trend toward smaller families—especially in urban areas, where the average among the affluent class is two children.

In addition, the Chinese and Indian governments have been making major investments, which are programmed through a series of five-year plans and which are designed to improve the lives of the people. In particular, as we will show in chapter 11, the governments, as well as individuals, have been investing heavily in education, knowing that this will serve as the grand escalator to greater opportunities and higher-paying jobs.

The bountiful optimism is leading Chinese and Indian consumers to believe, possibly for the first time, that they will be able to achieve their dreams—prosperity, security, and relative affluence. As part of our consumer sentiment work, we track changing values. In India, the family, education, savings, wealth, and the home are all seen as more important than they were two years ago. So too is "value for money," reflecting the enduring power of *paisa vasool*, which we investigate in chapter 12. Other rising values include status, convenience, and wellness.

In China, wellness, the home, the family, spirituality (but not religion), and savings have become more important over the past two years. Other rising values include the environment, conviviality, education, friends, and wealth. This underlines the continuing influence of the Confucian notion of a *xiaokang* society—translatable as a well-off, harmonious society. These values both reflect the confidence of people who have grown up in an era of economic liberalization and greater social freedom and underpin people's hopes and dreams. And, as we will see now, there are companies that are cashing in on this opportunity by providing better goods, more dependable distribution, and access to information about product safety and technical benefits.

Making Dreams Come True: Meeting the Needs of the New Consumers

Just as we started the book with a story of how a Chinese entrepreneur is serving the new appetite for haute cuisine, we will close the chapter with a story of how an Indian entrepreneur is serving the new appetite for healthy living.

Harsh Mariwala embodies the archetypical traits of an Indian entrepreneur—he is a man with an idea a minute, guided by a vision of growth and expansion and a sense that no barrier is too high. He joined Marico, his family business, in 1971, and today he is the chairman and managing director. He says he wakes up every day with the same energy that he had on his first day on the job. "I love the company, I love our achievements, and I love our future," he says.

Mariwala has lived a life obsessed with the needs of the new consumers. His goal has been to provide them with products that are convenient, easy to use, affordable, and healthy. "We have unlimited opportunities," he says, with animation. "We have always been a story about making decisions, taking action, thinking through the eyes of our consumers."

He handed us a copy of his book, *An Uncommon Journey*. He then told us his saga of creating a publicly owned consumer goods and solutions company in beauty and wellness over the past forty years. This was a time in Indian history when the country went from being regulated, restricted, and antibusiness to being free-wheeling and celebrating the spirit of entrepreneurs. He is particularly proud of his company's packaging innovations, investment in people and capabilities, new product lines, advances in point-of-sale information technology, and efforts to expand internationally. "Forty years ago, we set off on a journey armed with nothing but our dreams," he says. "We invented, we innovated, we twisted and turned to find supply, machinery, and distribution—and consumers who would buy our products."

When Mariwala began at Marico, it was a small producer of bulk edible oils. Today, the business is a leader in hair care products as well as edible oils, functional foods, instant starch products, and, most recently, skin care services. He and his family own 63 percent of the shares. Over the past ten years, it has been one of the top-ranked FMCG (fast-moving consumer goods) companies in India on the basis of total shareholder return—above Nestlé, Hindustan Unilever, and Tata Tea. Its success has been built on a far-reaching sales and distribution network: 3.3 million retail outlets.

Mariwala is full of facts about his company. "We are the leading consumer of coconuts in India. One out of every twelve coconuts produced in India is sold to Marico," he says. In the next sentence, he wants affirmation. "Haven't we created something exciting here? We're fast and decisive, and we know what our niche is." Two of the company's brands, Parachute and Saffola, are particularly successful. Parachute is a coconut oil packaged for a variety of consumer usages. Indians consume edible oils in prodigious quantities, and coconut oil is high in saturated fat. Saffola, an edible oil low in saturated fat, has been skillfully positioned as a product for a "healthy heart" and sells mainly to middle-class consumers.

Marico started as part of Bombay Oil Industries Limited, a company that has been in existence for more than sixty years. Only in the last three decades, under Mariwala's direction, has the company evolved into one of the largest fast-moving consumer goods (FMCG) companies in India. Sales were about $700 million in 2011. The company has expanded internationally, with a large presence in Bangladesh, Egypt, parts of the Middle East, Southeast Asia, and South Africa.

"We will certainly continue to grow both domestically and abroad," Mariwala says, beaming. "We won't chase the biggest markets. We will enter the markets with an emerging middle class. We will be there for their beauty and wellness needs."

Mariwala is proud that he has competed and won against Hindustan Unilever, a much larger consumer packaged goods competitor in the core oils business. To secure victory, he says, he "contemporarized" packaging, ramped up distribution, and improved quality. "It was the core business for us, so we had no choice but to win." In the end, Marico acquired the Nihar brand of hair oil from Hindustan Unilever. He calls it "an emotional and psychological victory."

"We will grow and expand the product line," he says. "We know how to stay out of the bright lights of the multinationals. We know how to exploit niches. We know that our power is our extensive distribution. India will grow and develop tremendously over the next decade—roughly 10-plus percent compound annual growth. When Indian consumers want to spend their extra money on personal care and healthy food products, when they want a fix on skin or hair, we will be there."

He says mind-set is critical—and he is a prime proponent of the accelerator mind-set, which we will explore in chapter 14. "Grow faster than you are comfortable," he says. "Never stop seeking new opportunities. Push the envelope."

"We have very high energy and amazing persistence," he says. "I love it here. Our rapid-growth days are still in the future. You need patience, perseverance, perpetual reinforcement, and no escape buttons."

The rise of the newly affluent consumers will have a double-edged effect. It will create new opportunities and, at the same time, give rise to a new era of competition. For those companies in the United States and Europe that are fast and resilient enough to take advantage of the market growth, there will be spectacular wealth: a share of the $10 trillion prize. For those that are not fast and responsive, there will be competitors that, having grown up in China and India, will attack with deadly force in Western markets with low-priced, high-quality goods.

To help companies, we have tried to fill *The $10 Trillion Prize* with an abundance of practical lessons and strategies. We believe that the newly affluent in China and India are different from those in the West. They grew up with nothing and suddenly find their lives filled with choice. They are careful buyers yet they want the recognition, respect, and sophistication conveyed by branded products. They are uniquely optimistic about the future. They expect to be richer and they expect to command a greater share of the world's resources and income.

To win these new consumers, it is necessary to win them over—to *captivate* them. You can do this by focusing on six emotions:

- Help fulfill their dreams—give them a moment of gratification and elevation.

- Help brand them as in-the-know—discerning, informed, visibly affluent.

- Help them live big, on less. Understand that they "work hard, spend hard"—every renminbi, every rupee, is precious and causes them angst as it leaves their pocket.

- Understand that painful memories still haunt them. Almost every consumer we have talked with in China and India has either firsthand or family memories of deprivation and personal risk. You need to respect their history and provide them with an optimistic view of the future.

- Earn their loyalty and reverence by aiding the advancement and health of their children.

- Listen hard. The new consumer wants to engage in a dialogue and is looking for your respect and appreciation.

PART I

The Rise of the New Consumer in China and India

TWO

The New Revolutionaries
The Rise of the Middle Classes

Who the new consumers are, how they spend their money, and what
companies should do to captivate nearly one billion people

OVIND SINGH SHEKHAWAT does not look like a revolutionary. A hardworking forty-something who holds down two jobs in the sleepy Indian desert state of Rajasthan, he has the broad smile of a man who is happy with life. Ma Guojun does not look like a revolutionary, either. Younger than Govind by about ten years, he is an engineer and teaches at a university in Qinghai province in western China. Yet they unquestionably are part of a revolutionary movement: the rise of the Chinese and Indian middle class.

Throughout history, China and India have been sharply polarized countries, with a small elite of very rich at the top and an overwhelming majority of very poor at the bottom—and nothing much in the middle. Most people, whether in the cities or the countryside, scratched out a subsistence living. Over the past ten years, however, this has been changing, and dramatically so. In the next ten years, these two countries will have a substantial middle class for the first time in their history. In his 1947 speech "Tryst with Destiny," Jawaharlal Nehru, the first prime minister of independent India, proclaimed that India "will awake to life and freedom." A mere two years later, in October 1949, Chairman Mao proclaimed, "China has stood up." In fact, it has taken more than sixty years for Chinese and Indian consumers to wake up, stand up, and start to earn and spend as never before.

As discussed in chapter 1, the number of middle-class households in China will nearly double during the current decade, rising to 202 million by 2020. This will be the largest group of middle-class consumers in the world. Likewise, in India, the number of middle-class households will nearly double to 117 million over the same period. These middle-class consumers will account for nearly half of consumer spending in the two countries by 2020 (figure 2-1). It is their newfound productivity and earning power that is underpinning the dramatic growth in consumer spending and providing people such as Govind and Guojun with their extraordinary ambition, drive, and optimism.

The level of household income defines this group of newly prosperous people—but it is not a homogeneous group. We segment households into lower, middle, and upper class. It is helpful to further segment the lower class into the left-behinds and the next billion, to segment the middle class into emerging middle and middle, and to segment the upper class into lower affluent and upper affluent. The *next billion* are people in the lower class who have some disposable money in their pockets for the very first time and have the energy and ambition to move up into the middle class—they work hard, they care about their children's education, and they choose better quality goods.

FIGURE 2-1

How the $10 trillion prize breaks down across classes

	China in 2020	India in 2020
Upper (income)	$2.8 trillion (>$31.3K)	$1.1 trillion (>$33.5K)
Middle (income)	$2.8 trillion ($9.9–$31.3K)	$1.8 trillion ($11.2–$33.5K)
Lower (income)	$0.6 trillion (<$9.9K)	$0.7 trillion (<$11.2K)

Sources: Euromonitor, Countries and Consumers; BCG City Income Database; BCG analysis.

FIGURE 2-2

Household income in China, 2010 and 2020

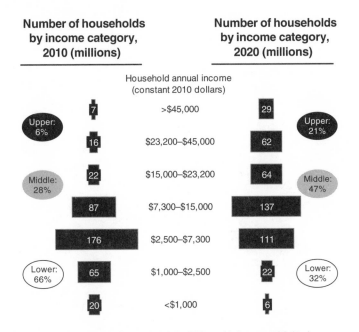

Number of households by income category, 2010 (millions)		Number of households by income category, 2020 (millions)

Household annual income
(constant 2010 dollars)

Upper: 6%	7 — >$45,000 — 29	Upper: 21%
	16 — $23,200–$45,000 — 62	
Middle: 28%	22 — $15,000–$23,200 — 64	Middle: 47%
	87 — $7,300–$15,000 — 137	
	176 — $2,500–$7,300 — 111	
Lower: 66%	65 — $1,000–$2,500 — 22	Lower: 32%
	20 — <$1,000 — 6	

Sources: Euromonitor, Countries and Consumers, Annual Disposable Income; BCG City Income Database; BCG analysis.

In China, the threshold for entry to the middle class, taking into account the lower cost of goods and services, is an annual household income of $9,750. But we put the threshold for entry to the emerging middle class at $7,300, while the ceiling for the richest members of the middle class is $23,200 (figure 2-2). Guojun, who earns around RMB 80,000, or $12,500, fits squarely into this category.

In India, the middle class has an income range of $6,700 to $20,000 (figure 2-3). We often subdivide this class into two groups: the urban and the rural. Govind is comfortably middle class, earning more than 500,000 rupees, or around $11,000, from his various business ventures.

But if income is a key segmentation factor, it is not the only one. Other factors include education, occupation, and geography—and, as we will see in this chapter, these differences influence consumers' attitudes and, importantly, their patterns of consumption.

First, though, we should meet the new members of the middle class.

FIGURE 2-3

Household income in India, 2010 and 2020

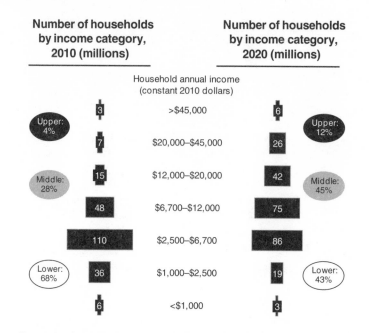

Number of households by income category, 2010 (millions)	Household annual income (constant 2010 dollars)	Number of households by income category, 2020 (millions)
Upper: 4% — 3	>$45,000	6 — Upper: 12%
7	$20,000–$45,000	26
Middle: 28% — 15	$12,000–$20,000	42 — Middle: 45%
48	$6,700–$12,000	75
110	$2,500–$6,700	86
Lower: 68% — 36	$1,000–$2,500	19 — Lower: 43%
6	<$1,000	3

Sources: Euromonitor, Countries and Consumers, Annual Disposable Income; BCG City Income Database; BCG analysis.

The Middle (Class) Kingdom: China's New Bourgeoisie

Ma Guojun is typical of this new class. Born near Xining, the capital city of Qinghai province, he grew up in a poor family, the eldest of three boys. His father worked for the local electricity company and dreamed that his son, if he studied hard, would rise up through the ranks of Chinese society.

As it turned out, Guojun performed only modestly in his *gaokao*, the national college entrance examination, and secured a place at a university in Shenyang, rather than Beijing. There, he studied for a degree in material science and engineering. But he did so well that he was able to go on to study for a postgraduate degree at a university in Beijing. For him, this was a big turning point.

Soon after completing his studies, Guojun got a job as a researcher at Advanced Technology & Materials Company (AT&M). This manufacturer of metallic products was founded by a state-owned research institute in the late 1990s. His annual salary was RMB 60,000, or about $9,400. This was double his father's salary and marked him as a member of the urban and emerging middle class. If Guojun felt special, he was not alone—many others were climbing the social ladder. In 2010, those living in emerging middle-class households or higher constituted 26 percent of the population. By 2020, this proportion will have risen to 50 percent. Much of this growth will take place in China's fast-expanding cities, where 75 percent of the population will enter the emerging middle class or higher by the end of this decade. Today, the emerging middle class accounts for about 15 percent of the general population and 26 percent of the urban population. Guojun fit the bill perfectly. But he was not ready to rest on his laurels.

In Beijing, the middle class has to cut corners and budget tightly in order to live the better life. For instance, workers must sometimes go as far out as the fourth ring—the expressway encircling the city more than five miles from the center—before finding affordable apartments. The commute to work can then take ninety minutes or even longer.

At that time, Guojun did not feel rich, even though he was, by the standards of his family. He lived in a small apartment of just forty square meters, which he rented with a roommate, and it was poorly furnished and miles away from his office. It took him more than an hour to get to AT&M's offices in the Zhongguancun Science Park, China's answer to Silicon Valley, and he had to get there on the crowded subway. It meant that there was very little time for recreation. As he put it, "Every day was work, work, work." Worse than this, he felt that even if he worked and saved for a lifetime, he still would not be able to afford a proper-sized apartment in Beijing.

At the age of twenty-seven, Guojun was lonely. He had fallen in love with a beautiful young woman in Beijing, but his modest financial income, together with the fact that he came from a city 1,250 miles from the capital, did not make him an attractive bet as a husband—or, more significantly, as a son-in-law. The girl's parents forced the couple to go their separate ways. As he explained, "Her mom said, 'This guy can't lead a good life for himself, so how could he give you happiness?'"

Status, as expressed by a nice house and a good job, is a big factor in China, as we will see in chapter 8. "A house doesn't only mean a place to live. It translates as a statement of affluence: security, health care, identity, and education," Guojun told us. "A lot of people growing up in Beijing had houses bought for them by their parents. But for me, as someone who had migrated from a rural area, I had to pay for a house myself, and that's almost impossible because of the high and rising costs of property."

As he searched for a new direction, Guojun's moment came when he stumbled across a job made for him: a lectureship in engineering at Qinghai University in his home city of Xining. Offered a comparable salary, he jumped at the chance to escape Beijing and return home. He knew his money would go further, he would stand a better chance of finding a wife and starting a family, and he would have a better life. This common migration pattern is driving the growth of the tier 2 and tier 3 cities in China.

Four years later, he has a wife, a one-year-old son, and an annual household income of RMB 80,000, or $12,500. He owns an apartment that is three times the size of the one he rented in Beijing—thanks, in part, to a gift from his parents—and he has many of the things that he wanted: a TV, a computer, and a new HTC smartphone that he bought on taobao.com, China's largest online market.

Like many middle-class consumers, he is actively online, spending around two hours a day on the Internet—often sending messages to fellow lecturers on QQ, the instant messaging service. He used to spend more time than this, but his infant son now takes up many of his spare waking hours.

He definitely wants more—more goods, more savings, more comforts. He wants his own car; currently, he travels by train or shares the university's car pool. He also wants to give his son every chance in life by providing him with the best education. He is busily putting money away to cover the cost of his son's schooling. In an effort to climb the career ladder and earn a bigger salary, he is studying part-time for a doctorate at Lanzhou University of Technology. Every night after his son goes to bed, Guojun turns to his books, working until the early hours. Periodically, he takes the two-hour train ride from Xining to Lanzhou to meet with his professors. He will earn his degree this year, opening more doors to advancement. When he completes his PhD, Guojun will be one of more than sixty thousand new PhD graduates this year—a sixfold increase in the number of PhD graduates in ten years. He wonders whether an MBA would also be a worthwhile investment to help him stand out from the crowd.

Guojun has, in his words, achieved "the first half of his dreams." In the decade ahead, he expects to continue to invest in himself and in his career. It is likely that his annual income will continue to rise as he opens more doors for himself and as his city of Xining becomes more prosperous. In so many ways, he is part of China's *middle class in motion*—a fast-changing and mobile group that is redrawing society.

Cars, Caste, and Class in India

The caste system still survives in India. Although it is less defining and rigid today than ten years ago, and an interventionist government is attempting to improve social and economic mobility, it still hangs in the air. Govind is a Rajput—the proud warrior caste that once ruled the princely states of northern India. He wears a dark moustache, a marker of his masculinity and his martial heritage. Yet what really distinguishes Govind are his possessions: for a man who started with nothing, these are the things that really count for him.

Born in 1971, some twenty years before the introduction of the market reforms that would signal India's reentry to the global economy, Govind was raised in a hut in Jhalana Dungri, one of the most deprived areas of Jaipur. Like Guojun, he was the eldest of three boys and, as such, was expected to help provide for the family from an early age.

His father, a painter, brought home about 50,000 rupees, or about $1,100, per year. Young Govind, offering his services as a day laborer and painter, was soon earning enough to help the family. "I started working when I was fifteen," he explains. "With the money I made, I was able to put myself through school and support my father."

He left school at nineteen and started full-time work. Very soon, he was earning around 35,000 rupees ($750)—about two-thirds of his father's income. His turning point came when he met his wife. "She's my great inspiration," he says. She was a student at the local college when a matchmaker first introduced them. She was studying for a degree in education in order to be a teacher. "I realized that being a painter's helper would not allow me to achieve what I wanted for my family," he explains. "I wanted to do something more than just be a painter or contractor."

This was the mid-1990s, and the Indian car market was just opening up. Until then, the Hindustan Ambassador, modeled on the stately 1950s Oxford III from the now-defunct British Morris Motor Company, was the classic Indian automobile—so much so that it was dubbed "King of the Indian Roads." Govind took a second job as a car-wash attendant, supplementing his income as a painter. "I used to wake up at four a.m. and clean cars for people and then start my day job at nine a.m.," he recalls. "And then, in the evenings, I learned to drive and earned a driver's license."

Handsome, well groomed, and physically fit, he was selected as the chauffeur for a prominent businessman in Jaipur. "I drove a white Fiat in those days," he recalls, "and I learned all that I needed to know about how cars work." This knowledge proved to be critical in his journey to prosperity. In his late twenties, he decided to start a small business selling secondhand cars, which he ran alongside his day-to-day work as a driver. "I bought a rundown car and put it into shape," he says. "I worked on it for nearly two months—working most nights from eight p.m. till midnight. I earned nearly 20,000 rupees ($430) on that deal."

This was big money for Govind, and he has not looked back since. He started dealing in cars—buying, repairing, and reselling them. Last year, he estimates, he completed as many as twenty such deals. With more money in his pocket, he was able to leave his job as a full-time chauffeur and become a free agent, driving people for special occasions: many Indians drive their car in the city but hire a driver for long-distance trips.

Today, his annual income is more than 500,000 rupees—about $11,000, a tenfold increase in twenty years. Middle-class status symbols of success are all around him: a TV by Videocon, a refrigerator by Godrej, a Suzuki car, and a Honda motorcycle. And then there is his house: a three-bedroom house in a middle-class district. It says a lot about Govind—not only his position in society but also his hunger for more. He is always on the lookout for ways to boost his earnings. At one point in our meeting, he leaned over and offered to buy our car. "I will make you a good deal," he said. We declined.

About twelve years ago, he bought a small plot of land, paying 100,000 rupees ($2,200). "No bank was willing to give money to a person like me at that time, so I borrowed small amounts from people I worked with and slowly paid them back over six years." In 2008, he started building, seizing on a time when he believed that the prices of steel and cement were relatively low. He invested in the contents as well as the construction of the house. He is especially proud of the two air conditioners that he had installed. Manufactured by General, among the most expensive brands, they provide cool air in the hot Jaipur summers. "It is the best Japanese brand, so it has to be good quality," he says. "It also uses less power than other brands."

Now, the house is worth 6.2 million rupees, or $130,000—a fortune for Govind. But it is not luxurious, at least not in the Western sense of the word. It is a simple, single-story, rust-pink building. The bathroom is basic: there is a faucet, which is used to fill a bucket for a makeshift shower; a small mirror that he uses for shaving; and a basic toilet, but no tissue. Also, the power supply is intermittent—electricity is routinely cut in the afternoon between 1 p.m. and 3 p.m. It is for this reason that he bought a direct-cool refrigerator that can keep food cold for four hours without electricity. He also has a washerman, who comes to his house to hand-wash and air-dry his clothing.

To further boost his income, Govind joined Gold Souk, a marketing firm, as a part-time, commissioned sales rep. In the last three years, he has earned more than 1 million rupees ($21,000) in commissions. For all his newfound wealth, however, Govind is still hungry for more—for himself and for his two children.

He dreams of taking his family on holiday to Dubai and Singapore. He also dreams that his children will achieve more than he has and all that they wish for. "I spend about 5,000 rupees ($100) every month for their education. My son is doing well in school—he got 90 percent in his exams. I hope that he becomes an engineer. I don't want him to go through the struggle that I had to go through."

As Govind talks, he chews tobacco. He doesn't smoke or drink alcohol. A serious man, he is rightly proud of his success, his hard work, and his ability, through his own endeavors, to pull himself up by his bootstraps. "When I was sixteen years old, I never thought that I would one day have a house of my own, a foreign-made car, and a motorcycle. But I've learned that with the right effort, one can achieve anything. I work fifteen to sixteen hours a day, seven days a week, and that's why I have reached this point. But I will still do anything to earn more money. I want to double my income every three or four years. I want to make sure that I am able to buy a better house, send my son to a good college, and provide my family with everything that I never had." (He does not talk about sending his daughter to college.)

He feels this passionately. When he said "double my income," he repeated it over and over again, jabbing his finger for emphasis. He is a man on a mission.

Consumption Curves: How Middle-Class Consumers Spend Their Money

Food, homes, household appliances, transport, education, health care, clothing: these are the things that middle-class consumers, enriched with higher incomes, are starting to spend their money on as never before. The number one item on the family shopping list is food. But if this is striking, expect growth that is even more spectacular in other consumer categories as more and more people join the middle class.

The second-biggest item on middle-class consumers' shopping list is housing and household appliances. In China, household appliances were the number one category that people wanted to trade up to in 2011, according to our annual survey: some 53 percent of consumers registered their intent to spend more on TVs, refrigerators, and computers.

These figures underscore Chinese and Indian consumers' extraordinary optimism about their future. As described in chapter 1, some 39 percent of Chinese consumers and 34 percent of Indian consumers expressed an intention to trade up. By contrast, only 18 percent of Americans and 16 percent of Europeans did so.

Yet, as they grow richer, they become even more optimistic, and their spending behavior evolves in a distinct way. In years past, the evolution of people entering the middle class and rising to affluence was hard to observe because so few people made the journey from poverty to prosperity. In the last ten years, however, the transition has been dramatic, like a fast-forward video of social transformation.

To monitor this transition, we use a tool we call a *consumption curve* to help us to establish how consumers change their spending habits as they earn more money. Different types of products have differently shaped consumption curves—which shows that consumer demand for different products changes at a different rate as income changes. Take two types of beverage, for examples: water and fine wine. As people's income increases, they do not actually consume that much more water, and so the consumption curve is fairly flat. By contrast, as a consumer enters the middle class, there is a tendency to drink better wine every now and then, as a special treat. Then, as the consumer becomes truly affluent, he or she begins to consume fine wine on a regular basis. So the consumption curve for wine is upward sloping, rising as income rises.

Using this tool, our analysis shows that once people have sufficient *disposable income* to enter the emerging middle class—typically when their household income reaches around $7,500 per year—they start spending on things that they could once only dream of having: fresh fruit and vegetables, manufactured ready-to-wear clothing, better housing.

Our research shows that consumers hit a second important threshold once they start to earn around $12,500 per year. At this point, they begin to invest in a first automobile, dabble with entry-price luxury goods and health foods, and spend more on beauty products, apparel and shoes, entertainment, and alcoholic drinks.

Then, as they become more affluent, with an annual income of $19,000, consumers cross another threshold. They start to spend money on travel, recreation, fancier household goods, and foods that are not everyday commodities, such as yogurt, chocolate, coffee, and wine.

For items such as household goods, the consumption curve is a sharply upward-sloping line, indicating a steady rise in spending as incomes rise (figures 2-4 and 2-5). Other consumer categories that rise steeply, if less so than household-related goods, are transport and communication, as well as education. Expenditures on health, another major category, only start to rise as people reach upper middle or upper class, with only the tail end of the consumption curve bending upward.

By contrast, the consumption curve for food follows a gentler upward trajectory and actually flattens out, as people get richer. You can only spend so much on food and consume so many calories.

Consumption Patterns in China

In China, people rising to emerging middle-class status focus on three core needs: food, clothing, and the household. When they were poor, they bought their clothes from street vendors, bartered for basic food, and endured subsistence-level living conditions. With more money, they visit modern retail stores to buy apparel; they go to supermarkets to select a broad mix of fruit, vegetables, meat, and dairy products; and they invest in basic household goods. In urban areas, more than 95 percent of households have a washing machine, a refrigerator, and air-conditioning units.

FIGURE 2-4

BCG consumption curves for different products in China

Categories fall into three groups based on their consumption curves.

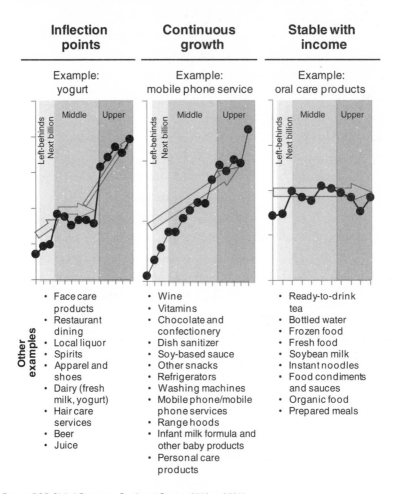

Inflection points	Continuous growth	Stable with income
Example: yogurt	Example: mobile phone service	Example: oral care products

Other examples

• Face care products	• Wine	• Ready-to-drink tea
• Restaurant dining	• Vitamins	• Bottled water
• Local liquor	• Chocolate and confectionery	• Frozen food
• Spirits	• Dish sanitizer	• Fresh food
• Apparel and shoes	• Soy-based sauce	• Soybean milk
• Dairy (fresh milk, yogurt)	• Other snacks	• Instant noodles
• Hair care services	• Refrigerators	• Food condiments and sauces
• Beer	• Washing machines	• Organic food
• Juice	• Mobile phone/mobile phone services	• Prepared meals
	• Range hoods	
	• Infant milk formula and other baby products	
	• Personal care products	

Source: BCG Global Consumer Sentiment Survey, 2010 and 2011.
Note: The consumption patterns are summarized according to annual spending per capita for fast-moving categories and spending per capita in the previous twelve months for durable categories.

As people enter the middle class, they switch their focus to consumer goods that enhance their quality of life far beyond subsistence. Food, clothing, and the home remain important, but they look for sophisticated products with advanced functionality and instantly recognizable international brand names. They also look for definably healthy products: juices, bottled

FIGURE 2-5

BCG consumption curves for different products in India

Categories fall into three groups based on their consumption curves.

Inflection points	Continuous growth	Stable with income
Example: Utensil cleaner	Example: Refrigerator	Example: Hydrogenated oil

Other examples

• Toothpaste	• Coffee	• Tea
• Toothbrushes	• Ketchup	• Edible oil
• Hair oil	• Processed cheese	• Washing
• Fabric whiteners/blues	• Glucose/sugar	powders/liquids
• Floor cleaner	• Butter	• Biscuits/cookies
• Toilet cleaner	• Instant noodles	• Milk powder/
	• Jam	dairy whitener
	• Branded soup	• Hair
	• Ready-made tomato paste	products (except shampoo)
	• Branded baby foods/ baby oil/disposable diapers	• Talcum powder
	• Fabric bleaches	• Washing cakes/ bars
	• All durables: washing machine, desktop, microwave oven	
	• Telephone	

Sources: India Reserve Service; BCG Global Consumer Sentiment Survey, 2010 and 2011.

water, vitamins, and other food supplements. This is a growing trend. For instance, we noted an increasing appetite for bottled water in China, with the purchase incidence rising from 67 percent in 2007 to 86 percent in 2011. Fearful that tap water may be polluted, the Chinese devote more of their income to safe products.

When Chinese people enter the upper class, their shopping behavior evolves as they trade up to premium products such as luxury items and prestige cars, as well as to life-enhancing activities such as dining out, going to the movies, playing sports, and going on overseas trips, especially long-haul flights to the United States and Europe. Today, these richer Chinese are buying a record quantity of fine wine from the vineyards of Bordeaux. In doing so, they are starting to appreciate, and not just consume, wine—a reflection of their growing sophistication.

As they become wealthier, Chinese consumers look ever more closely for branded products: some 70 percent say they trade up because of brand, a higher percentage than for consumers in most other countries (figure 2-6). In the United States, just 30 percent trade up to brands in this way, and in Europe, it is an even lower proportion, at just 19 percent. Chinese consumers emphasize brand mainly because they see it as an indicator of quality and functionality.

For some consumer categories—notably baby products (such as infant formula), luxury products, and designer labels—brand plays an especially important part in the purchase decision. For other categories, such as home decoration and entertainment, brand is less significant. There are also some categories for which foreign brands are coveted and others for which local brands are preferred. When it comes to clothing and consumer electronics, foreign brands are favored—notably Nike, Adidas, and Nokia. By contrast, for home appliances, local brands, which offer trustworthy products with good after-sales services, are preferred. For instance, twice as many consumers are aware of Haier refrigerators than of other brands, including famous international manufacturers of white goods.

Consumption Patterns in India

We segment the Indian middle class into emerging middle and middle, with particular focus on urban and rural distinctions. At the lower end, there is some overlap with the next-billion category, which includes some of the emerging middle class, while at the upper end, particularly with the educated professionals, there is some overlap with the rich or affluent classes.

Today, the middle class—including teachers, junior executives, factory managers, and village doctors—accounts for 28 percent of households and

FIGURE 2-6

Consumers' reasons for trading up, by country

Brand is still the leading reason for trading up in China and India, but technical differences and being healthier are emerging as common motivations.

Reasons for trading up	Respondents (%)						
	China	India	Brazil	Russia	U.S.	Europe	Japan
Because of the brand name	70	64	60	26	30	19	24
There are meaningful technical differences in the product or service quality (e.g., features, construction, materials, look)	65	61	70	60	52	45	6
Because it's healthier	65	65	73	68	49	38	6
These products/services give better results than the average or lower-price products or services	63	55	71	66	63	51	41
These categories of products/services are more important to me	53	57	76	63	44	34	13
I enjoy the feeling of using these products/ services	52	62	69	59	32	34	17
I can afford to	50	58	63	64	34	30	27
I deserve it	46	60	77	59	26	26	22
I enjoy the feeling of buying these products/services	47	55	68	54	26	27	14

Sources: BCG Global Consumer Sentiment Survey, March 2011; BCG analysis.
Note: Europe consists of Germany, the United Kingdom, Spain, Italy, and France.

some 44 percent of consumption.[1] As might be expected, the urban class has relatively higher spending, accounting for 8 percent of households and 11 percent of consumption. Educated professionals, a distinct group whose members include graduates working as managers and executives and whose income overlaps with the richer middle class, will see their share of household consumption increase from 16 percent in 2010 to 26 percent in 2020.

We estimate that the discretionary spending of the urban middle class is about 32 percent of their overall income. For the rural middle class, it is slightly lower, at 28 percent. For educated professionals, it is substantially higher, at 48 percent.[2]

Most Indians, even those with income of $3,000 or lower, consume basic products such as cooking oil, bathing soap, washing powder, and tea. As they get richer, they start to purchase durable goods, with the typical hierarchy being a TV, then a gas cooking stove, then a music system, then a refrigerator and washing machine, and then an air conditioner. Also, most will buy a two-wheeler, such as a scooter or a motorbike, for getting around.

Beyond this, their priorities are things relating to the family, especially children. We have calculated that 37 percent of the middle-class household's expenditure is devoted to children, mainly food and education. One young couple we met in Mumbai earned about 15,000 rupees ($300) a year and lived in a one-room *chawl* (a ghetto-like apartment). The couple spend nearly 1,000 rupees ($20) per month on school fees for their only daughter. "We want the very best we can afford for her," they explained.

By buying a private-school education, they are buying a branded product—one with quality assurance. Indeed, our research shows that, as with Chinese consumers, 70 percent of Indian consumers consider the brand to be an important criterion when making a purchase, with 64 percent saying it is a reason for trading up.

This buying habit affects a range of consumer categories and is becoming more widespread: for instance, since 2005, the number of households buying coffee, milk powder, biscuits, ketchup, toothpaste, washing powder, and even toilet cleaner from large or national brands has risen to well over 50 percent. According to one study, the top three brands in the country are Amul, a farmers' milk cooperative; LIC (Life Insurance Corporation of India), a state-run insurance company; and Nokia, the Finnish mobile phone manufacturer. D. Shivakumar, head of Nokia's newly formed India, Middle East, and Africa region, told us, "Rich people buy brands for vanity and poor people buy brands for security. India is a brand-led market, and the guy with the lowest price is not always the market leader."

Although there are broad buying habits shared by all of India's middle-class consumers, there are subtle differences in the way that the urban and the rural middle class spend their money. Overall, as we have seen, middle-class consumers spend the largest part of their budget on food; for the rural middle class, this eats up 35 percent of total consumption spending, compared with 31 percent for the urban middle class and 17 percent for educated professionals.[3]

For educated professionals, the largest category of spending is housing and consumer durables, accounting for a fifth of their budget. It is also a major outlay for the urban middle class, accounting for a fifth of their budget, too. For the rural middle class, the second-biggest priority after food is the education of their children, which accounts for 13 percent of this group's disposable income.

These spending priorities explain some striking differences in consumer attitudes about the future. Some 88 percent of educated professionals expect their lifestyle and finances to be even better in the next two years. The next-most-optimistic group is the urban middle class, with 70 percent reporting that they think they will be better off in the next two years. Behind them, some 64 percent of the rural middle class are optimistic about the future.

Their material wealth also reflects this abundant confidence. About half of the rural middle class have basic durables—a television, a DVD player, a pressure cooker, a refrigerator, and a scooter. An even higher proportion—66 percent—of the urban middle class have these necessities of modern life.

When it comes to more advanced durables, however, the numbers are much lower and they indicate significant room for growth. Only 28 percent of the urban middle class and 13 percent of the rural middle class own a modern oven, a dishwasher, a microwave, a camera, a plasma TV, or a car. By contrast, 42 percent of educated professionals possess these types of products.

There is also room for greater connectivity, as will be shown in chapter 10. Just 15 percent of the urban middle class use the Internet. Among the rural middle class, it is even lower, at just 4 percent. Moreover, nearly a fifth of the urban middle class and nearly half of the rural middle class do not have a bank account.

The data indicate that the middle class in India, as in China, is far from a homogeneous group—and different from the middle class in the United

States and Europe, as well. But, in their voracious appetite for a Western lifestyle, albeit with Indian or Chinese characteristics, middle-class consumers from both these countries are unrivaled.

Upwardly Mobile: The Lifestyles of the Middle Classes

Much is made of the migration from the rural districts to urban centers. But an even bigger migration is taking place from the lower reaches of the social pyramid to the next level of the pyramid. As you will see in part II, this migration is having a transformative impact on the demand for food and beverages, housing and household appliances, luxury goods, digital products, and education. But it is also having an impact on consumers' recreational lives. After generations of living at a subsistence level, millions of people are engaging in definably middle-class pursuits.

Take, for example, the new passion for driving on the newly built expressways that fan out from Beijing and other main cities. It used to be that only people who could afford chauffeurs owned cars. Now, however, there is a fast-emerging car culture, and proud owners are eager to sit at the wheel and take to the open road.

Driving clubs are popular, with many organizing self-drive tours. For instance, the Beijing Target Auto Club runs a seven-day excursion from Beijing to Hubei province in central China, and arranges visits to the Three Gorges Dam, one of the controversial wonders of modern engineering, as well as to a mountain forest famous for its fabled race of hairy ape-men.[4]

In India, too, the car trip has become a popular weekend activity. Rising incomes, together with much-improved roads between the regional capitals, have paved the way for the new passion for driving. As Govind, who spends his life with cars, told us, "It used to take me three days to drive from Mumbai to Jaipur, and the roads were terrible. Now the National Highway 8, which links Mumbai and Delhi, is a pleasure to drive on—and it takes me only eighteen hours to complete the 1,200-kilometer journey." And better roads are attracting a bigger variety of cars, he said. "A few years ago, all I would ever see were Ambassadors and Fiats. But now, I often spot Camrys, Accords, Skodas, and even the occasional Mercedes Benz and Audi."

Another sign of middle-class affluence, and one linked to the popularity of the self-drive tour, is the dramatic growth of the travel and tourism business.

According to our analysis, Chinese travelers made sixteen million overseas trips in 2010, two million more than the number of foreign trips made by Japanese travelers.[5] Over the next decade, we project that the number of overseas trips made by Chinese travelers will swell to fifty-three million. These travelers will account for 9 percent of foreign tourists in North America by 2020, compared with 3 percent today, and they will represent 19 percent of foreign tourists arriving in the European Union. Spending by Chinese tourists is surging by 19 percent a year and will reach nearly $120 billion annually by 2020.

Middle-class and affluent consumers, most of whom have never traveled overnight, are spearheading this travel craze. Today, around two hundred million urban Chinese consumers have taken an overnight leisure trip. But with an average of twenty-five million people taking their first-ever such trip every year, this number is likely to more than double by 2020.

If Western tourists typically go to see the sights, Chinese travelers go to shop. We have calculated that 40 percent of the money they spend abroad is spent on shopping—around twice the share that Japanese and U.S. tourists devote to the same activity. Affluent Chinese, in particular, buy luxury items abroad. For Chinese travelers of all income levels, hotels tend to be places to sleep, not experiences in themselves. When choosing a hotel, they look for cleanliness and the hotel environment—these are as important as price. Customer service, location, and brand matter much less to them. Hotel quality is more important for affluent Chinese, but even these travelers dislike spending lavishly on just a name.

Indian travelers are similar to Chinese travelers—with a focus on value. Yet even the ongoing global economic crisis has not reduced the readiness to travel far and wide. Destinations such as Switzerland, Dubai, New Zealand, and Singapore generate significant revenues from Indian tourists. As an example, the Singapore Tourism Board reported that Indians spent more than any other nationality on shopping in Singapore. Interestingly enough, the tourism boards of these countries have realized the power of the Indian film industry and provide incentives to Indian movie makers to film in their countries in order to generate tourist demand. Switzerland has seen thousands of Indian tourists make their way to Zurich, Geneva, and Interlaken to see the sights that they saw on the silver screen. Jungfrau, one of the top tourist destinations in Switzerland, with a cog railway and panoramic views of the Alps, now has an Indian restaurant—aptly called Bollywood.

If there are many other things that the new middle-class consumers are doing now that they have more money in their pocket, no coverage of this theme would be complete without some mention of the growing popularity of blogging—something covered more fully in chapter 10. The Internet is a craze, with people spending hours surfing the Web, and for newly affluent, property-owning consumers, it is a new channel for speaking out against corruption, incompetence, and the misuse of power.

This new political outspokenness is the other side of the demand coin. Better educated than before, and more confident, too, consumers feel entitled to articulate their views on everything from products to public policy. As property owners, they are angered by anything that threatens the value of their property; as consumers, they are angered by anything that threatens the affordability of their newly acquired lifestyles; as increasingly well-informed parents and children, they are angered by less-than-satisfactory access to health care and education; and as citizens, they are pushing for greater accountability and better governance. Pushing the boundaries, and raising expectations, these new middle-class consumers are on the march—and they do not want anything to get in their way, let alone push them back.

Implications for Business

The rising middle class is the most important consumer segment in China and India. In our work with companies, we have identified three strategies that should be mastered to achieve success with this consumer group.

First, it is imperative that products deliver *technical, functional,* and *emotional benefits.* Although the new middle-class consumers are optimistic and ready to spend money, they still have a natural inclination to keep their cash in their pockets. They worry that their newfound wealth could disappear as quickly as it arose—not least because there is no Western-style social safety net. This means that companies have to develop convincing products offering real value: products with technical and functional innovations. These consumers will become mini-experts in the finer points of the products, typically reading the lists of ingredients, studying the product manuals, and asking store clerks for more information. In the end, this is how they justify their purchases to themselves and to their friends. When consumers are able to articulate the functional benefits to their friends, they ladder up emotionally. They become advocates and apostles.

In India, for example, Maggi, a brand of instant noodles owned by Nestlé, the Swiss food company, has come to understand the technical, functional, and emotional needs of mothers. Nestlé has built up the Maggi brand over a decade. It started with "two-minute convenience" positioning for a quick snack for the child, but that did not resonate with mothers. To rethink its strategy, Nestlé engaged with mothers to determine their needs with regard to nutrition and local taste. It then created a variety of Indian flavors and offered whole-wheat nutrition—along with vegetables, as suggested by the mothers—to make a hearty snack. The result is that Maggi is now a $500 million brand with an 80 percent share of the instant noodle market.

Second, the full range of products offered should include *aspirational* items. Companies should price their products in a way that makes some items in the line just out of reach. Pricing that embraces the *good, better, best* range works well in the Chinese and Indian markets. In India, for instance, LG, the South Korean consumer electronics and handset manufacturer, has taken market-leading positions in a number of consumer categories, even though its products can cost more than a local branded product.

In an example of aspirational products in education, V. K. Bansal, an unemployed engineer with a passion for science and a need for money, decided to start tutoring young men for the entrance exam to the Indian Institutes of Technology in the early 1990s. He began with a small group of six in Kota, a medium-sized industrial city in the northwestern state of Rajasthan. Five out of the six earned a good rank on the exam, and very quickly Bansal's fame started growing. Slowly the numbers increased, from six to sixty and then six hundred students. Bansal Classes became renowned in nearby cities and soon all over India. Over a fifteen-year period, the program grew to more than five thousand students, and imitators started similar training academies. Kota now provides more than 25 percent of enrollment in the Indian Institutes of Technology (IIT), drawing test preparation candidates from as far as fifteen hundred miles away. Students now must take entrance exams to get into the top-rated preparatory classes. Middle-class parents who send their children to Bansal Classes (and others) and to live away from home for as long as two years dream about an engineer in the family.

As the third and final strategy, every product must have perfect *safety, reliability,* and *quality assurance.* Once poor, but now better educated and relatively well off, these new consumers will not tolerate shoddy products. They want to buy products that will stand the test of time. This is a large contributor to their preference for branded products: a good name is a guarantor of quality. The quickest way to a rapid market decline is to provide consumers with low-quality, unreliable, inconsistent, or health-threatening products.

The revolutionary middle class—320 million newly affluent households by 2020—represents the core growth market in China and India. Without them, there is no $10 trillion prize. They are consumers with incredibly high aspirations, irrepressible energy, and great confidence in themselves and in their children's future. There have been "I want more" generations before— notably the postwar baby boomers in the United States and Europe. But the new consumers in China and India are an "I want more" generation the likes of which has never been seen before. Most started life experiencing poverty and deprivation, and they can recount the stories of their parents' or grandparents' suffering through famine, war, or political repression. Most were born in rural communities and migrated to cities, where they found factory or service jobs and received enough education to capitalize on lucky breaks. Today, they have critical mass, recent memory of hardship and denial, hunger for the back story about brands and goods, and low levels of debt.

Right now, Chinese consumers have more disposable income than Indians do. In India, where the families are large and women are not encouraged to work, consumers have less money in their pockets for goods and services. But in both countries, consumers are more vocal than ever before—going online to blog about their hopes, dreams, and fears. In a political setting, this is revolutionary, especially in China. But it is revolutionary in a commercial setting, too. These consumers really do want it all: aspirational products that offer comprehensive and advanced features at a value price.

Companies will need to do everything possible to satisfy the needs of these nearly one billion consumers and grab the first-mover advantage. The consumers are careful purchasing agents—open to buying better food, better housing, better education, better cars, and all the trappings of the middle class. Companies that listen to their hopes, dreams, and needs and respond with products that elevate and certify the consumer's taste can expect to win a disproportionate share of the prize, garnering loyalty, advocacy, market share, and profits.

THREE

The Boom of the Superrich

The Millionaires (and Billionaires)

How ambition, persistence, luck, and timing create
a significant population of wealthy consumers

I N 2001, FIFTY YEARS AFTER Mao's revolution and Gandhi's triumph, there were just five billionaires in the two most populous countries in the world (figure 3-1). Back then, China's only billionaire was Rong Yiren, an eighty-five-year-old descendant of Wuxi traders whose close relationship with China's top leaders became a platform upon which he built a business empire. Three of the four Indians on the *Forbes* 2001 list were self-made entrepreneurs whose fortunes were transformed after the end of British rule. The fourth hailed from an old business family.[1]

Azim Premji, aged fifty-six in 2001, turned Wipro, originally a palm oil company, into one of the world's largest information technology (IT) services companies; Dhirubhai Ambani, then aged sixty-nine, started Reliance Industries, India's largest conglomerate; and Shiv Nadar, fifty-six in 2001, cofounded HCL at the age of thirty-one, which became India's second-largest IT company.[2] Finally, Kumar Mangalam Birla, a youthful thirty-four in 2001, ran Aditya Birla Group, another conglomerate, after his father's untimely death in 1996 at the age of fifty-two.

That there were only a handful of ultrawealthy people in these two countries told the story of the economic stagnation and isolation of China and India in the decades prior to the 1990s. It demonstrated that the economic reforms then under way had yet to create opportunities for massive wealth

FIGURE 3-1

Number of billionaires by country, 2001 and 2011

There has been a significant rise in the number of billionaires in China and India over the last decade; developing countries took three of the top five spots in 2011.

	2001 Country	Number of billionaires		2011 Country	Number of billionaires
❶	U.S.	269	❶	U.S.	412
❷	Germany	28	❷	China	115
❸	Japan	28	❸	Russia	101
❹	Italy	17	❹	India	55
❺	Canada	16	❺	Germany	52
	Hong Kong	14		Hong Kong	36
	Russia	8		Japan	26
	India	4		Canada	24
	China	1		Italy	14

❌ Rank

Sources: 2011: "The World's Billionaires," *Forbes*, October 2011, http://www.forbes.com/lists/2011/10/billionaires_2011.html; 2001: "The World's Richest People," *Forbes*, June 21, 2001, http://www.forbes.com/2001/06/21/billionairesindex.html.
Note: Net worth values are from June 2001 and March 2011.

creation in the private sector. Only a dramatic upward surge in domestic consumption and a dramatic deepening of capital flows between these markets and the world would make this possible—and, in the 1990s, these had yet to occur.

But by 2011, there were at least 170 Chinese and Indian billionaires. According to *Forbes*, they were worth $477 billion. China accounted for 115 of the billionaires, behind only the United States with 412. But India's 55 billionaires were richer. Individually, they were worth, on average, $4.5 billion—$2 billion more than the Chinese billionaires. And some were rich beyond imagination. Two—Lakshmi Mittal and Mukesh Ambani, the son of Reliance Industries founder Dhirubhai Ambani—made the world's top-ten richest list. Only the United States—with Bill Gates, Warren Buffett, Larry Ellison, and Wal-Mart's Walton family—had more top-ten billionaires. The highest-ranking Chinese billionaire was Robin Li, the forty-two-year-old chief executive of Baidu, China's answer to Google. He was number 95.[3]

But this list represented only a snapshot in the rise of the billionaire class. Six months later, it looked very different. No sooner had Li been anointed China's richest man, with a fortune of $9.4 billion, than another entrepreneur, Liang Wengen, chairman of Sany Heavy Industry, the construction equipment manufacturer, rose to the top of the *Forbes* China's richest list, his wealth soaring as China's construction market boomed.

Moreover, the number of Chinese billionaires increased to 146. In other words, 31 billionaires were "created" in China between March and September—more than 1 per week.[4] Collectively worth $60 billion, the top ten built their fortunes by pursuing business opportunities in some of the high-growth sectors of China's rapidly diversifying domestic economy, including the Internet, real estate, retail and consumer goods, home appliances, pharmaceuticals, and manufacturing. In India, most of the top ten are leaders of conglomerates with interests in diverse sectors ranging from commodities such as aluminum, cement, petrochemicals, and steel to service businesses such as IT, construction, and financial services.

These billionaires and multimillionaires are not just statistics. They are men and women with ambition, drive, energy, and vision. Adi Godrej, chairman of the Godrej Group, is one of them. His company, as he puts it, is 114 years young—having started out as a lock manufacturer. Today, it is a conglomerate with a presence in fast-moving consumer goods and durables, chemicals, and real estate. He inherited a small household products company nearly forty years ago. Since then, he has grown the company from $25 million in sales to $3 billion today. Now aged sixty-nine, he is still ambitious for his company and his country. "Today, we have just annunciated what we call a ten-by-ten vision—ten times bigger in ten years," he calmly says. He believes in this vision and says it is possible because India is at a "tipping point"—providing unprecedented opportunities for massive wealth creation and fertile ground for entrepreneurs. "I don't look at it as an unachievable goal," he says. "But it's going to be tough, and it's going to need not only strong strategic thinking but also excellent execution."

Godrej expects to see the company grow its share of the personal care, hair care, and household products markets. "We have leadership positions in some of these categories, so that will help us grow strongly," he says. "And there are underpenetrated categories, so the opportunity to get nonusers to become users is strong in a country like India." He adds, "In fast-moving consumer goods, we are very competitive with any producer anywhere in the world. In consumer durables, I would say the Chinese probably have an advantage over us because of scale, size, and volume."

Adi Godrej reflects the best of the accelerator mind-set that we see in China and India: successful business leaders who clearly see significant growth opportunities ahead and who have a well-formed vision and a strategy for capturing it. They possess a confidence to invest and to act—knowing that the markets are booming around them and that their own actions can spur the growth of the markets.

Many entrepreneurs in China see similar opportunities and have been busily building empires—while also envisioning more substantial growth ahead. One is Zhang Yue, founder and chairman of Broad Air Conditioning (Broad Group). This engineering company is headquartered on the outskirts of Changsha, a city of seven million where he was born fifty-one years ago. Zhang, with a fortune estimated at $780 million, has become a crusader against pollution and the emission of greenhouse gases. The company motto is "Champion of Earth."[5]

The corporate campus is called Broad Town. White-collar workers wear blue blazers, while factory workers wear blue uniforms and get free food (grown on company-operated organic farms and fishponds) and housing. Slogans designed to inspire the workforce are spread around the campus and include quotes from Winston Churchill, Abraham Lincoln, and Martin Luther King Jr.

Zhang, who trained as an artist and interior designer, has steered his company toward sustainable development. It is one of the leading manufacturers of air conditioners, and the nonelectric coolers use lithium bromide and natural gas. The company claims that the units are twice as effective as conventional air conditioners and yet have just one-quarter of the carbon dioxide emissions. One of his most recent innovations is the Broad sustainable building, or BSB for short. The BSB is an energy-efficient system for designing and assembling prefabricated buildings strong enough to withstand earthquakes. It took one of his teams just six days to fully construct a fifteen-story hotel; the video of this stunning demonstration of building prowess is on YouTube.[6]

We estimate that there were nearly four hundred ultrawealthy households—those with more than $100 million—in China in 2010. That put it eighth in the world ranking. The year before, it was thirteenth. If we add

Hong Kong's ultrawealthy residents to the list, China would surge into the world's top five, ahead of Russia and just behind the United Kingdom.[7]

Below this select group, there is a burgeoning number of millionaires. China boasted more than 1 million millionaire households in 2010, behind Japan's 1.5 million and the 5.2 million in the United States. The year before, China had recorded just 670,000 such households. India, ranked eleventh in the world, has 190,000 millionaire households.[8] Some of these will soon reach the billionaire threshold.

The key to success for many of these people has been working out how to serve the new domestic markets, while at the same time managing government stakeholders for necessary support. Robin Li's Baidu figured out how to overcome the challenges of developing a Chinese-language search capability and serving advertisers while ensuring a position as the government's preferred company in the Internet business. Likewise, Liang Wengen's Sany figured out how to deliver an ever-higher-quality range of construction equipment in a highly competitive market while ensuring sufficient government sponsorship in a sector where state-owned companies are the major buyers.

In each case, the business leaders secured positions on the crest of massive waves of growth: the Internet user base zoomed from tens of millions in 2000 to nearly five hundred million by 2011, and the construction sector has grown by 30 percent a year for a decade. Then, they turned to overseas stock markets to translate the sweat equity of their Chinese domestic businesses into globally tradable hard currency. The listing of Baidu on NASDAQ and Sany Heavy on the Hong Kong Stock Exchange created shares traded outside China in foreign currency, transforming the two founders into U.S. dollar billionaires on the world stage.

In India, the top wealth creators have a diversified set of businesses. Some of these, such as Nandan Nilekani, have decided to give something back to their country, taking on public-service jobs at no pay.

Nandan Nilekani: From Global Entrepreneur to Best-Selling Author to Public Servant

Nandan Nilekani is a man of the world. For thirty years, he was the public face of tech giant Infosys. He traveled the globe convincing companies that Indian engineers could deliver world-class programming at much lower prices. As the company moved from a start-up in 1981 to a global competitor with a market cap of nearly $30 billion, he served as chief operating officer and later CEO. Nilekani is also the author of *Imagining India*—a sweeping best seller that chronicles India's dynastic past, complicated present, and hopes for a bright future.

He is now an unpaid public servant and the mastermind behind a scheme to give every one of India's citizens an official identity. Three years ago, he began the third chapter of his life when he was asked by India's prime minister to create a unique identifier, a cutting-edge biometric identity system for all 1.2 billion Indians. This identity system is described in Nilekani's book and is his brainchild. He says his intention is to provide access to financial services, health care, government assistance, and education to the hundreds of millions who live an identity-free life—migrants in Indian society and the left-behinds. If successful, the system will also reduce corruption. A numeric identity will enable the poor and uneducated to open a bank account; obtain a passport; receive government-assisted wheat, rice, and oil rations; and directly participate in government minimum-income labor programs.

Nilekani was born in Bangalore, the son of a mill manager. In his town, there was no prep school for the IIT entrance exam. But he was convinced, like many of his peers, that engineering was a ticket to a good job. He still beams when he speaks of being ranked number 127 nationally on the admissions test and being able to graduate from IIT Bombay in 1978. He describes IIT as the defining break in his life. A cofounder of Infosys, he helped to take the company public on the NASDAQ stock exchange, a move that created great wealth for the cofounders and many employees.

"I succeeded beyond my wildest dreams," Nilekani told us, as he sat in the New Delhi office where he is chairman of the Unique Identity Authority of India. This office is a step down from the lavish headquarters of Infosys, where he enjoyed a breathtaking view of a beautifully landscaped campus built to celebrate the company's achievement and stature. Outside the present building, two dozen street vendors were aggressively soliciting Delhi's citizens to buy a winter coat on the coldest January day in recent history.

Nilekani is a rule breaker and a commanding presence in India. While many of his contemporaries left IIT for Silicon Valley, he chose to create an Indian powerhouse. "Creating a company here in India and creating jobs was more fulfilling for me," he says. "When we started Infosys, we believed software was a major play for India. We knew we had human capital and a global market. I knew it was going to happen. I was more confident as a young man. It was the arrogance of youth."

He says that running the sprawling global Infosys business is simple in comparison with public policy and running a new government agency. "In a company, you just need to convince yourself, a few of your colleagues, and your board—and then you make it happen," he says. "In India, we live in a diverse society. Everyone has an opinion and everyone voices it. You have to work to create consensus."

So far, the Identity Authority has enrolled 170 million people and is adding a million people a day across twenty thousand locations. "We hope to achieve a level of accountability and transparency," Nilekani says. "We will use the identification system to deliver services to millions of people. We know there will be many benefits to the people—they will get food rations, better health care, and education."

Nilekani is an inspiring communicator. Each of his sentences is delivered with animated imagery and quiet confidence. "The politicians are supportive because the people are supportive. The system opens doors for them. It is part of an inclusive society," he explains. "It will help bring money out of mattresses and bring productive capital to the market. But we have many more stakeholders—politicians, media, the judiciary, activists—a diverse and interested population. They all must be enrolled."

He continues, "We have been successful so far because Indians have had positive experiences from technology. They see how it has opened up markets to them. Indians have found technology liberating. The key to success in India is the same as the key to success anywhere. You need a purpose, a vision, and a tenacity to get things done. You need to overcome obstacles."

He says that while he pays close attention to the opinion of others, he is resolute in his mission. "The cacophony in India is high. It is a part of our lives and our historical roots," he says. "If you are in a position of leadership, you need to filter the noise from reality. Hyperindividualism is definitively Indian."

Nilekani remains a strong India booster. He sees his country as bringing four key advantages to the world stage: the globe's largest young, ambitious population; a culture of entrepreneurs; English as a common second language and ease of communication in global markets; and an ability to use diversity as a means to better problem-solving and integration. He believes that no single country can grow in a no-growth world, but he is confident that India will prosper over the next decade.

"We need to leverage the aspirations of the people," he says. "The speed of change is dizzying. We need to overcome government bureaucracy and boost development. We need to create a healthy and educated population, and we need a better, faster legal system. We need to build a platform to unleash the aspirations of the people. The biggest risk is not doing enough things fast enough. Our young population can get old and angry fast. Over the next ten years, we need to lay the foundation for better platforms."

He contrasts India and China by saying that each can learn something from the other. "The issue is bottom up versus top down. India is a bottom-up culture. China can get a road built in a week. It is a country that has had central command for a thousand-plus years. You need a minimum sustainable top-down approach for a bottom-up culture to work. Being exclusively bottom up is chaos. Being exclusively top down wipes out creativity and a spirit of independence."

Many of China's and India's billionaires have created new corporate empires and vast new fortunes. Between 2005 and 2010, the total market capitalization of stocks listed on the Shanghai Stock Exchange Index rose by 144 percent, and the Bombay Stock Exchange Index grew by 143 percent. By contrast, the London Stock Exchange rose by only 5 percent, and the Tokyo and New York Stock Exchanges actually fell by 21 percent and 6 percent, respectively.[9]

This buoyant stock market has also produced increasingly large numbers of wealthy individuals and families—large enough that they now constitute a major portion of the economy and represent important but diverse target markets. Understanding these broader segments of wealthy Chinese and Indians is essential for companies seeking to grow in these countries. We explore these groups in turn.

China's Superrich: The New Millennium Millionaires

In our work with China's superrich, we have identified some important features of this fast-expanding group: they are young, new to their wealth, and spread out across China.

In 2010, according to our research, most of China's nouveaux riches—people with more than $250,000 of annual income—had made their financial moves in the previous five years. About 70 percent of the 700,000 in this upper echelon, a half-million households, were not superrich in 2005. And the trend will continue: we expect another 800,000 households to join this rarefied group by 2015.

Another characteristic of this group is its relative youth. A striking 80 percent of China's rich are less than forty-five years old. By contrast, only 30 percent of wealthy people in the United States have not yet reached their midforties.[10] It goes to show that in a fast-growing market, it is relatively easy to turn an idea into a business and a business into a small fortune.

China's billionaires are a bit older than the rest of China's superrich—it takes a little longer to make the first billion. Of the top ten Chinese billionaires in 2011, only Robin Li and Ma Huateng, thirty-nine and founder of Tencent, the world's third-largest Internet company, were under forty-five. Even so, they are still relatively young.

A third common characteristic is that the wealthy are popping up across China, not just in a few locations. For example, the billionaires hail from forty-nine Chinese cities.[11] According to our research, Guangdong province boasts the highest number of rich households: 18 percent of the total. Shanghai, which is China's wealthiest city, has 12 percent. Further behind are the eastern coastal provinces of Zhejiang, Jiangsu, and Shandong, as well as Beijing; together these account for 28 percent of China's wealthy households. A further 30 percent were located in thirteen other tier 1 cities, and another 16 percent lived in twenty-three tier 2 cities.

As we will explain in chapter 5, the likely growth of the superrich population will take place in the cities that currently rank tier 3 or below—those with fewer than one million inhabitants. By 2015, we expect that 600,000 of the 1.5 million superrich households in China will be located in these smaller cities, compared with 200,000 in 2009.[12]

India's Superrich: The Rise of the Bollygarchs

Besides the billionaires, there is a small and growing superrich segment in India. This group can be divided into three subsegments.

First are the business families that are *old money*. These consumers have always been wealthy—though not at the billionaire level. Many of them are traditional and conservative in their social outlook—and they are comfortable with spending their money and displaying their wealth. One such consumer we talked to is Anjali. Born in 1969, she was raised in a traditional family and sent to an all-girls boarding school—as expected in those days. Her father, worth $11 million at the time, expected her to abide by the strict social norms and mores of the day.

To illustrate how her life has changed in the last twenty years, she takes the example of the apparel that she wears every day. When she won a coveted place at the best local college, she was still required to live at home and wear saris rather than jeans and a T-shirt. "Western clothes were off-limits," she says, "and we didn't have the guts to rebel against the family." But from the late 1980s onward, the restrictions started to ease. "As society started to get more Westernized, it became more acceptable to wear Western-style clothing," Anjali recalls. She gained a further measure of independence when she married a wealthy pharmaceuticals entrepreneur. "By this time, I was able to make my own decisions, and I didn't want to wear just Indian clothing anymore."

Today, she still wears clothes by some Indian designers, such as Vivek Narang and Bina Modi, as well as footwear from Joy Shoes, a Mumbai-based store (located opposite the Louis Vuitton store at the Taj Mahal Hotel) favored by Bollywood divas. But she has also seized the moment to buy big-name international luxury brands on shopping trips to Dubai and Fifth Avenue and Oxford Street. Her wardrobe now features clothes from Burberry and Shanghai Tang. In her choice of clothing, Anjali is an archetypal consumer from the upper echelon of the superrich consumer group. These consumers have money and they like to spend it—both in India and abroad. They are aware of brands—but pick and choose the brands with which they like to associate.

The second group is what we call the *educated rich*. These are typically professionals with a university degree who work in banking, private equity, professional services firms, and global multinational companies. Infosys alone has granted stock options worth $10 billion since its inception—creating hundreds of millionaires in the process. One of them is Chandra—an Infosys lifer. He joined Infosys nearly fifteen years ago after completing his engineering degree at the IIT in Delhi. He has lived around the world, and he is now back in Bangalore leading one of Infosys's distribution businesses.

For Chandra, who says his newfound wealth has been the natural product of his education and his effort, his top priorities have been a good house for his family, a nest egg for his retirement, and the best education for his children. He has earmarked about $1 million for his son's education in the United States (partly because he believes that the U.S. education system is the best and partly because he is not sure whether his son will be able to get into the ultracompetitive IIT system). Beyond this, he indulges in the best electronic gadgets, but only after a lot of research. For many other things—whether it is furniture or apparel—he and his wife favor functionality rather than global brands. In this, he is a typical "educated rich" Indian. Most grew up in middle-class homes and worked incredibly hard to achieve what they have today, so they are reluctant to consume conspicuously.

The third group consists of what we call the *emerging rich*. These people can be found in the top eight cities, but many also hail from tier 2 or emerging cities such as Coimbatore, Ludhiana, Surat, and Visakhapatnam. One of them is Nirlipt Singh (not his real name) from Ludhiana. Nirlipt has a successful midsized apparel export business—and he likes to display his wealth. He recently bought a BMW 7 series automobile and a Porsche. Alka, his wife, visits Dubai twice a year to buy her Gucci and Louis Vuitton bags. She has no interest in buying these items in India. As she told us, she finds the Emporio Mall in Delhi (which carries the same luxury brands) "a waste of time because it does not carry the latest collections and it is also more expensive."

The emerging rich are typically first-generation entrepreneurs who have set up small and medium-sized companies in manufacturing, services, or trade—and they have made it big as the economy has expanded. They travel widely and are influenced by what they see during their visits to Europe and the United States. They have high aspirations and are willing to buy international brands to announce to the world that they have arrived.

Implications for Business

China's and India's superrich will spend on modern houses, fast cars, complete luxury wardrobes, financial advisers, and servants to prepare their meals and clean their homes. They will travel, educate their children abroad, and, for the most part, live the dreams of the rich and soon-to-be-famous. A few will engage in social enterprise, helping their fellow compatriots (and the world) to achieve more.

They may be a small segment of the population, but the sheer number of millionaires in China and India and their rapid growth make them an important consumer market. As we will explain in chapter 9, China will soon be the world's top luxury market and India will soon achieve the critical mass of wealthy families necessary for a place on the global luxury map.

Serving these consumers requires a company to understand that they are not one homogeneous segment. To win, you must divide the groups into microsegments—and not just based on income. As we have shown, education, profession, and family background drive attitudes and behavior. It is also essential to develop the right go-to-market model—because large numbers of these consumers do not reside in the big cities. Successful segmentation models aggregate groups of consumers into targets that can be specifically addressed—with customized products, focused distribution, and advertising that is compelling and informing.

Moreover, you must stay true to the rules of new luxury consumption. Deliver the following, and the large China market and the emerging India market can be yours:

- Technical, functional, and emotional benefits

- Rich and graphic consumer targeting

- A continuous stream of innovation

- A deep and broad product line

- A communication strategy that engages the core consumers to just say *yes*

- A map of the needs and dissatisfactions of each segment and how to respond to them

- An environment that matches their need for exclusivity, privilege, and catering

- The back story of the brand, which defines the reason to believe

FOUR

The Next-but-One Billion
The Future of the Left-Behinds

The poor and the left-behind—why they should not be overlooked, and how
companies can serve them and create second and third waves of growth

IMAGINE *ALL* OF THE PEOPLE in the United States and Western Europe
living on less than $1.25 per day—about one-third the price of a large cap-
puccino from a coffee shop. It is hard to picture. Yet, at last count, there
were nearly 665 million people in China and India living below that poverty line: 455 million in India, or 38 percent of the population; and 208 million in China, or 16 percent of the population (figure 4-1). These are the *left-
behinds*—people who are extremely poor and disconnected from the rapid
prosperity of their countrymen. But over time, they will enjoy trickle-down
benefits as a by-product of economic growth in their countries, and because
of their sheer numbers, the multiplier effect of very modest income growth
will translate into markets worth hundreds of millions of dollars.

As you travel through China and India, you see two countries of
contrast—rich and poor, educated and illiterate, healthy and sick. Many of
the most impoverished are locked in a vicious cycle, with no money for safe
and nutritious food, proper housing, or medicines. In the case of India, where
there is limited access to birth control and a high fertility rate, many children
are born into poverty. With no funds for a proper education, they are forced
to work for a tiny cash income before the age of eight or nine. Right now,
many of these people have no way out, and no way to break the cycle.

FIGURE 4-1

Number of people living in poverty in China and India, 2010

Left-behinds still account for a large percentage of populations, particularly in India.

Country	Population living below the international poverty line (millions)		Population living below $1.25/day (%)
	<$1.25/day	<$2/day	
China	208	473	15.6
India	455	828	37.9

Sources: Central Intelligence Agency, *The CIA World Factbook 2010*, https://www.cia.gov/library/publications/download/download-2010/index.html; World Bank, World Development Indicators; United Nations Development Programme (UNDP), *Human Development Report 2009*; Japan Health, Labor and Welfare Ministry; BCG analysis.
Note: The international poverty line is adjusted for purchasing power parity measured in 2005 dollars.

Remarkably, over the next ten years, some of these people will rise to afford entry-level consumer goods, providing companies with second and third waves of growth. By 2020, some 200 million Chinese and 280 million Indians are expected to rise out of poverty. They will claw their way up from the bottom rung of the social ladder, taking any job that comes their way, saving a small amount, and receiving a small set of benefits from the government. This will still leave as many as 220 million in continued dire economic straits. But it will be progress.

The newly somewhat affluent will surge into the classes above, filling the new lower middle class with strong optimism and a voracious appetite for consumer goods. For the first time, they will appreciate the little joys of life—they will have a wide-eyed wonder about the technical and functional attributes of goods, and they will become brand advocates for products they like, spreading a positive message by word of mouth.

In 2010, by our calculation, there were 260 million Chinese households in the lower classes—those with annual incomes of less than $7,300. This amounted to 66 percent of households. By 2020, this number will have shrunk to 138 million, or 32 percent of households. Likewise, there were 152 million Indian households in the lower classes, amounting to 68 percent of households. By 2020, this number will have fallen to about 110 million, or 43 percent of households.[1]

But even those who are left behind over the next ten years should not be discounted as consumers. We are careful to distinguish between two types of lower classes: the truly poor who are often penniless and without hope, and the aspirant poor with real prospects for income improvement—the next billion. They have jobs and varying levels of education, but below-average incomes. In China, their annual income ranges from $4,800 to just over $7,000. In India, the scale ranges from $3,000 to $6,700 (taking into account the different purchasing power in different parts of the country).

As we will describe in this chapter, a few companies are fully engaging these consumers' hopes and dreams by actively developing customized products and services. The companies aim at entry-level price points and high quality. To do this, companies first find out how these consumers live, what they want, what their priorities are, and how to deliver fully to their expectations. Then, they construct distribution systems to put the products within arm's reach at the right price, create product development programs that deliver something at a predictable pentameter, and engage all types of media.

India's Next Billion Consumers

Sushil Kumar was a humble data operator from Bihar, a state in the northeast of India that borders Nepal, until the fateful day in November 2011 when he appeared on India's version of *Who Wants to Be a Millionaire* and, in a story reminiscent of the Oscar-winning film *Slumdog Millionaire*, won 50 million rupees, or about $1.1 million. It was a life-transforming moment. During the TV show, he earned (after taxes) what would have taken him some 487 years to earn on his annual salary of $1,460.[2]

But it is what he did next that speaks volumes about the new generation of consumers. Often, in the West, lottery winners, speaking amid the sound of champagne corks popping in celebration, announce their intention to go on a world cruise or buy a new car. But not Kumar. Instead, he unveiled his plan to repay his loans, build a home for his family, and prepare for his country's ultracompetitive civil service examinations.[3] In other words, he wanted to fulfill his dream of becoming a member of the respectable middle class.

Millions of others are experiencing transformative events in their lives—if on a much more modest scale—and working hard to do so. One is Bharat Kumar Patel, a thirty-three-year-old cotton farmer from a village near Mehsana, some forty miles north of Ahmedabad, the largest city in Gujarat.

Five years ago, Bharat produced *jowar*, a wheat-like grain, and *urad*, a kind of lentil. These grew well in Mehsana's climate, and Bharat found a ready market for his produce. Farming a five-acre plot of land with no tractor, Bharat relied on bulls to plow the field. It was hard, sweaty, menial work and delivered only a modest income of 50,000 rupees ($1,100) per year.

Then Bharat's village near Mehsana was connected to Gujarat's electricity supply, which gave farmers access to a ready supply of power to move water. For Bharat, this created a significant new opportunity. Suddenly, he was able to contemplate growing cotton—a more lucrative crop.

At the same time, he heard about a new type of cotton—Bt cotton, a genetically modified version designed by Monsanto, the U.S. agricultural company that has pioneered genetically modified seed for higher yield and greater resistance to pesticides. Cotton plants with the *Bacillus thuringiensis* (Bt) protein are toxic to insects and harmless to humans. The result is higher yields and less need for pesticides—reducing costs and increasing profits.

Near Bharat's home, Monsanto had developed a demonstration farm, and after one visit Bharat decided to shift his focus to cotton. It was a life-changing decision. The Bt cotton seeds allow him to generate five to seven times as much income as either *jowar* or *urad*. This, plus the rise in cotton prices, means that Bharat now earns 150,000 rupees ($3,300) per year, or three times his former income.

This increase has transformed his lifestyle. He lives on the same plot of land, but he has turned his home into a three-room *pucca* house, made with bricks and concrete. Gone are the mud-brick building and the thatched roof. Gone, too, is the outside toilet. "We renovated our house in the last six months," he says. "It cost us 200,000 rupees. This was expensive, but the house really looks good now."

Bharat, who is married with an eight-year-old son, has purchased a refrigerator, which he displays proudly in the living room, and a color TV. He watches two Hindi broadcasters, Zee TV and Star TV, but he also likes to watch the local Gujarati station.

The extra money has also allowed him to buy new clothes. He now goes to Mehsana every couple of months to buy them. Before, he would go once a year, if that. "I used to buy clothes from roadside stalls," he explains. "Now I go to a shop." His favorite clothing store is Vimal, an old Indian brand owned by the Reliance Group. He wears these garments when he travels to the local *mandi*, the marketplace where he sells his produce to local cotton traders.

If his clothes have improved, so, too, has his diet. Before, he rarely ate fresh fruit or vegetables and seldom bought any provisions for the week ahead. "We used to buy what we needed on a daily basis. Now we fill up our bags and store food grains in large quantities. We also keep a fifteen-kilo tin of oil."

No longer living hand to mouth, Bharat and his family can afford to go to Mehsana for day trips. "There we like to shop, eat out, and enjoy ourselves," he says, with the wide-eyed enthusiasm of someone for whom this is a new experience. "Sometimes, we even watch a movie."

Looking ahead, Bharat is optimistic. "I really dream of owning a tractor," he says. Now, having dispensed with bulls, he rents a tractor during the harvest time. If he owned a tractor, he could rent it out himself, earning even more income. He also wants his son, who studies at a local private Gujarati school, to go to college and, eventually, migrate to the city. "I'd like him to get a real job in the city someday."

These are big ambitions for someone who, five years ago, was a humble farmer without much of a future. And he knows it. "I don't worry too much in life," he says. "I am happy with what God has given me, and I really do believe that things will only get better with time."

Surplus income, technology, and careful capital investment are combining to raise the lot of many of the lowest-income Chinese and Indians. The resulting optimism is reflected in the attitudes and spending habits of the aspirant poor. As with the middle class, we divide the next-billion or aspirant poor into those in major cities and those in small towns or rural districts.

The second group—from small towns and rural areas—constitutes 24 percent of Indian households and accounts for a quarter of India's private consumption. The first, smaller group, the urban poor, constitutes 6 percent of households but accounts for 8 percent of the country's consumption.[4] In many ways, these urban dwellers are more optimistic and better off than the slightly wealthier consumers in the countryside.

As an example, 56 percent of the large-town next billion own basic durables, compared with 49 percent of the rural middle class. We have also found a difference in the ownership of more sophisticated products, such as bigger-screen color TVs, double-door refrigerators, digital cameras, and secondhand cars. Approximately 16 percent of the large-town next billion possess these more advanced durables, compared with just 13 percent of the rural middle class.

We have found that city dwellers have much greater access to and ability to use the Internet, a greater commitment to particular brands, and a greater financial maturity—taking out loans and utilizing mobile and Internet banking. Indeed, the promise of dramatic growth in financial services is coming to life, as consumers establish themselves as good credit risks and open their first savings accounts.

China's Next Billion Consumers

In China, there is a similarly distinctive group of aspirant consumers within the lower strata of society. These people constitute about one-fifth of all Chinese and well over a quarter of the people in the cities and towns.

As we described in chapter 2, we have observed a striking rise in consumers' willingness to buy products as their income rises above subsistence levels. Monitoring consumption patterns across hundreds of product categories, we have found that these consumers start to buy healthy products—such as juice, fresh food, yogurt, and vitamin supplements—as well as personal care products and the various accoutrements of modern life, including electrical appliances and more stylish, branded clothing with familiar and visible logos.

One such household is the Chen family from Chongqing, a municipality of thirty-two million people that lies on the Yangtze River in the hot and humid heart of the country. This great city was the provisional capital of Chiang Kai-shek during the Sino-Japanese War in the 1930s and 1940s, and it was during this time that it earned the epithet "City of Heroes." The city was also the home for Bo Xilai, the once-rising star of the Chinese Communist Party. Today, its fortunes, which were boosted by the opening of the controversial Three Gorges Dam, rest on its position as a major manufacturing and transportation hub.

Chen Ronghui, a thirty-three-year-old beauty shop assistant, and her husband, a salesman, have a combined annual income of $5,280. In the past five years, they have seen a striking improvement in their standard of living. Five years ago, they were earning a little over $3,000, having just moved to the city from Changshou, fifty miles from the center of Chongqing. Living in a cheap dormitory and paying $29 in monthly rent, they struggled to pay for goods at the local market and had very little, if any, surplus income for recreational activities or entertainment. But as their salaries have increased, they have been able to put a largely subsistence life behind them.

First, they bought their own apartment for the princely sum of $24,190, taking out a mortgage that costs them $90 per month, three times the rent of their old dormitory. For the down payment, they turned to family, extended family, and friends.

Second, they started to shop in fancier locations, buying their groceries from Yonghui, a local chain of superstores that specialize in fresh produce bought directly from farmers. Founded in 1995, headquartered in Fujian on China's southeast coast, and listed on the Shanghai Stock Exchange, Yonghui now operates more than 180 stores modeled on Western-style supermarkets with their service-oriented culture.

Third, the couple invested in some household goods for their new apartment, mainly selecting affordable Chinese-branded products. They have a color television by Konka, one of the best-known national brands in the country; a refrigerator by Wuxi Little Swan, another renowned company that won a Reader's Digest "trustworthy brand" award; and a laptop from Lenovo, which bought IBM's personal computer business.[5] The only foreign-branded product is a washing machine from Whirlpool, a U.S. corporation. The washing machine is made in a factory in Zhejiang. However, this is part of a joint venture with Hisense Kelon, a major Chinese white goods company.

The couple have not altogether left their troubles behind them. They fear getting ill, as they would not be able to afford the medical bills. They also still feel like outsiders. As Ronghui says, "We grew up in the countryside, and it seems that we are, by nature, country folk." They could apply for a *hukou*—a residential license that would give them more privileges in Chongqing—but it would mean giving up their small plot of land in Changshou. They do not want to do this, just in case things do not work out and the cost of living becomes too high.

Yet, for all this uncertainty, life is good. "Although we feel some pressure," she says, "we still think the future will get better." They have plans to start a business, and over the next five years they expect their income to double to more than $12,000, which would put them firmly in the middle class.

"I dream that my son can go to a great school, that I can have a decent career, and that we can live a better life." With the extra income, they expect to be able to move into a larger apartment with a study for their nine-year-old son, upgrade their electrical goods to more international brands, and buy an automobile.

These are big goals. They reflect a view that we heard over and over:

- "My life will be better."

- "We will earn more money."

- "Wages will increase."

- "I won't be able to afford *everything* ... but I will get a better home, better food, provide education for my family."

- "My hard work and effort will pay off."

Such optimism stands in sharp contrast to the plight of the trapped poor in China and India who have been left out and left behind by the march of the two countries.

China's Left-Behinds: The Marginalized Migrants

Changhua Zhang and his wife, Chen Suqin, wait to catch the train back to their ancestral village so that they can celebrate the Chinese New Year with their children. It seems that everyone is on the move, and tickets are a treasured commodity. Day after day, they wait patiently at the station in Guangzhou, the country's third-largest city, which sits on the banks of the Pearl River some seventy-five miles northwest of Hong Kong. Each morning, they hope that they will get a coveted ticket, but as the afternoon wears on, they sense disappointment, and by the evening, they are disheartened, having lost out yet again in the rush for the few unsold tickets. Their faces show the agony of disappointment and the countdown to the day when it will be too late to go home—when the holiday is over.

After five days, their luck turns, their patience is rewarded, and they join the crowded train and the biggest annual migration of human beings on earth. It is, however, a bittersweet moment. The train is overloaded, the cabins are cramped, and the long journey home is slow and tedious.

This story, told in *Last Train Home*, a moving documentary about the plight of the poor migratory worker in China, is an all-too-common one.[6] Once a year, many of the 150 million rural migrant workers return to their homesteads in the countryside to celebrate Chinese New Year with their families. It is as if the whole of Russia were to leave home and go on a journey—all in the space of two days.

The need to provide for their families has forced many rural parents to go to the cities in search of employment. Often, they do not see their loved ones for a whole year at a time. Changhua and Chen work in a garment factory making jeans for "big and tall" Americans at piece-rate wages—the more hours they put in, the more money they earn. It is still not enough to pay for a guaranteed seat on the train, which is why they have to endure the uncertainty of waiting for tickets. They eventually make it home, where they have left their two children with the children's grandmother. Full of resentment and anger, Qin, their teenage daughter, greets them with disapproval. She is upset by their long absences—even though her parents are working in the sweatshops of a distant city in order to give her better prospects in life. She argues with her father, and the two shout angrily at each other. It is a painful tale of personal sacrifice, alienation, isolation, and a life of toil with no window for escape.

The irony is that these migrant workers power China's urban economy. Without them, China would not have become the world's manufacturing hub. Yet while they constitute one-third of the urban population, they are not participants in city life in any meaningful way. They are forced to live in company dormitories or temporary housing on building sites or, if they are less fortunate, share a dingy room in one of the shantytowns. They struggle on average wages of around RMB 1,800 ($430) per month—28 percent less than the typical salary of an aspirant poor worker in China.

In the near term, there is little prospect of this changing. The divisions in China's urban community are entrenched by the local system of registration known as a *hukou*. As we saw in Chen's story, this is, in effect, a kind of internal passport, and it limits people's freedom to settle somewhere other than where they were born.

In 2010, four in every ten city dwellers had no local registration. Consequently, they did not have access to local health care or social security, and they did not have the right to educate their children in local schools. This was why Changhua and Chen had to leave the children with their grandmother.

But the Chinese government, keen to promote social harmony, has made urbanization the centerpiece of its twelfth five-year plan, which runs from 2011 to 2015. It is also encouraging employment in central and western China, the home of two-thirds of Chinese migrant workers. The purpose is to persuade workers to live in the local towns and low-tier cities. Foxconn, a Taiwan-based company and the world's largest manufacturer of electronic components, has established a recruitment booth at the train station in Zhengzhou to tempt local workers to stay rather than leave for the factories on the prosperous eastern seaboard. In time, these migrant workers will need to be able to settle in the cities, so that they, and the broader Chinese economy, can reap the benefits of their potential.

India's Left-Behinds: The Story of Sahabpur

Ghulam does not know his own age. He thinks he is around forty years old. He looks older, perhaps fifty or fifty-five. But he does not really dwell on the past. For him, and his family, life is a struggle. He takes each day as it comes.

He lives in Sahabpur, a village of about five thousand inhabitants that is located three miles from the four-lane highway to Lucknow, the capital of Uttar Pradesh. Most people are farmers, producing rice and wheat. A few are artisans. But Ghulam is neither. He spins and dyes cloth, using his only substantial possession: a spinning wheel (worth less than $40).

If this conjures up images of a rural idyll and the memory of Mahatma Gandhi, it shouldn't. Ghulam endures a grim, hopeless, downtrodden existence very far from the gleaming cities with their rising middle class.

He lives in a small brick structure originally earmarked as the village's public toilet. "We were not doing well," he told us, sitting meekly on the floor and almost whispering his words. "But the village headman understood our problem and allowed us to stay here."

Ghulam's work is intermittent, and he typically receives about 110 rupees ($2.42) a day for his services. All told, he earns around 40,000 rupees ($900) per year—a pitifully low income and not enough to feed his large family. He has nine children between one and sixteen years old. His wife has been almost constantly pregnant for the past decade and a half. She is a picture of frailty, thin and emaciated. She wears no jewelry, and the only makeup she wears is a small red *bindi* on her forehead. Even though the family is Muslim and the *bindi* is Hindu in origin (it is worn in the middle of the forehead on the *ajna*—the sixth chakra, which is supposed to be the exit point for *kundalini* energy), many Muslims in the South Asian subcontinent wear it, partly for good luck and partly for decoration.

Two of Ghulam's teenage children help to supplement the household income, working in the cloth-dyeing trade and bringing in an extra 30 to 40 rupees (less than $1) per day. Four of the others do odd jobs, too, although they are not paid. None of the children attend school, even though the village has a small government primary school. "We don't have money for their education, but at least by working they can help with the upkeep of the household," says Ghulam.

Nor is there enough money to pay for his wife's medicines. Her multiple pregnancies, plus the family's meager diet, are taking their toll on her health. Severely anemic, she suffers agonizing pain from the waist down. The village doctor prescribed a month-long course of pills, but Ghulam could only afford enough for four days. "These cost me 75 rupees, and the four days went like that," he explains, clicking his fingers to show how three-quarters of his daily income seemed to disappear in an instant.

As an act of goodwill, the doctor passed along some free sample pills that he receives from the pharmaceutical company. Ghulam also found some extra work, just to be able to buy a few more pills. Even then, it was still not sufficient for her to recover from her chronic illness. "If I had the money, I would have bought all the pills in one go, and she could have benefited from that."

The only things that Ghulam buys are food and clothing—the fundamentals of a subsistence life. His "home," better described as a shelter, is rent-free. Most of his children sleep outside, on coarse matting. Only the youngest children sleep with a roof over their heads. There are no furnishings. Other than the spinning wheel, Ghulam owns only some cooking utensils and the clothes on his back. There is no oven. When his wife cooks, she goes in search of firewood, returning to make a meal of *roti*—an unleavened bread—and a mixture of grains, pulses, and potatoes bought from a street vendor. If she is lucky, and the price has fallen, she will purchase onions to flavor the food. But this does not happen very often.

If there is any silver lining in this bleak story, it is that Ghulam does get some support from the government, thanks to his friendship with the village headman, or *panch*. A fellow Muslim, the headman not only found him a shelter but also secured him a BPL card, short for "below poverty line." It is a much-sought-after card among India's poorest citizens. Not everyone gets one. One of Ghulam's neighbors, a Hindu casual laborer who earns half as much as Ghulam does, has only an APL, or "above poverty line," card.

The Gram Panchayat, the ruling body of a village, led by the *panch*, decides and certifies who gets a BPL card. With a BPL card, Ghulam is entitled to two types of benefits. One is preferential treatment when it comes to getting a job through the government employment scheme. Under the Mahatma Gandhi National Rural Employment Guarantee Act, registered individuals are guaranteed one hundred days of employment at 120 rupees ($2.60) a day. Ghulam does not participate, because he knows that local officials siphon off a significant percentage of the money. He describes it as a tax. He has concluded that it is better to work as an independent agent than as a government-registered employee.

The second benefit is access to heavily subsidized grains, sugar, and kerosene. This benefit he does use, and it makes a difference. Even so, he is apprehensive about the future. "I have a lot of worries," he says. "I think that if only someone gave me work, I could make some money and move ahead. I hope for this in my heart."

With little to look forward to, Ghulam peppers his conversation, which is halting and largely monosyllabic, with a Hindustani phrase: *Allah ki marzi hai*, or "That is God's will." He accepts his fate. There are millions of other Indians with the same mental model of acceptance and resignation.

Most of these people reside in rural districts, but many others suffer a bleak existence in city slums. One of the worst slums is Dharavi, in the very heart of Mumbai, India's commercial capital. Half of the city's population—roughly thirteen million people, as many as live in London—squeeze into the city's slums. About one million of these people live in Dharavi, the location for *Slumdog Millionaire*.

The stench, emanating from open sewers and steaming garbage dumps, is hard to escape. The electricity is intermittent, a few televisions glimmer in the dark, and a few people carry mobile phones—but in so many ways Dharavi is reminiscent of a Dickensian scene. Trade exists, with estimates suggesting that there are ten thousand small businesses with gross domestic product in excess of $600 million.[7] But when compared with the people living in the gated communities rising up across Mumbai, the slum dwellers might as well be living on a different planet.

Implications for Business

On the face of it, the left-behinds, even those classified as aspirant poor, are not a tempting prospect as potential customers. Yet they should not be overlooked.

In our work, we have identified several key strategies for tackling this group of largely untapped consumers. These include creating what we call *fit-to-constraint products* with the right price; developing ubiquitous distribution; promoting educational and advocacy marketing; investing time in creative collaboration and partnerships; and capitalizing on government regulations. Given the challenging market environments, it is important to test and pilot these strategies before scaling up.

1. *Create fit-to-constraint products for different price points.* Marico, the Indian beauty and wellness company, has shown how to do this. Renowned for products based on coconut oil, the company has shrunk the size of the products so that it can sell to the bottom of the pyramid. For instance, Parachute, its popular shampoo, can now be bought in four-milliliter blister packs instead of the traditional hundred-milliliter (a little over three fluid ounces) bottles. Meanwhile, in China, Procter & Gamble has also developed an approach for the $2-a-day consumer in an effort to find the fortune at the bottom of the pyramid. A bottle of Rejoice, its cheapest shampoo, costs RMB 9.9 ($1.50). For some families, it marks a step up from using laundry soap flakes, which leave hair lank and greasy. "It's a myth to say poor people want only function," says one of P&G's top scientists, working at the company's $70 million R&D facility in Beijing. "They care about beauty—just like everyone else."[8]

2. *Develop ubiquitous distribution and reach.* In other words, you need to go to the customer. That means having myriad points of sale and distribution. Hindustan Unilever is one company that has done this well. In an effort to reach millions of rural Indians, it devised the so-called Shakti Entrepreneurial Program, drawing on the Hindi word for "power." Its purpose is to help the very poor set up small businesses as direct-to-consumer retailers and, in the process, create new markets for its products among the large group of low-spending consumers. It is a kind of Amway for rural India.[9]

Initially, Hindustan Unilever mapped every village in the country. The goal was to reach small, scattered settlements with next-to-no infrastructure. In doing so, it calculated that some 630,000 villages had no direct way of getting its products—and, with nearly five hundred million people without a TV, there was no easy way to ensure mass promotion. The company then launched the Shakti program with the aim of reaching these new consumers. It was a bold move. When asked what he was most proud of, Nitin Paranjape, CEO of Hindustan Unilever, told us, "I am proud of what we have been able to achieve in Project Shakti. We have reached the real rural India through this effort—villages with less than two thousand in population. We have forty-five thousand Shakti Ammas (women) and twenty-five thousand Shaktimaan (men) who reach millions of new consumers directly. But more than the reach and access, it is what we have been able to achieve in terms of income and employment generation, which is most remarkable. They earn between 800 and 2,500 rupees [$18 and $55] per month." Hindustan Unilever now has a new market for a range of products, including Pureit, a water purifier; Wheel, a detergent; Brooke Bond tea; Lux and Lifebuoy soaps; and Sunsilk shampoo. Indeed, it has seen its business grow by 10 percent, thanks to the program and its efforts to penetrate the lowest class.

3. *Promote educational and advocacy marketing.* Hindustan Unilever's Shakti Ammas and Shaktimaan have been critical not only to ensure the physical distribution to rural areas but also to educate the five hundred million who had not been exposed to many of these products and had limited access to mass media. Godrej, too, has used this strategy to great effect. Its unique refrigerator Chotukool (literally, "small cool"), priced at $60, was developed for the next-billion market, recognizing the constraints of small, cramped houses; low affordability; and irregular electricity supply. It is not sold through mainstream channels but through small entrepreneurs and nongovernmental organizations (NGOs) that can explain the benefits to first-time users.

4. *Invest in creative partnerships.* Godrej's Chotukool could not have been built alone. Its creation was made possible by collaboration with a U.S.-based company that has codeveloped the cooling

technology (without using compressors), with NGOs for marketing, ˎ and even with India Post, which runs the largest postal network in the world and which has started retailing the tiny refrigerator. As Jamshyd Godrej, chairman of Godrej & Boyce, told us, "Chotukool is something we have developed through a small separate team of three or four that focused on disruptive innovation. We believed that it was possible to address this segment, and we cocreated this refrigerator, observing the requirements of the segment very closely and testing and retesting what worked in the field." The Chotukool mini-refrigerator is aimed at the 70 percent of Indian consumers who have no refrigeration at home.

5. *Understand and respond to government regulations.* The poor are a top priority for the Chinese and Indian governments as they endeavor to promote greater social harmony, and countless initiatives and subsidies are designed to alleviate the worst problems—especially those relating to health. For example, in China, there is a project to promote iron-fortified soy sauce to counter the prevalence of anemia among the poor. In India, one government program promotes the use of iodized salt in food in order to tackle health problems such as goiter.

These and other government programs are unleashing more consumers new to branded products. We estimate that these consumers will spend $160 billion more than current levels over the next ten years in China, while the new entrants to the lower middle class in India will spend $75 billion more over the same period. These fast-growing markets are too large to be left behind.

FIVE

Finding the New Consumer
The Urban Centers and Rural Communities

Where to look for the newly affluent consumers, why smaller cities will turn out to be even more promising than the big cities, and how to prosper from the infrastructure and agricultural revolutions that will drive incomes and service availability up

I F YOU GO TO SHUNHEZHUANG, a two-hour drive from Beijing, near Gao-beidian, you will find a small village. Its population is about a thousand. Farms are small—about an acre or less. The farmers typically plant wheat and corn, rotating them on an annual basis.

Deep in the northeastern province of Hebei, this corner of China is no rural idyll. The summers are hot and humid, and the winters are harsh. There are next to no wild animals, and birdsong is a rarity. Dust storms have destroyed crops and swept away the already-thin topsoil. It does not help that decades of environmental neglect have denuded the land. A tall, mature tree planted in the 1970s is almost unheard-of. Most trees have been cut down in the past for firewood and building materials and to clear farmland.

Yet the villagers have undergone a radical transformation over the past twenty years. In the 1980s, and even the early 1990s, rural life focused on farming, and it was a hard existence: most people were grindingly poor and lacked basic amenities, including decent schools and health care, paved roads, and a reliable power supply.

Fast-forward two decades, and life is much better. Nearly everyone has access to electricity, about 95 percent of towns and 80 percent of villages have paved roads, and some 96 percent have access to basic health care. Incomes remain low, relative to those in the city: average disposable income per person amounts to RMB 5,000 ($760), which is about one-fifth of the income in tier 1 cities. On the other hand, incomes are on the rise. In 2005, average income was $407. Four years later, it was $845—a 20 percent compound annual growth rate. And while only 34 percent of the rural population earned more than $882 per year in 2009, this proportion is expected to reach 54 percent in 2015.

The big reason for this improvement in living standards is the diversification of employment. If it was once all about farming, now it is a great deal more: forestry, fishing, construction, and the production of bricks and cement. The improvement in living standards is expected to continue as the Chinese government undertakes a substantial and sustained effort to reinvest in the rural communities—to promote growth and social harmony.

In Shunhezhuang, only 20 percent of the villagers' income is derived from farming. Another 30 percent comes from the wages of people working in the factories of nearby towns and cities, and a full 50 percent comes from local businesses. Since 2007, when we first started visiting this village, farming has declined significantly, and yet the average income has risen by 74 percent.

Not all of the growth is attributable to this trend away from agricultural work. The price of corn has risen, helping to boost income. Also, greater investment in irrigation and the use of fertilizer have helped increase productivity and profits by 40 percent. But the development of other sources of income has been the single biggest factor. Over the past ten years, average daily wages for a factory worker in nearby Gaobeidian have tripled from RMB 30 (less than $5) a day to RMB 90 (nearly $14) a day. The village head told us, "Everyone can live a good life as long as he or she is willing to work."

WX Liu is a typical resident. She was born in 1953 and was a child during the epic famines of 1959 to 1961. She is literate, although she had only three years of primary education. Her life has been a long, hard struggle. She has short cropped hair and a preference for blue work clothes, and her hands are calloused and muscular—a reflection of her working in the field for as long as she can remember, learning how to farm on her parents' small plot of land.

Since 2000, her family has seen a sixfold increase in its income—thanks to her hard work, good corn profits, and the growing contribution of her children. She lives with her husband, whom she met when he moved to the village, her son and daughter-in-law, and her granddaughter. Her son, who works in a local factory, and his wife, who works in a gas station, contribute more than two-thirds of the family income.

Liu's life is busy. She starts the day at 6 a.m., preparing the family breakfast. She then goes shopping, works in the field, does some babysitting, prepares the main family meal when they return from work, and only starts to wind down for the day at around 9 p.m. This is a round-the-clock existence, and the time in the field is not well rewarded. Farming wheat and corn is a low-margin business. She says wheat returns only RMB 660 ($100) in annual profit, after accounting for the costs of seeds, fertilizer, irrigation, pesticides, and reaping (figure 5-1). Corn is more profitable, yielding nearly RMB 3,000 ($450) in profit per season as a result of higher market prices, with similar input costs. We calculate that the profit per hour of labor on the one-acre farm is roughly RMB 1 to 1.25, or $0.15 to $0.20 per hour.

Despite her hard life, Liu is very good-natured and smiles during most of the time we talk with her. Her responses to our questions come in short, animated sentences. She is grateful for the changes in her life, particularly her new home, her new kitchen, and her courtyard. Liu would like to advance further economically and is ambitious for her grandchild to have access to the things she did not. She has sometimes pondered diversifying into other crops—especially vegetables—which have the potential for higher profit, but because she has no experience with these alternatives, she does not want to take the risk. She explains, "I have heard that some people are growing peanuts and vegetables now, but I don't know how to grow them … and I don't know where to sell them, either. So I'm carrying on growing wheat and corn."

If her family were dependent on the farm business, they would not have seen much of an increase in their income over the past five years and they would not have been able to afford her pride and joy: her new house. Back in 2009, she decided that the family needed to move into a new house with more modern amenities. She borrowed money from friends and relatives and set about designing the house: its construction, its size, and its furnishings.

FIGURE 5-1

Corn provides the bulk of Liu's income

Liu's family can only earn approximately RMB 3,700 ($560) per year by growing wheat and corn on six mu (approximately one acre) of land.

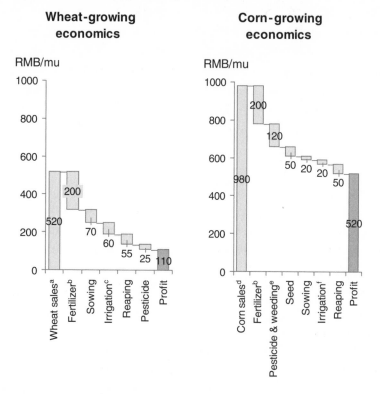

Sources: BCG rural interview in Hebei province; BCG analysis.
Note: Liu's household has six *mu* (about one acre) of land. The family grows wheat in the winter and corn in the summer.

a. Liu can harvest 650 *jin* (325 kilograms, or approximately 715 pounds) of wheat per *mu*; the price of wheat is RMB 0.8 per *jin* (approximately $0.12 per pound).
b. Twice per year, at RMB 100 ($15) each time per *mu*.
c. Five times per year, at RMB 12 ($1.80) each time.
d. Liu can harvest 1,300 *jin* (650 kilograms, or approximately 1,430 pounds) of corn per *mu*; the price of corn is RMB 0.76 per *jin* (approximately $0.11 per pound).
e. Four times per year, at RMB 30 ($4.50) each time.
f. Twice per year, at RMB 10 ($1.50) each time.

Today, after much labor, the new two-story brick house is complete. It has a courtyard built around one of the few old trees in the village, and two bedrooms. It is about two thousand square feet. It cost roughly RMB 150,000 ($23,000) to build and RMB 30,000 ($4,500) to decorate. "We borrowed a lot of money from friends and relatives for building the house," she says.

"So I always tell my son to tighten the belts and pay the debt first. But I do believe that we can pay off the debt in a few years."

The house is an investment—and speaks of her optimism for the future. Until recently, it had two power outlets for air conditioners—but no air conditioners. Now, her son has bought two secondhand units. It also has a garage for two cars, with rolling aluminum doors. As yet, she cannot afford one car, let alone two. But she thinks the time will come—one day soon.

"I am pretty satisfied with my life now," she says, in her rapid-fire, no-nonsense way. "It's so much better than it was just a few years ago." Her one big concern is her health. She suffers from hypertension and diabetes. With her extra income, she is able to pay the rural cooperative medical care unit a monthly fee of RMB 300 ($45) for regular checkups at the township clinic, where they check her blood pressure and blood glucose levels. But her life has improved dramatically since the days when farming was her family's only source of income, and the dark days of the 1950s seem a lifetime away—which indeed they are. As she says, with one of her trademark smiles, "I live a life of luxury."

Finding Liu was not easy. She lives in a remote village, off the beaten track. But for a company to locate her—and the millions like her in China and India—it must segment the two countries into specific urban centers and rural communities.

These are battleground markets where a significant growth opportunity lies in the next ten years and beyond. Our analysis shows that more than half of the $10 trillion prize will be won in China's cities (figure 5-2). In the not-too-distant future, some of the now hard-to-pronounce cities will roll off the tongues of executives in the United States and Europe: in China, these cities include Nantong, Xuzhou, Luoyang, Guiyang, and Baotou; in India, these are places such as Bhavnagar, Visakhapatnam, Bareilly, Sonipat, and Coimbatore.

But although the major trend is urbanization, there is nevertheless a significant effort on the part of the Chinese and Indian governments to reinvest in their rural communities. And our analysis suggests that 15 percent of the $10 trillion prize will be won in India's vast rural districts. To win a share of this market, companies will need to reach out to consumers with very different tastes and appetites.

FIGURE 5-2

How the $10 trillion prize breaks down between urban and rural markets

Market	China in 2020	India in 2020
Urban	$5.2 trillion	$2.1 trillion
Rural	$1.0 trillion	$1.5 trillion

Sources: Euromonitor, Countries and Consumers; BCG City Income Database, 2011; BCG analysis.

On the face of it, the rural population seems to offer limited interest to companies, as people increasingly migrate to cities. In China, for instance, we calculate that the rural population will fall from 53 percent of the total in 2010 to 45 percent in 2020, with rural households' share of the country's disposable income falling to about 15 percent, down from 25 percent today.[1] In India, the rural population will shrink, albeit at a slower rate—from 70 percent in 2010 to 65 percent in 2020. Meanwhile, we predict that rural households' share of disposable income will fall from 56 percent in 2010 to 41 percent by 2020.[2] But as we showed with Liu, the rural markets have pockets of rising wealth. And as this chapter will discuss, underpinning the transformation of the urban and rural communities are two revolutions: one relating to infrastructure, the other to agriculture.

When companies enter the Chinese market, it is important to keep the Chinese sense of identity in mind. To those living outside China, the name of the country is translated as "middle kingdom." But the Chinese characters for *China* convey a very different meaning. A more accurate translation is a country that is central to the world, wealthy in resources and capabilities, and well protected—spiritually and physically (figure 5-3). This symbolic categorization reflects comments that many of our interviewees made: they

FIGURE 5-3

A unique Chinese self-identity: central, protected, wealthy

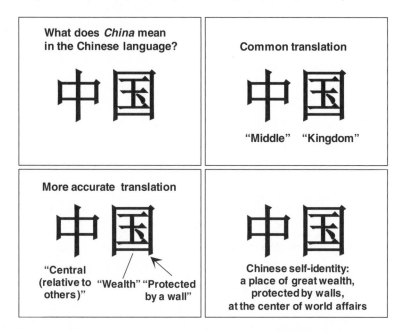

view themselves as players on the world stage who are in control of their own destiny. They have a sense of prosperity, strength, and momentum. They hope for an even better future.

Urbanization: Understanding the Cities

If you look at a satellite picture of Shenzhen circa 1980, it shows a sparsely populated former fishing village isolated from its neighbor Hong Kong—then still British controlled. Hong Kong's New Territories were directly across the Shenzhen River but separated by a high barbed-wire fence from Shenzhen and its 330,000 inhabitants. By contrast, Hong Kong had a population of more than 5 million, including many who had fled mainland China, some by swimming across Shenzhen Bay. The formal border crossing at Lo Wu checkpoint saw little traffic.

Thirty years later, the satellite picture shows Shenzhen as a built-up and bustling metropolis, a massive expanse of office towers, industrial parks, and residential areas—a new Chinese megacity of more than 10 million people, far surpassing the population of its once-larger neighbor, Hong Kong. The vast majority of Shenzhen's residents migrated there, either from rural areas or from other Chinese cities. The Hong Kong–Shenzhen border crossing has become the world's busiest, with millions of crossings every week (and indeed a rapid and fully automated crossing for residents carrying the right identity documents). High-speed trains routinely roll right across the Shenzhen River bridge, not stopping until they have completed the hundred-mile journey between Hong Kong and Guangzhou, at the upper end of the Pearl River Delta.

One consumer whose life embodies this urban transformation is Zhang Chi, who was just eight years old when his family moved to the city in the 1990s. By then, Shenzhen, the first Chinese city to be designated a special economic zone, had more than 2 million inhabitants. Chi remembers a place that was still underdeveloped: "You could still see farmland near downtown Shenzhen. The residential buildings were simple, and when I walked along Dongmen Street, it was nasty and crowded and full of street vendors, and I had to squeeze in and out of them just to go from one end to the other."

Today, Dongmen Street, one of the main commercial thoroughfares, has been completely upgraded, with office towers, hotels, and shops above, and a gleaming new subway line beneath. "Every time you look up to the sky," he says, "you see a skyscraper."

If Shenzhen was one of the first of China's new-growth cities, it is not alone. Across China and India, sleepy towns and villages are being transformed into great commercial centers as millions of people move from fields to factories in an unprecedented migration that dwarfs even the great European migration to North America in the late nineteenth century. For companies targeting the middle classes, these hundreds of cities—the big ones and especially the small ones—are the places to be over the next ten years. These cities are growing because they offer lower-cost and higher-quality living, and the government is directing job growth their way.

The development of cities is crucial to the two countries' growth. Urbanization is perhaps the most powerful transformative force—especially in China. As people move to cities, they typically find the kinds of job opportunities that make them far more productive. No country has achieved sustained economic growth or rapid social development without urbanization.

Liu He, a Chinese economic adviser, calculates that each percentage-point increase in China's urbanization rate adds 0.4 percentage points to its GDP growth.[3] Meanwhile, India's two largest cities contribute some 11 percent to national GDP, with only 3 percent of the population. China's two largest cities contribute 7 percent to national GDP, more than double what they could have expected to contribute, given the size of their populations.[4]

In 2008, the majority of the world lived in urban areas for the first time in history—and the growth of China's and India's cities was a major contributor to the passing of this demographic milestone. Today, according to the National Bureau of Statistics of China, 51 percent of China's population, or 691 million people, are living in urban areas.[5] In India, the percentage is a somewhat lower 31 percent.[6]

Over the next two decades, the cities are expected to grow dramatically, turning predominantly peasant societies into progressive metropolitan communities. But the growth rates are quite different. In China, some 824 million people (about 60 percent of the population) are expected to be living in cities in 2020, an increase of 188 million. That is 1.5 million new urban residents *every month* over this decade. By 2030, according to our research, there will be around 270 million more new urban residents in China. In India, the cities will grow more steadily. By 2020, we expect 35 percent to be living in urban centers, and by 2030, 40 percent of the country's population will be city dwellers.[7]

The pattern of urbanization is also different in China and India. The majority of China's urban population is located in midsized cities ranging between 500,000 and 5 million people. By contrast, most of India's urbanites live in smaller cities ranging between 100,000 and 500,000 people.

China's Urban Centers

When advising companies on the differences among the urban communities, we take them on a virtual guided tour, separating the cities into seven tiers. In China, the tiers break down into the following numbers:

- 12 tier 1 cities, projected to have more than 2.5 million middle-class and affluent consumers by 2015

- 25 tier 2 cities, with 1 to 2.5 million

- 30 tier 3 cities, with 500,000 to 1 million

- 88 tier 4 cities, with 250,000 to 500,000

- 200 tier 5 cities, with 100,000 to 250,000

- 199 tier 6 cities, with 30,000 to 100,000

- 96 tier 7 cities, with less than 30,000

Shanghai is China's richest city, with average incomes amounting to $23,000 per year, putting its people on par with the residents of oil-rich Saudi Arabia.[8] Typically, and perhaps not surprisingly, U.S. and European companies entering China have focused on the tier 1 cities of Beijing, Shanghai, and Guangzhou. But we tell them that this is a mistake. There are pockets of wealth all across the country, and the wealth is spreading deep into the country's western provinces.

By our calculations, a company needed to achieve strong positions in 60 cities to reach 80 percent of the country's middle and upper classes in 2005. Today, they have to be in 340 of them. And by 2020, they will need to be in 550 urban locations to reach that same percentage of the middle- and upper-class population.[9]

Right now, we estimate that there are some 148 million middle- and upper-class consumers—with 65 million in tier 1 and 2 cities and 83 million in tier 3 cities and below. By 2020, the number of middle- and upper-class consumers will have grown to 415 million, with 127 million in tier 1 and 2 cities and a staggering 288 million—69 percent of the total—in tier 3 cities and below. Significantly, by 2020, we estimate that some 268 cities will have average income levels that are equal to or higher than those enjoyed in Shanghai in 2010. We can regroup the cities into a series of four categories: megacities, cluster capitals, specialist hubs, and horizon towns.

In China, there are two *megacities*: Beijing and Shanghai. These cities, each with more than 10 million residents, are important for many reasons: one, they serve as international entry points to the country, and, two, by being trend setters for consumption habits and high-end brands, they constitute important stepping-stones for companies wanting to reach deeper into national markets. They are effectively the two gateway cities to China.

Yet across China, there are eight cities with more than 10 million people. There are ninety-three cities with more than 5 million people. To put this into context, the United States has only one city with more than 5 million people—New York. Over the next ten years, these cities will emerge as real consumer markets, as the urban population grows from 636 million to 824 million and as the urban middle class grows by an extra 110 million.

Beyond this group are what we call the *cluster capitals*. These include Changshu, Daqing, Dongguan, Fuzhou, Tianjin, Wuxi, and Zhengzhou. These are trade hubs surrounded by smaller satellite cities. The cluster capitals are large and therefore important in their own right, but their strategic proximity to a significant number of tier 3 and 4 cities makes them doubly important. Wuxi, for example, is the capital of a group of six cities within a thirty-mile radius in Jiangsu province: Jingjiang, Zhangjiangang, Changshu, Jiangyin, Changzhou, and Suzhou. On its own, Wuxi has a population of 2.3 million people, including 572,000 middle-class consumers. Treated as part of a cluster, however, it becomes the center of a market with 6.9 million people and 1.5 million middle-class consumers.

Besides the cluster capitals, there are important *specialist hubs*—tier 3 cities whose growth is often closely linked to the development of local natural resources or industrial hubs. These cities include Anyang, Bozhou, Chengdu, Lu'an, Suizhou, Xinxiang, and Yongzhou. And then there is a profusion of *horizon towns*, the hundreds of small, geographically dispersed emerging-market cities. Although hard to reach, they offer ripe market opportunities—consumers here usually have more basic needs than those of their counterparts in the bigger cities, but they also have a strong willingness to selectively trade up.[10]

We have encountered quite remarkable distinctions between people who, on the face of it, have the same take-home pay. A popular TV program—*Wo Ju*, or "Narrow Dwelling"—dramatizes how Shanghai's middle-class consumers are increasingly being squeezed by the burden of sizable mortgages. A very different picture is emerging in the smaller cities, where middle-class consumers have been more insulated from the ravages of real estate development and speculation. What is more, there has been considerable government investment in the smaller inland cities. As a result, many workers who would have emigrated to the coastal cities in earlier times have found work closer to home.

As described in chapter 2, Ma Guojun wearied of working in Beijing and hurried back to the northwestern province of Qinghai as soon as the opportunity to do so arose. But others have not found it so easy to escape the difficulties of life in the big city. We talked to several people—all with broadly the same income—to understand their contrasting lifestyles.

Zhang Wei is thirty-four years old and lives in Shanghai with her husband and nine-year-old daughter. An accountant for a textile company, her monthly income is RMB 6,500 ($1,000), which puts her at the lower end of the middle class.

Xue Ping, four years younger than Wei, lives in Xuzhou, which is a tier 3 city to the north of Shanghai. Married and with an eight-year-old daughter, she works as a clerk in a telecom company, and her family has a combined monthly income of RMB 5,800 ($880). Ping is part of the emerging middle class.

For Wei, living in Shanghai, the cost of necessities—including food, utility payments, education, transportation, telecommunications, and health care—comes to RMB 3,860 ($580), or about 60 percent of her household income. This means that she cannot afford to buy a house.

Her predicament, which is common in China, directly influences her behavior as a consumer. With larger discretionary budgets and more spare time to go shopping, those in small cities—tier 3 and smaller—have greater consumer confidence.

In tier 1 cities such as Shanghai and Beijing, some 37 percent of middle-class people say they are willing to trade up—a sure sign of consumer confidence. In tier 3 cities, some 45 percent of people in the same income bracket declare a willingness to trade up.

For certain product categories, the percentages are higher and the differences between consumers starker. In the case of home appliances, for example, some 52 percent of middle-class and affluent consumers in tier 3 and tier 4 cities said they intended to trade up in this category. By contrast, just 43 percent in tier 1 and tier 2 cities expressed such an intention.

There is an even bigger difference when it comes to home decoration, with 57 percent of those in small cities declaring their intention to trade up, compared with just 43 percent of those in big cities. Other categories in which middle-class consumers in the smaller cities showed a greater willingness to trade up than those in the bigger cities were consumer electronics, apparel and shoes, and skin care and cosmetics.

Aurangabad is a small city in Maharashtra, the home state of India's president at the time of this writing. Until October 2010, the city was little known and not much talked about. And then a group of businessmen, in a flamboyant gesture of wealth, purchased more than 150 Mercedes Benz automobiles from the local dealer, paying $15 million. "In and around Aurangabad, there are companies worth a thousand crores [an amount of Indian rupees equivalent to about $225 million]," said Sachin Nagouri, a property dealer, in an interview. "But Aurangabad is not known even in this state. There is plenty of money here. We just need to show it."[11]

The transformation of the urban centers is much slower in India than in China—and so the task of getting recognition is much harder. Remarkably, just thirty years ago, India's urban population was bigger than China's, and even twenty years ago, the figures were comparable: 26 percent in India, 27 percent in China.

There are other Aurangabads across India, but the country remains largely a nation of villages. It is because there are fewer urban communities that our segmentation of the cities is broader. We divide them into four tiers: those with more than 4 million inhabitants (8 cities), those with 1 to 4 million (38 cities), those with 500,000 to 1 million (45 cities), and those with 100,000 to 500,000 (407 cities).[12] As with China, bigger is not always better—at least from a commercial point of view. We also regroup these cities into megacities, cluster capitals, specialist hubs, and horizon towns.

The tier 1 cities are Delhi, Mumbai, Kolkata, Chennai, Bangalore, Ahmedabad, Hyderabad, and Surat. This is up from just two tier 1 cities twenty years ago. Today, these are among the world's biggest—and the first two rank among our list of megacities. They are also among the densest cities. Indeed, Kolkata, with nearly 60,000 people per square mile, is the world's densest city; Mumbai is close behind, with nearly 50,000 people per square mile.[13]

Beyond these, there is a myriad of cities whose names are rarely heard in the United States and Europe. But we expect that over the next twenty years, they will become altogether more familiar, as the country overtakes Japan to become the world's third-biggest economy, behind the United States and China.

By 2021, we estimate that the number of tier 2 Indian cities will have jumped from 38 to 51, with tier 3 cities increasing from 45 to 48 and tier

4 cities growing from 407 to a staggering 497. Together, the tier 3 and 4 cities are the emerging cities and constitute 29 percent of India's urban population, or 108 million people. Another 32 percent are based in the tier 1 and 2 cities—60 million in each tier. The remaining urban population—145 million—resides in towns of 10,000 to 100,000 people.[14]

Today, these top 498 cities generate just over 45 percent of India's GDP, with a significant proportion generated by people in the emerging cities. Tier 1 and 2 cities collectively generate $338 billion, while tier 3 cities generate $77 billion per year and tier 4 cities a remarkable $179 billion.

On average, people living in tier 1 cities are about 30 percent better off—in terms of household income—than those in tier 4 cities. But the pattern is not uniform, and there are several tier 3 and 4 cities that have higher average household incomes. For instance, Kalol (home of General Motors in Gujarat), Ambala Sadar (a center of India's glass-making industry), and Sonipat (headquarters of Atlas Cycles, one of the world's biggest manufacturers of pedal bikes), are tier 4 cities. Yet they have average household incomes in excess of 500,000 rupees ($11,000), making them middle-class cities. By contrast, Delhi's average household income is 360,000 rupees ($8,000).

These emerging cities are places where modern India and traditional Bharat—the traditional name for the country—come together. These contrasting cultures are seen in the choices made by consumers. Typically, people are more conservative when it comes to financial affairs, they display a pronounced affinity for local culture, and they like to shop the old-fashioned way: at small general stores and marketplaces. Also, as expert hagglers, they are primary proponents of *paisa vasool*—they are always searching for good value for their hard-earned money.

One such consumer is Omkar Trivedi. Age forty-two, he runs a small grocery store, or *kirana*, in Mehsana, a tier 4 city located fifty miles north of Ahmedabad, a former capital of Gujarat. Once known as the "Manchester of the East" for its booming textile industry, Ahmedabad now hosts major chemical and pharmaceutical industries.

Mehsana itself is a center for the oil and gas industry and the dairy business: Dudhsagar Dairy, one of the largest in Asia, produces everything from *ghee* and *dahi*, types of butter and yogurt, respectively, to ice cream and sweetened condensed milk. These are some of the products that Omkar sells in his store.

He set up his shop ten years ago, after working as a salesman at Charak, a pharmaceutical company specializing in traditional Ayurvedic medicines, which he had joined after completing his degree in Ahmedabad. When he left his job, he was earning about 8,000 rupees ($175) per month, so he had to take out a loan to buy his store—a 250-square-foot building with a counter that opens out onto the street. At first, he was not sure that he had made the right decision in abandoning a steady job: his shop made profits of around 7,000 rupees ($150) per month, and most of this went into paying off a bank loan. "Those early days were very tough," he recalls. His wife had to go out to work to help support the family: two children and Omkar's mother.

But today he earns a comfortable 50,000 rupees ($1,100) per month. "I have come a long way in the last ten years," he says, with an air of satisfaction. "I feel much richer, and I am able to afford what I want. Just a few years ago, we would have basmati rice just once a week—now we can afford to have it every day. Also, we could not afford to eat out very often. We might go two or three times a year—and then, only for special occasions. But now we go as often as once a week."

Indeed, consumers in tier 3 and 4 cities have much in common with those in nearby rural communities. Together, these cities and communities present companies with abundant commercial opportunities.

Commercial Opportunity in the Infrastructure Revolution

We estimate that there is a cumulative need for infrastructure investment amounting to $40 trillion across all emerging-market cities over the next twenty years—and China's and India's needs are greatest. For instance, it takes thirty hours to travel 1,000 miles by road in India, which has 2 million miles of road (figure 5-4). In China, the same distance, traveled along its 2.2 million miles of road, takes twenty hours. By contrast, it takes U.S. travelers just fourteen hours to go 1,000 miles along its 4-million-mile road network.

China and India are investing heavily in infrastructure. In China, the government is projected to spend $113 billion per year on trains and railway infrastructure. The new high-speed line connecting Shanghai to Hangzhou, which opened in late October 2010, cost $4 billion and took just two years

FIGURE 5-4

Infrastructure investment by country, 2010

Though the pace of infrastructure investment has increased, India and China still lag far behind the United States.

Parameter	U.S.	China	India
Total length of road, 2007 (1,000 km)	6,544	3,584	3,317
Paved road (%)	65.3	70.7	47.4
Time to travel 1,000 miles (hours)[a]	14	20	30
Air passengers (per 1,000 pop.)	2,308	147	43
Rail track length, 2008 (km)	227,058	77,830	63,330
Railroad density (km per 1 million pop.)	752	60	56
Quality of port infrastructure[b]	5.7	4.3	3.5

Sources: Central Intelligence Agency, *The CIA World Factbook 2010*, https://www.cia.gov/library/publications/download/download-2010/index.html; World Bank, World Development Indicators; Economist Intelligence Unit Market Indicators, Transport, Travel and Tourism; NationMaster, http://www.nationmaster.com/statistics; U.S. Department of Transportation, Federal Highway Administration.

a. At an approximate average speed of 75 miles/hour (U.S.), 50 miles/hour (China), or 35 miles/hour (India).
b. 1 = extremely underdeveloped and 7 = well developed and efficient by international standards.

to build—an astonishingly rapid rate, given the glacial pace at which large infrastructure projects proceed in the West. Even larger investments are pouring into housing, waterworks, mass transit systems, power plants, natural gas distribution networks, and electric grids.

Meanwhile, the Indian government is making significant investments in road and rail infrastructure as well. The Golden Quadrilateral, which is a highway network connecting India's four largest metropolises—Delhi, Mumbai, Chennai, and Kolkata—required building 3,633 miles of four- to six-lane express highways at a cost of $11 billion. The rail industry is also busy, with $43 billion reserved for the building of a metro rail system across thirteen cities over the next ten years.[15]

We calculate that China needs to make an investment of $17.3 trillion between 2010 and 2030: around 40 percent on housing, 27 percent on water infrastructure, 16 percent on roads and railways, 13 percent on electricity networks, and the rest on telecommunications, ports, and airports. Meanwhile, India needs to make an investment of $5.7 trillion: around 35 percent on water infrastructure, 26 percent on housing, 22 percent on roads and railways, 16 percent on electricity, and the rest on other infrastructure.

Housing will be the biggest investment—with some 10.7 billion square meters of housing likely to be built in China, and up to 5.2 billion square meters in India. New types of housing—especially high-rise multifamily residential housing—will be required. In this regard, Shanghai may be something of a leading indicator—the number of stories and the floor area of high-rise buildings there have increased threefold since 2000, along with population density.[16]

Commercial Opportunity in the Agricultural Revolution

In 2010, when the price of onions rose as a result of bad weather and the resultant shortages, the poor population took to the streets in Mumbai. Meanwhile, in China, there were literally thousands of riots and other *mass events*, as they are called, as the left-behinds protested rising food prices and other escalating costs.

With just one-tenth of a hectare of arable land for each person (one-fifth the amount in the United States), China will be able to feed its bulging population only through major agricultural reform. China and India need to create larger farms with fewer workers using more irrigation, more equipment, better-quality seed, and better methods. In a study conducted with the Confederation of Indian Industry, we estimated that up to 40 percent of the supply of fruits and vegetables rots before it reaches consumers, because of poor refrigeration, time languishing in depots, and mishandling during transportation.[17]

These problems mean that China and India need to drive a step-change improvement in agricultural productivity if they are to deliver the growth we forecast. A cycle of prosperity requires farm consolidation, investment in modern farm equipment, and the deployment of better technology, irrigation, and seed. Fertilizer, pesticides, and other expensive yield-enhancing tools need to be used wisely and sustainably, too.

Together, these reforms add up to an agricultural revolution, which would help ensure self-sufficiency in foodstuffs, permit people in rural districts to take higher-paying factory and service jobs, and address the dangers of social unrest. In the remainder of this chapter, we show that these reforms are under way. We share four stories of ambition, innovation, and entrepreneurship: farmers who have used crop choice and modern farming to improve their net returns; a New York private-equity fund helping to make China's milk safe to drink; an Indian company driving micro-irrigation to increase yields, save water, and drive a doubling of farmer incomes; and a mobile phone technology that increases farmer incomes by helping them to get better prices for their product, cut out middlemen, and increase their net yield to market.

Mastering Modern Farming Techniques—and Reaping the Profits

WX Liu, the farmer discussed earlier in this chapter, has enjoyed a rapid rise in her standard of living as a result of the outside jobs held by her son and daughter-in-law. Also, she has increased her hourly yield on labor on her one-acre farm sixfold in the last ten years. "My life is so much better," she says. But she remains worried about each season's production. Farmers in China and India bet money every spring in the form of seed, fertilizer, and pesticides that there will be sun and rain to grow a good crop.

When we met her in 2011, the summer in Hebei province had been unusually dry. By late August, the thin topsoil was parched and the year's harvest on her small plot of land—about the size of a football field—depended on the right combination of rain, sun, and luck in the next month. Liu had made an unusually large expenditure on fertilizer, her single largest farming expense. The fertilizer bet is among the biggest of many gambles that Chinese farmers must make every year. They have no choice but to buy it at the start of the growing season, hope that it is not counterfeit, apply it in the right amounts, and trust that it works. Together with another fundamental purchase that can sometimes be counterfeit—the seeds—fertilizer is key to success, and the price has soared in these inflationary times. Isolated from information and technology, but not insulated from market and climate volatility, Liu has anxieties that are common to millions of Chinese farmers.

In India, Bapurao Laxman is fortunate to have a medium-sized plot of land for an Indian farmer—a full seven acres—but he also faces great uncertainty. As he rests under one of the few shade trees on his acreage, he reflects on the most important risk that he has taken this year: the decision to plant more cotton and less corn. Last year's bet on corn did not play out as he had hoped. He discovered that corn did not take well to his unirrigated soil, and one particular brand of corn seed proved particularly disappointing. After careful study of his neighbor's experiences, and visits to a demonstration farm used by one of the big seed manufacturers to promote its products, he has shifted a few acres over to cotton.

Cotton is a difficult crop to grow and harvest. Bapurao dreads the physical pain that will come from the torturous days of the harvest. Picking cotton by hand has already left his knuckles deeply scarred, as the razor-sharp cotton bolls often cut through his old gloves, and his back aches at the days spent moving half-hunched through the cotton rows, dragging the heavy bag of harvested cotton buds with him in sun-drenched Maharashtra, one of the states in western India. But the more days of pain and the heavier the harvest bags, the higher the income for the year.

Even so, for all the similarities between Liu and Bapurao, the two farmers represent peasant nations that have taken different paths in agricultural development. In recent years, China has had much higher agricultural output than India, producing 40 percent more rice and wheat than India on a similar amount of arable land. At the time of China's Cultural Revolution, India was more productive in crops such as wheat. But starting with the reforms of the late 1970s, China's yield improvements have outpaced India's. Even in cotton production, where India has made impressive strides, China boasts much higher output and yields. These productivity differences matter enormously to farmer incomes and poverty levels. This is especially crucial for India, given that half its workforce is employed in the agriculture industry and the majority of its population is in the countryside.

China has outpaced India in rural infrastructure, agricultural R&D, fertilizers, and farming techniques such as double cropping. In both countries, the use of farm machinery is limited by farm plot size, although here again, China has been reforming with the creation of much larger farms in certain sectors such as livestock raising.

The lack of rural infrastructure in India contributes to inefficient distribution systems, as do some archaic regulations that artificially constrain these markets. Such rules limit entrepreneurial investment in logistics and storage. This is especially damaging for fruits and vegetables requiring modern cold storage and transport.

In both China and India, major changes are required in agriculture in the years ahead. Without change, it will be impossible to meet rising urban food demand while also improving the incomes of farmers and rural residents. In general terms, the required areas of change include the following:

- Enhanced education and technical training

- Improved investment in rural infrastructure, farm mechanization, and irrigation

- Improved R&D in advanced crop science and new farming techniques

- Continued land reform to enable the formation of more productively sized farms

- Rural job creation in nonfarm sectors to diversify the income stream

- Greater use of information technology and mobile communications to empower farmers

Luckily, many of these changes are already starting to happen in both countries.

Making Money in Chinese Dairy

KKR, the U.S.-based private-equity investor, might seem an unlikely company to co-own 110,000 Chinese milk cows. It might be an even less likely investor in the restructuring of China's scandal-plagued dairy industry—an industry that rose to global infamy in the baby milk powder tragedy in 2008. Yet KKR, together with other private-equity heavyweights, has piled into China's dairy sector, collaborating with the Chinese government and local entrepreneurs to clean up the industry. Their aptly named company, China Modern Dairy (CMD), is growing rapidly and is aggressively transforming the sector.

The rise of China's middle class has propelled China's dairy market forward. Diets have changed, distribution and retail networks have improved, and consumers value the benefits of dairy products. Dairy product consumption grew at an annual rate of 18 percent between 2005 and 2008 to more than $20 billion. And with per-capita consumption still quite low, there is much more growth ahead.

The need to transform this sector became clear to the world in 2008, when hundreds of babies became ill after consuming melamine-tainted baby formula. Because regulations called for milk to be tested for protein content, farmers and wholesalers had a strong incentive to add chemicals such as melamine that would trigger a higher protein reading. As price controls in the industry squeezed margins, the corrupt process of tainting milk expanded significantly.

In response to this tragedy, the Chinese government introduced a series of new rules and policies to strengthen regulations on food safety for dairy products. These policies included much stronger controls on the dairy supply chain, a new food safety law with much tighter standards and inspections, and a range of incentives to promote large-scale cattle breeding and farming. This was a dramatic shift from the previous one-cow-per-farmer policy and opened the door for the formation of large dairy-farming businesses.

Investors jumped into the sector to finance the major new integrated dairy companies that would be needed. One such company that attracted investment was named Modern Farm, which had established a dairy farm in Anhui province in 2006 and had expanded to Inner Mongolia and Shandong. In 2008, a group of investors, including KKR, took over Modern Farm through investment company CMD. By 2011, CMD had become the largest dairy-farming company in terms of herd size, as well as the largest raw milk producer in China.[18]

The company had its initial public offering on the Hong Kong Stock Exchange in November 2010, and as of June 30, 2011, CMD had approximately 110,000 dairy cows in seventeen large-scale dairy farms—each designed and constructed with a capacity of up to 10,000 dairy cows per farm.

By November 2011, CMD's market capitalization exceeded $1.1 billion, putting KKR's stake at nearly $375 million, more than double its original $150 million investment. CMD's revenue growth has been explosive, rising from $27 million in 2008 to $172 million in 2011, an annual growth rate of 82 percent. CMD plans for continued aggressive growth, aiming to double its operations again by 2015.

Monsoons, Droughts, and Wells

India suffers from the dual curse of too much and too little water. An intense monsoon season drowns the subcontinent for part of the year while leaving the land parched for months as well. Farmers with small plots of land and little capital are unable to afford large-scale irrigation systems to help manage this curse. But a new generation of micro-irrigation systems companies is delivering solutions that enable small farmers to control water usage, with dramatic improvements in yield and stability. Jain Irrigation Systems is at the forefront.

In 1963, Bhavarlal Jain launched a modest business selling kerosene from a pushcart in Jalgaon, a city in western India. Some 7,000 rupees ($150), representing the cumulative savings of three generations of his family, financed his business. Meeting with success, he expanded into selling two-wheelers, automobiles, and automobile accessories. Seeing the many needs of farmers, Jain then expanded into agricultural supplies and began trading a full range of farm equipment. By the late 1980s, Jain had become interested in new irrigation techniques and entered the business of micro-irrigation. Systems of simple plastic piping enable precise application of water drops to the plant root.

Farmers use micro-irrigation to plant earlier in the season, ensuring that their plants are well established before the heavy monsoon rains arrive. They also use it to safeguard crops against unexpected drought and to save groundwater for future use.

Now, Jain Irrigation is India's largest producer of micro-irrigation systems, with about half of the total market. Its products sell to 2.5 million small farmers, 90 percent of whom have less than one hectare of land. A family-owned business, Jain Irrigation makes a range of drip and sprinkler irrigation systems, as well as plastic pipes and wood-substitute plastic sheets. The company also sells dehydrated vegetables, tissue culture banana plants, and hybrid and grafted plants, not to mention greenhouses and biofertilizers. Total sales were $820 million in 2010.

Sustainability is a fundamental philosophy of the company, according to Anil Bhavarlal Jain, the chief executive. His mission—to "leave the world better than you found it"—dates from when his father built an agriculture input business. The business has moved on considerably since then, but the family philosophy and commitment remain the same—to have a positive impact both on the environment and on farmers' livelihoods.

The company—whose rhyming credo is "Serve and strive through strain and stress; Do our noblest, that's success"—has developed a drip irrigation system designed specifically for small farmers. Tailored to smaller incomes and more primitive farming conditions, it reduces water usage considerably. Recognizing that technology is only part of the answer to water conservation, the company works closely with customers to teach "precision farming," which optimizes the balance between fertilizers, pesticides, water, and energy to increase output. Farmers learn that using less water can actually increase yields.

Even so, says Anil Bhavarlal Jain, "India is a large country. There are hundreds of millions of farmers, so we need more people to convey knowledge to them." The company runs training programs for stakeholders, such as governments and lenders, to promote micro-irrigation and to expand its use in rural communities.

To help small farmers sell their products in export markets, Jain Irrigation has developed Jain Good Agricultural Practices, a version of the Global G.A.P. standards for certifying agricultural products. Small farmers in India were previously unable to participate in this certification. Jain Irrigation Systems customers are now able to participate in the global economy with the alignment of these two certifications.

Providing Farmers with Real-Time Data to Increase Net Price Realization

Farming is an information-intensive business, yet the small farmers of China and India have typically lacked timely and accurate information regarding many aspects of their work. Information about market prices, agricultural techniques, and new crops is often in short supply. Some farmers have also lacked the ability to verify that key purchases such as seeds are not counterfeit. But the mobile phone is changing this situation drastically. An array of mobile information services has arisen, tailored to farmers. It is the most rapid shifting of the digital divide in history.

In China, services such as Nongxintong, introduced by China Mobile, are empowering farmers with information and connectivity. Nongxintong is a farming information service that runs on a Web- and mobile-based platform, allowing subscribers to receive text or audio messages updating them on market prices, buyers, sellers, and job opportunities—all tailored to their needs. The service had fifty-seven million subscribers by 2010. China's massive efforts to provide physical mobile network coverage throughout rural China enable the service.

By the end of 2010, for example, China Mobile's Connected Village program had extended coverage to more than eighty-nine thousand small Chinese villages, reaching 100 percent coverage of China's officially registered villages.

China Mobile has also deployed mobile technologies to support farming techniques such as drip irrigation. In China's arid Xinjiang region, wireless systems remotely monitor drip irrigation networks and control the temperature and humidity of vegetable greenhouses. They also link eleven hundred remote meteorological monitoring stations.

By 2011, more than 600 online businesspeople were running approximately one thousand online shops in Shaji, in eastern China's Jiangsu province. Their suppliers include more than 180 furniture producers, ranging from traditional household workshops to modern factories. According to the Xinhua News Agency, online shops in Shaji recorded RMB 300 million ($45 million) in sales in 2010.[19] "We farmers have begun to make city dwellers work for us," said one official.[20]

In India, many new mobile services for farmers are coming to market. One such service from Tata Consultancy Services known as mKrishi offers farmers information on everything from weather and crop diseases to where they can sell their produce. In one of the mKrishi applications, farmers can use cell phone cameras to take and transmit pictures of their crops. Advisers from agricultural universities can analyze the photos and offer advice to the farmers via text messages and voice mail.

Other services, such as Nokia Life Tools and Reuters Market Light, provide customized solutions for Indian farmers using mobile platforms. Such services seek to overcome low literacy levels among farmers by using voice-response technology, graphical icons, and simple interfaces.

ITC, an Indian conglomerate, has successfully run its e-Choupal (which means "village square" or "gathering place" in Hindi) project since 2000. The innovative digital tool empowers small farmers in rural India with a host of services relating to farming techniques, sustainable-agriculture best practices, timely and relevant weather information, the transparent discovery of prices, and job opportunities, among others. Information is delivered in the local language through Internet kiosks and augmented with services through trained *sanchalaks* (local lead farmers). ITC e-Choupals not only connect farmers with markets but also allow for a virtual integration of the supply chain to create significant efficiencies within the traditional system.

As smartphones and mobile access become cheaper in the years ahead, many other innovations are likely to sweep through the rural communities of China and India, connecting them to national and global economies for the very first time.

Implications for Business

The rise of the cities and the revival of rural communities represent highly significant opportunities of the $10 trillion prize. But while the promise is vast, the complexities are daunting. Never before have companies been faced with the challenge of doing business simultaneously in hundreds of cities and villages across continent-sized countries. Those that manage to do so—and succeed—can expect to see significant growth in the future.

Reaching Liu, Omkar, and the millions of consumers like them will require innovative business models, vision, serious investment, and an appetite for risk. It also must be done quickly, because the huge consumer class of the future is forming brand preferences now. As corporations stick to the more familiar markets in the megacities, their local and multinational competitors are building the scale and breadth that will determine the global winners and losers.[21]

For this reason, we have synthesized a set of actions that companies should consider when preparing to reach the different consumers across China and India:

1. Rank and prioritize. Decide which markets to enter, when, and with what business models and organizations, because there are many highly diverse markets. Also, given the rapid changes in economic geography, the answers to these questions change rapidly and regularly—so they frequently need to be reevaluated. The best companies operate in two time frames—playing today's game while also planning for the different winning model needed in the next thirty-six months.

2. Be a first mover. As consumers rise up the income ladder, they get attached to different products and different brands—and these preferences often stay with people as they get richer. Companies

with the strongest presence and the most attractive product offerings will be well positioned to win in these markets. As we will explain in chapter 7, the presence of Yum! Brands, Inc., in more than 720 Chinese cities gives the company a competitive advantage in restaurant location, local market knowledge, talent sourcing, and supply-chain capabilities—an advantage that is extremely difficult for others to replicate.

3. Understand the consumers' needs and desires—and how they live their lives. For example, in today's high-end urban kitchen in China, there is unlikely to be a cappuccino maker, a food processor, an oven, or an automatic dishwasher. On the other hand, there may well be an expensive soy-milk machine, a high-end rice cooker, a modern gas range with a sophisticated ventilation hood, and possibly a built-in drinking-water filtration system. These elements of the modern Chinese kitchen reflect a combination of local cuisine (rice, soy milk, and fried rather than baked foods), local economics (a low-cost maid is likely to be more affordable than the space needed for a dishwasher), and local environmental concerns (water purification is a must). Companies wanting to win consumers in these markets must go to market with solutions based on these very specific types of insights.

SIX

The Power of the Purse
The New Female Consumers

Who they are, what they want—their dreams and desires—and what China and India need to do to foster a faster-growing female economy

LIU YITING'S MOTHER, WEIHUA, TESTED her at the age of three to see how her young prodigy was progressing. For three years, Weihua had been working on Yiting's education at home, beginning when Yiting was just fifteen days old. From the start, her parents would never use baby talk. They studied pictures, listened to music, and spent hours on language development with their child. But they would do much more. Over the next fifteen years, Yiting combined her raw intelligence with extraordinarily hard work to become a poster child for the next generation of women of Chinese descent. For the past decade, she has been a household name in China. She is better known as "Harvard Girl"—thanks to the book written by her parents, *Harvard Girl Liu Yiting*, about how they raised her and helped her secure admission to Harvard College in Massachusetts. The book has sold more than two million copies.

We met Yiting in New York. At twenty-nine, she is slender with a warm smile, high cheekbones, and shiny brown hair that falls to the middle of her back. Her eyes are big, bright, and dark. She dresses like the affluent Manhattan professional woman that she is—black leather pumps, a black cashmere cardigan, a black and white print sheath dress, pearl jewelry, and an oversized black leather handbag slung over one shoulder. She is a person who seems to have it all: brains, beauty, a top-notch résumé, a loving family and friends, and relentless drive and ambition. She is an example of the one-generation leap for talented women in China.

Some might think Yiting is a classic product of a Tiger Mom. But she is quick to counter this view. "My parents don't consider me a prodigy or a genius," Yiting says. "My mother is not a tiger mother. My education was fun, not rigid and oppressive." Together with her mother, she has done numerous interviews with the local Chinese media, and her parents have answered thousands of letters and calls. It is her work ethic, intelligence, and good fortune that have translated into a life of affluence and influence.

The female economy is strong in China today. Women work, have equal access to education, and have increasing access to top jobs. Child care is also usually available and affordable. Over the next decade, women in China are likely to flex their economic muscle, with young professional women breaking into middle and top management and fueling the next round of luxury spending. We expect Chinese female earnings to grow from $1.3 trillion in 2010 to $4 trillion by 2020, up from $680 million in 2005 and $350 million in 2000. That is more than a tenfold increase in twenty years.

By contrast, India's female economy is more fragile. Only the most affluent and urban women have a taste of equality. For the rest, there is significant gender discrimination, limited access to education, low rates of participation in formal labor, and low relative wages. Female labor-force participation rates in India have been stuck at 32 or 33 percent since 2000. Female wages have actually declined to 26 percent of men's wages. In 2010, some 134 million working women earned $280 billion. By 2020, we expect some 158 million working women to earn $901 billion. But despite this increase, relative earnings (the ratio of female wages to male wages) are expected to decline by 1.5 percent per year from 2010 to 2020.[1]

India really needs a political and economic revamp for women to lift off. The country needs to drive much higher normative female labor participation rates, freer access to education (particularly in rural areas), parity wages, and a dramatically different mix of occupations.

But if Chinese women are better off than Indian women, they are all underserved by companies. This creates a drag on growth in the two countries—educated females who do not experience gender discrimination can dramatically contribute to GDP growth. To realize their true potential, however, China and India will need to substantially change their mind-set. Our analysis suggests that a steady growth in female employment plus gradual increases in relative wages could open up the Indian economy to hundreds of millions of dollars in growth. This is over and above the $10 trillion prize.

Harvard Girl, Dong, and the New Chinese Woman

In 1955, Mao Tse-tung declared that "in order to build a great socialist society it is of the utmost importance to arouse the broad masses of women to join in productive activity. " He urged the country to "enable every woman who can work to take her place on the labor front, under the principle of equal pay for equal work." Mao's original purpose was to solve labor shortages. "China's women are a vast reserve of labor power. This reserve should be tapped in the struggle to build a great socialist county."[2] He was not motivated by thoughts of gender equality. His government was dominated by men who served with him in the war against Japan and the revolution.

There is, of course, still an old-boy network at play in China, with most top government positions filled by men—most over fifty years old—who started at the bottom in party politics, worked their way up slowly, and achieved prominence and stature partly as a result of longevity. In many of the big urban cities, however, women have closed the gap on wages, occupations, average education, and advancement.

For mothers all over China, their one child—whether son or daughter—is their hope and dream. They take the child for lessons and arrange for private school and coaching. They push the child to study hard, test best, and reach full potential. It is common to spend as much as 30 to 40 percent of household income on the child's education, private tutors, and special classes.[3] Liu Yiting's early years in Chengdu in Sichuan, a province in southwest China, were not easy. "I can remember at the start of the week, my mother had to plan when we would have to have tofu and when we would get chicken, using government vouchers to get rice," she told us.

Yiting and her parents kept reaching higher—they wanted to maximize her learning, push her upward. When they were unhappy with their initial choice of elementary school, they went to family and friends to raise the

RMB 30,000 ($4,500) for the tuition needed to enter a better school. Relentless studying and working filled each day. "Students in China work extremely hard. I really don't remember having a lot of time for extracurricular activities," Yiting says. In 1996, she entered Chengdu Foreign Languages School, one of the best high schools in Sichuan province. It was well known for sending students to top colleges in China, but Yiting dreamed of an education outside her home country.

Determined to get the best possible education, Yiting became the first person at her high school to apply to a U.S. college. She submitted eleven applications to elite American colleges, learning more than three thousand new English words in two months in preparation for the Test of English as a Foreign Language (TOEFL). She completed her U.S. applications while continuing to work hard at school and prepare for the gaokao—the national college entrance exam—just in case she was rejected in the United States. "I still say that is the hardest I've ever worked in my life," she says. "I remember one day sitting over those application essays late at night, and I just started to cry because I was so exhausted."

Yiting's hard work paid off. She was accepted to Mount Holyoke, Wellesley, Columbia, and Harvard. So she never needed to take the gaokao. She matriculated at Harvard and started on full financial aid, worth approximately $30,000 each year, in the fall of 1999.

Until Harvard Girl, there was a gap in the Chinese market for books to help children gain entrance to a top global university. Numerous spinoff books have since been published, detailing Chinese children's successful paths to Yale, Columbia, Oxford, and Cambridge—but Harvard Girl was the original answer to parents and children with limited resources but infinite drive, energy, and ambition.

Since graduating from Harvard, Yiting has worked in a number of strategy- and finance-related positions, including two years as an associate at The Boston Consulting Group. Most recently, she and two partners founded an investment management firm, Ray Shi Capital Group, which focuses on small and medium-sized companies in China. Yiting's personal definition of success is holistic: she does not just want to run a profitable business; she wants that business to help change its surrounding society for the better. With Ray Shi Capital Group, she is hoping to move closer to that goal. "The small and medium-sized companies we invest in are creating jobs and contributing to the economic development of China," she explains. "Business is not the same thing as charity, of course, but you can be helping people while doing business."

Yiting is certainly not the only child from China to study in the United States. According to recent data, there are more than 156,000 Chinese students in American colleges and universities.[4] Each one of these students is pursuing the dream: the best education, the best credentials, the opening up of a lifetime of opportunity. They start with a high IQ, ambition, a strong push from their families, persistence, drive, and increasingly good information about their options. They choose depth of topic—a standout skill in one or two areas—as their card to admission. Admissions counselors at the major U.S. colleges and universities say they could fill their ranks with China's most elite students.

In general, women in China are more optimistic and feel more secure than women in the West. According to BCG proprietary research, 88 percent of Chinese women feel secure in their current financial position, whereas only 62 percent of Americans have that level of security. Eighty-seven percent of Chinese women feel secure in their current job, compared with 44 percent in the United States.

Seven of the top thirteen richest self-made women are from China. Four of the wealthiest are under the age of fifty. These include forty-seven-year-old Wu Yajun, a real estate developer with property in ten cities and an estimated net worth of $3.9 billion. She worked as a factory worker and a news agency employee before becoming a real estate developer in her hometown of Chongqing. Then there is Xiu Li Hawken, a forty-eight-year-old who is the largest shareholder in Renhe Commercial Holdings, a shopping center developer. She graduated from Heilongjiang University in 1986 with a degree in Chinese literature. This list also includes Chu Lam Yiu, a forty-one-year-old cigarette maker with an estimated net worth of $2.1 billion. Her company also makes flavorings and fragrances. The four others on the list include another property developer, a paper producer, another real estate magnate, and a medical supplies producer from Tibet with a degree in physics.[5]

Dong Mingzhu runs Gree Electric, China's largest manufacturer of air conditioners. Her book, *Regretless Pursuit*, is her story of rising from star salesperson to company leader. At thirty-six, she joined the company as a sales manager in the poor Anhui region. She helped grow regional sales to 10 percent of company revenues within eighteen months. In 1994, she became sales director. In 2001, she became the CEO and helped drive revenues to $6.4 billion. She brings to her job an amazing work ethic. In a *New York Times* interview, she talks about not having taken a holiday for twenty years. "I'll rest when I retire," she says.[6]

Dong Mingzhu is attempting to empower women in China. She is a member of many women's organizations in China and has taught business classes at a university. In her company, women are entitled to twenty-four weeks of paid maternity leave, twice the norm in China. But there is a long way to go. Women hold only one in five seats in the National People's Congress. There has been little change in this distribution over the past decade. The World Economic Forum ranks China 57 out of 135 countries on political empowerment gender equality.[7]

In rural China, there is significant discrimination against women. Jon Huntsman, former ambassador to China and a GOP leader, took up the call for women while he served in China. In a diplomatic cable posted by WikiLeaks, he decried an imbalance between birth rates and female child mortality. These two factors, he said, result from selective abortion of girls and a high mortality rate of baby girls. He says there are 32 million Chinese men under twenty who will be unable to find a female partner and refers to these men as "bare branches."[8] The ratio of boys to girls at birth in China is 119 to 100. In India, the story is similar, with a ratio of 110 to 100.

Understanding the Female Consumer: What Women Want in China and India

BCG's proprietary survey of women consumers, first completed in 2008, was updated in 2011. Through the survey, we learned both qualitatively and quantitatively what women want in China and India.[9] We surveyed more than twenty thousand women in twenty-one countries across a range of incomes.

Women in China

In China, women told us that they want a trifecta of "a happy home, rising, secure income, and good health." One participant in our survey put it this way: "I want a stable income and work that makes me happy; a loving husband, all family members who are healthy and happy. Also a big dream: world peace." Another participant said she wished "to live in a good environment with fresh air and social order; to find the love of my life; to have success in career; to have a comfortable life free of worry and anxiety; to have good health for the whole family; to see my child's studies go smoothly and result in success; and to live a happy number of golden years." Another called out material and emotional goals: "a bigger car, a bigger house, harmony in life."

We found that Chinese women have significant concerns about health, income, and an old age with no social security. In rank order, the biggest fears are health and longevity, financial security, and family well-being. Women point to these fears to explain their voracious appetite for savings. In China, women hold most of their savings (62 percent) in a bank account.

Besides big fears, Chinese women often have low self-esteem. In our global survey, only 15 percent of Chinese women described themselves as very attractive. This compares with 37 percent in the United States, 51 percent in Russia, and 48 percent in India and Turkey. A Chinese woman is the least satisfied user of health care across twenty-one countries.

We talked to Cara, the twenty-two-year-old daughter of an army engineer, about her hopes and fears. She is a senior at Peking University, where she is studying advertising and economics. She is slender, stands about five foot five, and wears her hair straight back. Her wireless glasses frame her face, and she is not shy about direct, sustained eye contact.

When she was growing up, getting into a top college was "the only goal." "You have to live up to the expectations of your parents," she says. Now, she has some new goals. Her ideal life? "I would like to achieve some career goals: to be a successful businesswoman, to establish my own company. Making a lot of money comes along with success. Money means freedom because you can do more things you want to do."

Also, her ideal life involves marriage and two children. She explains that the government is relaxing the one-child policy and that parents who are both only children can have two children. "I don't want to have an only child," she says. "There is too much pressure on that child. I feel it every day. If you don't study very hard, you can't get a good job. I feel insecure most days. It's a struggle."

In the course of our work, we asked many other Chinese women to describe their dream day. Most often, they described leisure time, sharing a meal with friends, relaxing, and shopping. "To laugh satisfyingly, to feel relaxed and really good inside, and to be able to share this with family and friends," one woman told us. "I would cook, go out and shop, rest and relax. I would enjoy the moment."

They talk about big breakfasts, time at a spa, shopping, having dinner out, going to the movies, leisure time with boyfriends or husbands. They contrast their dream day with their reality: regimented workdays where they have long commutes; intense and busy work; and then significant responsibility at home for food preparation, service, cleanup, housework, laundry, and child rearing.

Most Chinese women rank family as the top priority. They place their parents, husband, and child ahead of themselves. Many women feel that their daily obligations prevent them from feeling completely fulfilled. They have too many demands on their time and feel challenged to manage their households and find time for themselves. Nearly 50 percent are unsatisfied with their daily stress levels.

But Chinese women believe they will overcome. They are among the most confident about the future—and with a very strong job participation rate and higher education, they expect to close the earnings gap for similar work.

With this extra money, they expect to go shopping for branded products. The best and favorite brands are often Western, which provide a certainty of quality. Among the most cited brands were Adidas, L'Oréal, Apple, Nokia, Lancôme, Chanel, Samsung, Johnson & Johnson, and two Chinese brands: Li-Ning, a sports company, and Haier, a white goods company.

Women in India

India's urban middle-class women have similar notions as to what drives their happiness. They rank a successful career and accumulating possessions as their top two wants. They can often get paid help to relieve the burden of household responsibility. Moreover, they are among the most optimistic when it comes to women's political, social, economic, and professional futures, and they are twice as optimistic overall about the future of their external world.[10]

One woman surveyed said, "I would like to buy my dream house in Goa, to live a successful life. I want to become a good life partner. I want a happy and peaceful life. I want a home of my own with all facilities. I want a husband who is loving, caring, and can provide a fulfilling life with all my needs taken care of. My ambition is to lead a settled life without any financial problems." Another woman said, "I want more time for myself and the things I would like to do: to be my own boss and have my own firm, to work at my own pace and time, and to give back to society in a small way."

The three top emotional objectives are happiness, peace, and satisfaction. Money, food, and shopping are Indian women's highest sources of happiness. They rank themselves seventh on the priority list, behind their parents, husband, money, children, job, and education. But the women we surveyed also said they had many unfulfilled wants from their spouses. Among other desires, the women wanted their husbands to be better listeners, better savers, and better financial planners and to spend more time at home. In contrast to Chinese women, roughly half of Indian women said they are very attractive physically, ranking second-highest among women from twenty-one countries. They said they are close to their ideal weight and self-rank themselves second on emotional health compared with the other countries.

Indian women consider money essential for their lives, calling it "important," "a necessity," "indispensable," "essential," "crucial," and something that "can take you to the top of the world." "Money is a like a godfather for me," one woman told us. "To survive, you need money." Another commented, "Money is the oil to make the machines work. I can't live on next to nothing. Poverty is not my favorite pastime." Another respondent said, "It's absolutely essential for independence."

Today, women in India say they control less than half of total household income—the fourth-lowest among twenty-one countries. In other words, they do not hold the purse strings. As mentioned above, they wish their spouses were better financial planners, and the women are also dissatisfied with financial services providers.

Indian women spend more time shopping—and shop for food and household items more frequently—than women in the rest of the world. Middle- and upper-class women are willing to pay as much as they can and somewhat more for a large swath of categories, including food, clothing, housing, hair care, restaurants, and kitchen appliances. Favorite brands include Nokia, Sony, and Levi's. Attachment to the Nokia brand appears profound—Nokia is described as having incredible value, being strong and durable, and having high resale value.

Indian women's fears center on health and longevity, family well-being, and financial security. "I fear being bankrupt or sick, or losing my husband," one woman said. "I also fear terrorist attacks." Said another, "My biggest fear is losing those I love," which echoed comments made by many of the respondents. In a society where the man is dominant at home, there is fear of divorce and family crisis.

We met a nineteen-year-old named Shruti who attends one of the Indian Institutes of Technology. She was number 3,000 on the IIT admissions test—a far cry from the brilliant student we call Mr. Number 19, whom we will discuss in chapter 11.

"This place is 90 percent boys," she says. "I am the odd one out. Most of the boys are socially awkward and geeky. They have studied their whole lives and, prior to coming here, didn't know many girls." But there are benefits to being the odd one out. "I have my pick of the smartest boys," she says, smiling.

She studies textile engineering. "It is a good major," she says. "Just think about how fast demand is growing for clothing. I see a career of growth where people go from very modest consumption to buying every week. The education here is good, but the professors are only moderately interested in me. They spend less time with me because they say I will become a mother and not work. I intend to make a difference, however." She adds in a determined voice, "I am here because I want a career. My life will be a series of challenges to overcome."

Indian women—especially those in rural communities—face some major challenges. In BCG's proprietary Worldwide Women's Index, India scores in last place. This is driven by a low level of enrollment at tertiary school, a high maternal mortality rate, low female life expectancy, a low incidence of paid parental leave, a low relative income ratio, a very low level of membership in India's Parliament, and a very low presence in professional and technical jobs. And although female representation in the Indian Parliament has doubled since 1990—and, of course, the current president is a woman—it is still only 10 percent. Meanwhile, the World Economic Forum ranks India 113 out of 135 countries on its political empowerment gender equality index.[11] Among the biggest changes India could make are increasing the per-capita income of women and reducing the death rate for pregnant women, estimated at 450 per 100,000 births—or 150 times the mortality incidence in Sweden, the country with the lowest rate of infant mortality.

Yet, for all these grim prospects, Indian women are, like Chinese women, very optimistic—and there are rays of hope. The latest census shows an increase in female literacy levels—from 54 percent to 65 percent. The so-called Women's Reservation Bill, which reserves 33 percent of all local government positions for women, has resulted in the election of more than one million female officials. There are moves to expand this to cover the national Parliament, too. Moreover, in the business community, women are beginning to prosper. Currently, 11 percent of large-company CEOs in India are female, compared with 3 percent in the *Fortune* 500.[12] The CEOs of two of the three largest private-sector banks, two of the three largest multinational banks, and four state-owned banks are women. Two of the top six executives at Hindustan Unilever are women. Also, 29 percent of students at the Indian School of Business are female, a number comparable to that of Harvard Business School (39 percent) and INSEAD (33 percent).[13]

Reflecting these developments, some 81 percent of the women we surveyed believe their personal life will be better five years from now, and 86 percent believe they will achieve more economically and professionally in ten years—the highest of any country surveyed.

When asked about their dream day, there is a joy in the response. They say they want time to relax and time for themselves, time with family and a good meal. Their ideals are often centered on home and family. "I would wake up, get dressed, get my family ready, shop for happiness, smile in the mirror, and be happy for what I have done and what I have to cherish all my life," one respondent stated.

In some places, young women are beginning to band together to fight gender discrimination. In September 2011, in Satara, a rural district in Maharashtra, a state in the west of India, more than 200 mostly teenage girls with given names like Nakusa or Nakushi—names that translate into "unwanted" in Hindi—picked new names. The chosen names were about beauty, strength, and power. In this Indian state, there are 883 girls per 1,000 boys under seventeen, with the gender difference due to gender-selection abortions. Public officials called the ceremony a new beginning for the girls—a first step to providing them with social and educational security and status.[14]

For China and India, growth in the female economy will stimulate growth in the overall economy—and provide a new wave of consumers for companies. But for this to happen, women will need to enjoy the benefits of better education, a better range of jobs, a greater political voice, and changing social mores. In India, this means the government promoting female literacy. In both countries, it means the governments promoting university attendance. It also means promoting guaranteed maternity leave and gender pay parity.

PART II

Preferences, Appetites, and Aspirations

SEVEN

Food and Drink

Acquired Tastes: Cookies, Wine, Whiskey, and Tea

The fast-growing appetite for food and drink, the companies creating products for local tastes, and the recipe for becoming a favorite in China and India

W X LIU HAS NEVER BEEN more than fifty miles from her home village of Shunhezhuang in the northeastern province of Hebei. But as discussed in chapter 5, she has enjoyed a rapid increase in her standard of living over the past decade. Not only has she bought a new house, but her diet has also taken a tremendous turn for the better.

Ten years ago, the family income was less than RMB 5,000 ($750) a year. It was a stretch to buy fertilizer for her crops, to keep the roof on their dilapidated home repaired, and to even imagine fresh vegetables every day at dinner and pork or chicken once a week for the main meal. Today, with her family pulling in RMB 30,000 ($4,500) a year, she is able to afford much better food.

Liu's kitchen is relatively sparse. It has a propane cylinder gas burner, an electric baking pan, a rice cooker, and a coal stove used for cooking and heating the kitchen in the winter. She is a modest woman, and she and her family live on a simple diet—"farmer food," as she puts it. Breakfast consists of chopped green onions with millet porridge. Lunch is usually pancakes, fried cabbage, and fried celery. In the evening, dinner might be as light as onion rolls and pickles. Another favorite is shredded marinated tofu.

"My family enjoys simple food," she says. "The longer it cooks, the more flavor there is. The secret is to use spices and fresh ingredients. I have time to go almost every day to the local market for onions, scallions, and mushrooms. And I buy meat three or four times a week."

As a family treat for breakfast, she might make egg bubble soup. She heats her wok, drops chopped scallions on hot oil or lard, and then tosses in beaten eggs until they bubble. The secret is adding water and simmering with salt, monosodium glutamate (MSG), and pepper. For a very special family dinner, she will make braised pork hock, slow-cooked in a sweet-and-sour sauce. When served, the meat falls off the bone and separates easily with chopsticks. For a casual occasion, she will cook chicken and vegetables in her wok, adding nuts, rice wine, garlic, chili pepper, and peppercorns. Spices, oils, rice, and noodles of various kinds fill her cupboard.

For festivals, she sometimes splurges on homemade beef dumplings. This requires her to make dough from flour, turn the dough into round cakes, roll them out, and then carefully place beef, cabbage, onion, pepper powder, sesame oil, and salt into the dumpling. The dumpling is carefully rolled and then cooked in boiling water and served hot. It takes about one hour of active preparation.

Today, Liu shows all the signs of a healthier diet. With some pride, she says that she has gained ten pounds. But she is not alone in enjoying a more abundant, higher-variety diet. As we will describe in this chapter, Chinese and Indian consumers are trading up when it comes to food and drink. What's more, the food and beverage market will be worth some $2.3 trillion in 2020 (with housing a close second) (figure 7-1). Several companies are already seizing this new opportunity—including Amul, Yum! Brands, PepsiCo, Cofco, LVMH, Pernod Ricard, and Kraft. But first, let's explore the factors driving the growth of the food market.

Food, Glorious Food .

Curry, noodles, rice—these have become staples of cooking around the world, and they testify to the observation that China's and India's culinary traditions, stretching back thousands of years, are among their most successful exports. Now, however, the new consumers are acquiring the

FIGURE 7-1

How the $10 trillion prize breaks down by product sector

Food and housing are the two largest sectors for consumer spending.

Category	Total spending in 2020 ($ billions)[a]		
	China	India	Total
Food	1,390 ←——————→ 913		2,303
Housing and household goods	1,479 ←——————→ 774		2,253
Transport and communication	763	618	1,381
Education and leisure	890	360	1,250
Health	444	184	628
Clothing and footwear	359	189	548
Other	862	546	1,408
TOTAL	6,187	3,584	9,771

Sources: International Monetary Fund, Data and Statistics; Economist Intelligence Unit, Market Indicators and Forecasts, Consumer Spending Patterns; Euromonitor, Countries and Consumers, Consumer Behavior; Project Landmark consumer research (December 2010); BCG analysis.
Note: Expenditure on food includes spending on alcoholic beverages and tobacco but excludes food sold by catering services such as restaurants, hotels, and kiosks.
a. In nominal dollars at constant 2010 exchange rates.

taste for more expensive fare, as well as the food and drink more commonly prepared in the kitchens of the United States and Europe.

In China, the amount spent on food by people with middle incomes will nearly triple by 2020, from $233 billion to $626 billion (figure 7-2). The increase among those with higher incomes will be even more dramatic: from $94 billion to $502 billion.

FIGURE 7-2

Household spending on food in China, 2010 and 2020

Growing middle and upper classes lead to increases in food consumption of nearly $750 billion annually in ten years.

	2010			2020		
Income class	Number of households (millions)	Household spending on food ($)[a]	Total spending on food ($ billions)	Number of households (millions)	Household spending on food ($)[b]	Total spending on food ($ billions)
Upper	24 ✕	3,944 ⊜	94	91 ✕	5,541 ⊜	502
Middle	109 ✕	2,140 ⊜	233	202 ✕	3,104 ⊜	626
Lower	260 ✕	1,213 ⊜	316	138 ✕	1,899 ⊜	263
			643			1,390

Sources: Economist Intelligence Unit, Market Indicators and Forecasts, Demographics and Income; U.S. Bureau of Labor Statistics; Euromonitor, Countries and Consumers, Annual Disposable Income; BCG Consumer Sentiment Survey, 2011: China Trading Up and Trading Down; BCG analysis.
Note: All spending figures are in nominal dollars at constant 2010 exchange rates. Includes spending on alcoholic beverages and tobacco but excludes food sold by catering services such as restaurants, hotels, and kiosks.
a. Average household spending on food in 2010 is $1,635.
b. Average household spending on food in 2020 is $3,230.

In India, the upward trajectory is even steeper. Those with middle incomes will increase their spending on food from $124 billion in 2010 to $447 billion in 2020, while those with higher incomes will spend some $215 billion on food—up from $34 billion (figure 7-3).

This growing appetite is reflected in an increasing intake of calories: China's is rising from 4,256 billion per day to 4,856 billion per day, and India's is rising from 3,022 billion to 3,908 billion per day. It is not only the *quantity* but also the *quality* of the food that explains the growing calorie intake.[1] The shift in quality can be seen in China in the trend toward more meat in the diet (figure 7-4).

In our consumer sentiment survey, conducted in 2011, some 51 percent of Chinese respondents reported that they were trading up in fresh food, while 46 percent were trading up in dairy products. Also, more than 40 percent said

FIGURE 7-3

Household spending on food in India, 2010 and 2020

Gains in household wealth generate $585 billion in additional annual food spending by 2020.

	2010			2020		
Income class	Number of households (millions)	Household spending on food ($)[a]	Total spending on food ($ billions)	Number of households (millions)	Household spending on food ($)[b]	Total spending on food ($ billions)
Upper	9	✕ 3,642	＝ 34	32	✕ 6,824	＝ 215
Middle	63	✕ 1,976	＝ 124	117	✕ 3,813	＝ 447
Lower	152	✕ 1,120	＝ 171	110	✕ 2,277	＝ 251
			328			913

Sources: Economist Intelligence Unit, Market Indicators and Forecasts, Demographics and Income; U.S. Bureau of Labor Statistics; Euromonitor, Countries and Consumers, Annual Disposable Income; BCG Consumer Sentiment Survey, 2011: China Trading Up and Trading Down; BCG analysis.
Note: All spending figures are in nominal dollars at constant 2010 exchange rates. Includes spending on alcoholic beverages and tobacco but excludes food sold by catering services such as restaurants, hotels, and kiosks.
a. Average household spending on food in 2010 is $1,463.
b. Average household spending on food in 2020 is $3,525.

they were trading up in organic food, an increase of 5 percentage points over the year before. Fresh fruit and vegetables, fish and seafood, and fresh meat were all separately ranked as "essential" consumer categories. Likewise, Indian consumers ranked dairy products and fresh food as their top food categories for trading up: some 53 percent reporting their readiness to do so. Organic food is less popular, with 34 percent ranking this as a trading up category. On the other hand, Indians do value healthiness, and vitamins and food supplements constitute their third-most traded-up category.

In China, the average person's consumption of meat will rise from 45 kilograms in 2010 to around 53 kilograms in 2020—an 18 percent increase. Across the country, this will translate into an increase of 36 billion kilograms—from 98 billion to 134 billion. Dairy products will grow in popularity, with each person increasing his or her intake from 25 kilograms

FIGURE 7-4

Composition of the Chinese diet over time

Makeup of the Chinese diet is shifting dramatically toward meat and away from vegetables and grains.

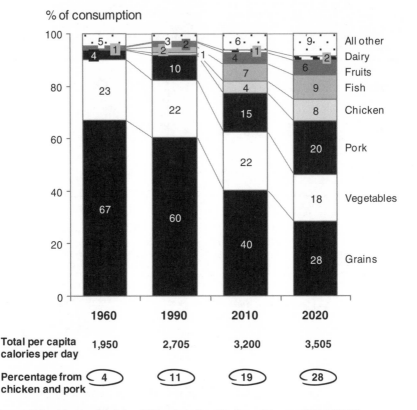

% of consumption

Sources: National Bureau of Statistics of China, Agriculture, http://www.stats.gov.cn/tjsj/ndsj/2011/indexeh.htm; United States Department of Agriculture, Economic Research Service, Data Sets, http://www.ers.usda.gov/Data/; Economist Intelligence Unit, Market Indicators and Forecasts; Euromonitor, Industries, Food-Related Industries.

to nearly 34 kilograms. In India, which is, because of Hindu strictures, a predominantly vegetarian country, meat consumption will rise only modestly—from 5.5 kilograms to about 8 kilograms per person. The big increase in the Indian consumer's diet will be dairy products, rising from 86 kilograms in 2010 to 102 kilograms per person.[2]

Two other factors explain the growing expenditure on food and drink: a predilection for healthy foods and, paradoxically, for Western-style fast foods—mainly in the expanding urban centers, where Western lifestyles have surged in popularity. Eating out, especially in restaurants and Internet cafés, has become the hot thing to do.

China, in particular, has long been acquainted with French fries, fried chicken, and sugar-rich carbonated drinks. Coca-Cola arrived in 1979 and enjoyed revenues topping $3 billion in 2010; KFC arrived in 1987 and pulled in revenues totaling an eye-popping $5 billion in 2011; McDonald's entered China in 1990 and reported revenues of $1.5 billion in 2010; and Starbucks arrived in 2000 and had nearly five hundred stores in mainland China by 2011. As we will describe later in the chapter, Yum! Brands, which owns KFC and Pizza Hut, has enjoyed enormous success.

These outlets have continued to prosper as lifestyles have continued to follow Western traditions and as the pressure of work has limited the time available to cook. Chinese people work longer hours than any other people in the world. In 2010, it was calculated that they work, on average, 2,200 hours every year. By contrast, people in the United States work just 1,610 hours.[3]

Chinese fast-food chains have also prospered—offering quick-service products such as pot noodles. Tingyi, the instant-noodle, beverage, and bakery giant, has seen astonishing growth. From 2005 to 2010, the company's revenues doubled to nearly $6 billion. In late 2011, it negotiated a contract with Pepsi for distribution of the U.S.-based company's soft drinks and, ultimately, the integration of the bottlers in the Pepsi network. Analysts have speculated that the independent beverage-distribution company owned by Tingyi, Pepsi, and Asahi Breweries could be worth $15 billion.

It is a big move for Tingyi. In 1992, the Taiwanese company, founded by four brothers, started selling instant noodles, and this business now has a market share of nearly 60 percent.[4] Four years later, it launched its ready-to-drink tea, bottled water, and juice business, which now generates $2.5 billion in revenue. But Tingyi's rising fortunes have not followed a straightforward upward trajectory.

In 1991, after one business venture—selling egg rolls and cooking oil—failed, Wei Yin-Heng, one of the brothers, felt disheartened and took a trip back to Taiwan. And then, returning to China, he noticed something that would change his life. "Every time I took out my dinner on the train, I would attract the attention of all the passengers in the compartment," he recalls. "People were so fascinated by the smell of my tasty food and so curious about where to buy similar products." What was he eating? "It was just the instant noodles I brought from Taiwan—and I sensed a huge business opportunity from this."

He launched the Master Kong brand—today China's biggest noodle brand. In Chinese, *kong* means "healthy," while *master* suggests professionalism, amiability, and responsibility—all good attributes in modern China. The noodles now come in a wide variety of flavors—more than one hundred—to suit different regional tastes: in the northern and eastern regions, the noodles are saltier; in the Shanghai region, they are sweeter; in the southern and eastern regions, Tingyi sells vermicelli noodles; and in the southwest, the company adds chili.

FIGURE 7-5

World's largest soup players: Tingyi versus Campbell Soup

Tingyi valuation increased from $1.1 billion to $17.2 billion in fifteen years.

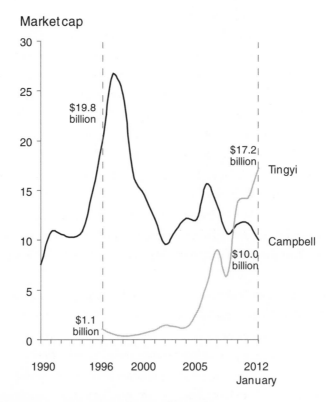

Sources: BCG Value Science Center; Yahoo! Finance; BCG analysis.
Note: To calculate market cap, Tingyi stock prices are converted to dollars at average annual exchange rates.

To get these products to the consumer, Tingyi has a network of five hundred sales and distribution offices, sells through nearly six thousand wholesalers, and boasts more than seventy thousand direct retailers.[5] It is a formidable operation, and not surprisingly, it was valued at $17.2 billion at year-end 2011, having doubled in size since 2007. In fact, a comparison of Tingyi and Campbell Soup, the venerable company based in Camden, New Jersey, shows very different stock price performance (figure 7-5).

Amul: The Taste of India

Every morning across India, millions of families wake up to a breakfast with milk, butter, yogurt, and other dairy products carrying the most famous brand name in the country: Amul, which means "priceless" in Hindi.[6]

In September 2011, as India prepared to launch its first Formula 1 Grand Prix, Monisha Kaltenborn, the Indian-born chief executive of the Sauber F1 Team, whose racing cars are supported by the dairy brand, said, "Amul products are present in practically every household. Having spent my childhood in Dehradun, India, I have fond memories of Amul, especially the Amul butter."[7]

Launched in 1946, Amul was initially the product of two village dairy cooperative societies that together produced 247 liters of milk each day. Today, more than three million farmers in sixteen thousand villages produce nearly twelve million liters of milk each day under the Amul brand, which is managed by the Gujarat Co-operative Milk Marketing Federation (GCMMF).

Amul is now a $2.5 billion business whose success is attributable to a number of factors. One is the evolution of a variety of dairy products—from pouched milk to milk powder, ice cream, and products processed with ultra-high temperatures (UHT). R. S. Sodhi, managing director of GCMMF, told us, "We were a milk and butter company. Then, in the 1990s, we added ice cream to our portfolio. And in 2000, we entered the fresh products market—for example, *dahi* [yogurt]."

Another factor is cost-effective marketing. If sponsorship of a Formula 1 racing team sounds expensive, the GCMMF spends just 1 percent of revenues on marketing—about $25 million—compared with the 10 percent spent by most food and consumer products companies.

A third factor is Amul's extensive distribution. From 2010 to 2011, it opened one thousand new Amul Parlours, taking the total to six thousand. These retail stores, offering the full range of Amul products, are located in bus and train stations, airports, tourist spots, colleges and universities, and government institutions. In an effort to increase its presence in rural districts, it has also created so-called super distributors: 30 so far, spread across eight states and covering 520 smaller towns. The plan is to increase these to 150, covering 3,000 small towns. Another retail venture is the Café Amul. This is a quick-service restaurant, piloted in Ahmedabad and serving Amul products: butter *pavbhaji*, pizzas, cheeseburgers, sandwiches, ice cream scoops, sundaes, and milk shakes. It is now being extended to other tier 1 cities.[8]

But if these factors are important, there is one other reason for Amul's success. As Sodhi told us, "The biggest reason for winning is taste. We *know* the taste of India. We *are* the taste of India."

KFC, Yum! Brands, and Duoduo's Birthday Party

Li Duoduo is six years old and lives in Jiangmen, a coastal city in southern China. By Chinese standards, she lives a privileged life and is already trading up. She attends a private school, takes English classes Tuesday through Friday, goes to a painting class on Saturday, and learns to play Go, an ancient board game, on Sunday. She is the daughter of two thirty-five-year-old civil servants with a combined household income of just over RMB 230,000 ($35,000) per year. The family spends a third of its income on its mortgage and saves another third. The rest goes to food, health care, transportation, and education. Duoduo and her parents live in a 1,300-square-foot apartment in downtown Jiangmen. When Duoduo's mother asked her where she wanted to have her sixth birthday party, the answer was instantaneous: "KFC."

At Kentucky Fried Chicken—which opened its first Chinese restaurant in Beijing in 1987 and which is now the largest restaurant chain in the country, with more than four thousand restaurants—a child's birthday party is a special responsibility. "It's a big, international brand with clean restaurants, quality food and service, and no surprises," Duoduo's mother says. The family dines at KFC twice a month. The Chinese restaurants are different from those in the United States and Europe. They have two to three times as much space, in addition to more extensive menus. Duoduo's favorite food is French fries, but equally important are the facilities: she loves to play in the store playground.

Duoduo got the idea to have her birthday party at KFC after she attended the party of one of her best friends. Mom said yes to this special treat. The party is free with the purchase of meals. Duoduo and her mother invited five families, including six other children. Unfortunately, Duoduo's father was unable to attend because he was working that Saturday.

The day was set: September 24. The big party began at 11:30 a.m. On hand to help was an employee known as a "KFC big sister," a female employee assigned to each party. The restaurant, which opened two years ago along Gangkou Road, has a bright blue, beige, and brown color scheme. As you enter, you can smell the aroma of fried chicken.

Upon arrival, the families were shown to a decorated party area. Duoduo wore her favorite pink princess shoes and insisted that her mother do her hair—with curls and matching bows. Most of the guests at the party feasted on fried chicken, French fries, and ice cream. Duoduo had a "burger"—a chicken sandwich. She could also have chosen KFC's version of Chinese food, including such exotic fare as Cantonese egg tarts, winter soup, oven-roasted wings, seasonal vegetables, and *congee*—a traditional Chinese soupy rice dish. Catering to China's widely varying appetites, KFC offers food that spans eight major Chinese cuisine types. On the menu are New Orleans roasted burgers, shrimp burgers, dragon twisters, milk tea with red beans, a breakfast pastry-puff sandwich, and Chinese Sichuan-flavored burgers. Many stores are open twenty-four hours a day and offer home delivery.

After devouring the meal, the children played organized games with the KFC big sister: a Chinese version of "Simon Says," a Chinese-character recognition game, and the equivalent of pickup sticks. The parents sat at a separate table, relaxing and drinking tea. For an extra RMB 3 (about $0.40), each child got a KFC prize. Duoduo, as the hostess, received a comic book. Her friends gave her gifts, including a pencil case, a headdress, three plastic dolls, and a building kit. Two of her friends begged their parents to duplicate the party for them when their birthdays rolled around.

This party was no accident.

Yum! Brands—the New York Stock Exchange–listed restaurant chain—owns KFC. David Novak, the company's CEO, is incredibly proud of his company's accomplishments in China. "Shortly after we were spun out from PepsiCo and I became CEO of the newly founded company, I visited China," he told us. "It was 1997, and we had a hundred stores in China. I was waiting in a long line at a KFC. The store was packed. A woman told me in Chinese, 'Build more stores.' It was the best advice I have ever gotten."

He encouraged a predominantly Chinese management team to develop best-in-class site development capability, an integrated supply chain, and local recipe innovation. Sam Su, the chairman and CEO of the China division of Yum! Brands, is credited with much of the company's success in China. A Taiwanese-born chemical engineer who graduated from the National Taiwan University before completing an MBA from Wharton and working at Procter & Gamble, Su embarked on a building spree in the late 1990s.

The first KFC opened in Tiananmen Square in 1987 and featured seating for five hundred customers. It then took the company another twelve years to reach three hundred outlets. Su's mission, to open one or more outlets every day, was ambitious—particularly because the outlets are typically twice as large as U.S. restaurants. But to get help in doing it, he created a build-out team of 450 people. "We clearly exceeded expectations," says Novak. "We looked at the business model and unit economics and we put the pedal to the metal. It was a good, profitable business. We worked hard at becoming local."

Novak considers China the number one plank in his company's growth strategy: "If Ray Kroc could do things over again at McDonald's, he would have had chicken, Mexican food, and pizza. But they came to that conclusion too late. China is at the ground floor of every category. There are just three restaurants per million in population versus sixty per million in the United States. We have more than four thousand restaurants and a $5 billion business. But we plan to be an $18 billion business in China in 2020 with ten thousand restaurants. We will be in every major category of restaurants."

True to his word, Yum! Brands announced the purchase of Little Sheep, a hot-pot restaurant operator, in November 2011. The deal, which was approved after a year of consideration by the Ministry of Commerce, was valued at $860 million. Little Sheep specializes in a meal called Mongolian hot pot, where patrons dip raw meat and vegetables into boiling broth. At the end of 2010, the company had 458 outlets in China.

Novak is bullish on India, too, but he is a realist about the requirements for duplicating Yum! Brand's success in China: "We are investing in India.

We have a hundred and forty KFCs and two hundred Pizza Huts. It's a youth franchise. We have created a vegetarian product line. But India's infrastructure is at least thirteen years behind China's."

Yum! Brands has certainly experienced rapid growth in China. Over the past five years, KFC's sales have risen at a compound annual rate of around 30 percent. Part of its success has been timing: a case of the right product and right vehicle at the right time. Chicken is the fastest-growing and, after pork, the most popular meat in the Chinese diet. KFC got to China early, and it hired local before anyone else.

But Yum! Brands also provides a complete example for adapting to the growing demand of China's consumers, building out stores across each city tier, and delivering very high profits. KFC offers consumers a good value proposition: a meal including two pieces of chicken, a side of French fries, and a drink costs about $2 in China. The restaurant also promotes itself as a provider of healthy food—consumers can replace Coke and French fries with juice and fruit. And two new products are unveiled every month, designed by the company's food lab for product development.

Yum! Brands has a broad network of restaurants, covering more than 720 cities, nearly half of them either tier 3 or below. And it has local staff who deliver on the one thing that really matters in quick-service restaurants: fast execution.

Moreover, each KFC is very profitable, achieving $1.2 to $1.3 million in annual sales and delivering a cash margin of 25 percent or more.[9] Investment is only $550,000 per store. Unit economics are as good in tier 2 cities as they are in top cities. New units are cash-flow positive in their first year. It is, therefore, not surprising that KFC is widening the gap with its big rival—McDonald's—especially in the smaller, lower-tier cities.

Just behind KFC in China is Yum! Brand's other business, Pizza Hut. The pizza chain was a first mover in the casual dining experience. It is positioned as a full-service restaurant; menus are extensive, running to more than thirty pages. Its sales and profits are similar to KFC's: for example, in a tier 3 city such as Wuhu, sales grew from $2 million in 2006 to more than $11 million in 2010, with profits growing from well under $1 million to over $3 million.

Novak says, "We're on the ground floor of this amazing country that's taking off. There's no question that it's the best restaurant opportunity in the twenty-first century. We expect that China will become our first billion-dollar-profit business within the next couple years."

Novak's first book is called *The Accidental CEO*. He tells the story of his humble beginnings and seizing opportunity as it came along. His new book, *Taking People with You*, is about leadership. He cites China as a classic example of all the principles of leadership success. Understanding the ambition of consumers—the desire to trade up—is vital. "Both the Chinese and the Indian people are very much in the pursuit of the American dream," Novak says. That American dream is what we hear from consumers across the two countries. They want more now.

Young Duoduo loved her birthday party, and she and her mother vowed to hold another party and to continue their bimonthly visits to this favorite restaurant. The child says she loves KFC and hopes to frequent KFC for the rest of her life.

Pepsi Kurkure: Indianizing the Product Portfolio

In the swanky hotel bar at the Hotel Oberoi in Gurgaon, businessmen were asking for another bowl of Kurkure to accompany their $20 Ballantine scotch and sodas. Far away, in the modest one-room home of a next-billion consumer in rural India, Kurkure came out again.

This salty, spicy, tangy snack—invented by PepsiCo—is a brand that has penetrated the top, middle, and even parts of the bottom of the income pyramid. Launched in 1999, Kurkure has reached revenues of more than $200 million and continues to grow by double digits. It has now become one of the flagship brands for PepsiCo in India.

PepsiCo reentered India in the 1990s (having first entered in the 1980s). At first, the company promoted its potato chip products, through the introduction of its global brand, Lay's. But changing food habits is difficult, and the American-style potato chip competed with local brands and more filling snacks such as samosas, *pakoras* (vegetable fritters), and biscuits.

Manu Anand, chairman and CEO of PepsiCo India, recalls, "In the mid-1990s, we realized that category creation takes time and we would not be able to build a business only on Lay's. We needed to have other products, and so we decided to Indianize our portfolio."

The obvious choice was to enter the *namkeen* market (*namkeen* in Hindi means "salty," but it also refers to Indian savory snacks), which PepsiCo did through the Lehar brand. By the end of the decade, however, the company found that namkeens were not providing a differentiated proposition or sufficient distribution velocity (the number of units sold per store per week).

"We tried our extruded portfolio," Anand says, "but consumers felt that Cheetos, with its corn and rice composition, was too light. We heard comments like, 'This is good for kids but I want something different and more filling.' The consumers were also saying, 'Don't give me more namkeen in a packet.' So we began looking for what we could do to find something to bridge the gap between the traditional namkeen and potato chips. We threw a challenge to our two-person R&D team to find something that filled this gap. The team started out testing various combinations and recipes. We had some unused assets in our factory in Channo and decided to use those as the base for whatever we did. The Lay's 'magic masala' flavor had proved to be a hit a couple of years back, so we knew what flavors worked in India."

Kurkure combines *besan* (ground chickpeas), which gives the snack its substance, and masala spices, which gives it zing. The product's name came about almost by accident. "Everyone was ideating on what the brand should be called," says Anand, "but when someone said 'kurkure' ('crunchy') in Hindi, the name stuck. It just felt right! We felt that we had the right product and the right brand. Consumers loved it and were coming back for more and more."

The in-store merchandising used for Kurkure was critical to its success. As Anand told us, the in-store racks were a new concept at that time. They allowed impulse purchases.

The initial success of Kurkure provided momentum for PepsiCo in India. It permitted the company to build a volume business to drive the snack's distribution, with Kurkure as the base load. Affordability has been a major factor in the snack's success. Kurkure started with three price points: 5, 10, and 20 rupees ($0.10, $0.20, and $0.40) for 25-gram, 50-gram, and 125-gram packs, respectively. These prices were about the same as those for potato chips sold under the Lay's brand, but the Kurkure packs contained 50 to 70 percent more volume by weight. Kurkure's success is a unique story of localized consumer insight and intrapreneurship—managers at a global company acting like Indian entrepreneurs on a shoestring budget.

A Sparkling Business: From Baijiu to Champagne, Bordeaux, and Whiskey

Zhang Jing and Li Demei stood in the Royal Opera House in London's Covent Garden in the fall of 2011—and smiled. The winemakers had just become the first Chinese to win viticulture's equivalent of an Oscar for their red Bordeaux.

Alongside Châteaux Lafite Rothschild, Margaux, and Latour, the name He Lan Qing Xue hardly trips off the tongue. But this winery, which Zhang, a thirty-four-year-old mother and banker's wife, runs in the mountainous northeast region of Ningxia, is now being talked about in this same distinguished company. Its Jia Bei Lan Cabernet dry red wine—the 2009 vintage—picked up the international trophy for Best Bordeaux Varietal over £10 at the Decanter World Wine Awards.[10]

Yet perhaps this should not be so surprising. The Chinese are now the world's biggest importers of French Bordeaux, having overtaken the United Kingdom in 2010.[11] More broadly, they saw their wine consumption double between 2005 and 2010. It means that China is now the world's biggest market for wines and spirits, accounting for about 40 percent of global consumption.[12] Trophy Bordeaux is a much-wanted gift in China. It is used as "grease" to ease and speed decision making. It often cycles back to Hong Kong's wine auctions, where the gift is easily converted to cash.

In the mid-2000s, nearly all the wine consumed in China was produced locally, and not all of it was pure grape juice. As Li Demei, the consultant who advised Zhang on her red Bordeaux, explains, "What I grew up calling wine was actually grape juice mixed with some other sort of alcohol." It was only later, when he studied horticulture in college and his lecturer, fresh from a trip to France, created a laboratory to make wine, that he tasted the drink for the first time. And his reaction? "I didn't like it. For me, it was too acid."

But now, Chinese consumers have certainly acquired the taste for, as they put it, "grape wine." When the 2008 Mouton Rothschild chose a Chinese artist for its label, wine merchants said the futures prices for the vintage increased overnight. The artist will receive six cases of the wine—worth close to $100,000—when it is released. Rothschild printed this message on the label: "The role of a great wine as a link between people and cultures, from one hemisphere to the other." At the Christie's auction in Hong Kong, a single six-liter bottle of 1961 Latour sold for $216,000.

Such is the demand for wine—especially red wine, which commands 90 percent of the market—that companies are waking up to the commercial opportunities. There is plenty of room to grow. Although China is the world's biggest wine market, it remains remarkably undeveloped; on average, Chinese drinkers consume just one liter per year, compared with twenty-three liters in Western Europe.

Cofco: A $100 Billion Company?

One of the companies seizing the opportunities in the fast-expanding alcohol business is China National Oils, Foodstuffs and Cereal Corporation—better known as Cofco. This giant state-owned conglomerate is China's largest food processor. Frank Ning, the chairman, who studied for an MBA at the University of Pittsburgh before returning to China's state-owned business sector, is building the company's future on China's growing demand for food and drink. "If China eats, we will grow," he says quite simply. "We are at the center of their plate—rice, dairy, snacks." A tough-minded, acquisition-oriented businessman with a lust for growth, he thinks he can turn Cofco into a $100 billion food and beverage company.

Before the Reform Trading Policy of 1987, Cofco was the only sanctioned importer and exporter of food, grain, and edible oils in China. Monopolies generate a lot of profits and can cover up weaknesses in cost structure and market responsiveness. In the early 1990s, the company experienced competition for the first time. According to Ning, the competition made Cofco tougher, and it reorganized by line of business. Cofco looked at line-of-business profitability and cut out failing parts of the business. It was capitalism with a purpose—profitable growth.

But Ning says Cofco still works hand in hand with the government. His office is located in a modern Beijing office tower within an easy walk of the government agencies with which he needs to interact. "This is a managed economy, and the government is a good partner," he says. "During the next ten years, we will apply the Western model to our economy. The Chinese economy will continue its fast-growth momentum in the next ten years. We need to deliver stability—political, social, balance between rich and poor, urban and rural. If we do that, our opportunities are unlimited."

In 2010, Cofco bought a major wine maker in Chile. Then, in February 2011, the company bought Bordeaux-based Château de Viaud, a small wine producer with vineyards at Lalande-de-Pomerol. This deal, like others, was driven by the theory that Chinese consumers will trade up to better quality and that companies should control the full value chain. It might seem incongruous that the company that holds the biggest bottling contract for that other great Western drink, Coca-Cola, should be suddenly so interested in the luxury drink. Yet Cofco has actually been in the wine business since the 1980s and was named the official wine supplier at the Beijing Olympic Games in 2008. Its flagship wine is the Great Wall brand, which it even exports to France. But the newly purchased Château de Viaud will allow Cofco not only to import the winemaker's own Bordeaux but also to learn much-needed skills in fine viticulture. This will be important, as the wine market is preparing for some unprecedented competition.

The acquisition also takes Cofco in a new direction. Ning has put much thought into the company's vision and direction. Its bright future is suggested by the corporate logo, which symbolizes a "broad sky, dazzling sun, fertile land, early spring." He wants to break out of the mold of the state-owned enterprise. "Chinese companies are mostly in low-profit areas of the value chain," he explains. "Every time Ralph Lauren sells a shirt, it enhances its brand value. However, every time Chinese companies produce a shirt, their equipment depreciates." With wine and other branded products, he thinks he can change this: "We want to be an innovator."

LVMH and the Market for Celebration

The last two letters in LVMH's name refer to its beverage businesses: the M for Moët, the company that owns such coveted champagne brands as Dom Perignon and Veuve Cliquot, and the H for Hennessy, the iconic cognac brand. China, and to some extent India, are proving to be major markets for the legion of beverage brands owned by the world's biggest luxury company. Indeed, in 2010, China was LVMH's second-biggest market for wines and spirits, accounting for 25 percent of its beverage business. Only the United States, with 45 percent of the business, was bigger.[13]

In May 2011, LVMH entered into a joint venture with Ningxia Nongken, a state-owned agribusiness, to produce Chinese sparkling wine within three years. This new product will be sold under the Chandon label, a secondary brand that currently markets wines from non-French domains in California, Brazil, Argentina, and Australia.[14] Officially, it will not be called Champagne, a name reserved for wine produced on the much-treasured eighty thousand acres of French *terroir* some one hundred miles to the east of Paris.

LVMH sees an opportunity in India, too. In Nashik, a city 105 miles southwest of Mumbai that has been dubbed the country's wine capital, the company is building a sparkling wine production facility. The market is considerably smaller than the Chinese market, with just 1.5 million cases sold every year, or approximately 13.5 million liters.

But LVMH faces some familiar competition. Château Lafite Rothschild, one of the most revered names in winemaking, has partnered with CITIC, China's largest state-owned investment company, to create a *grand cru* on a sixty-acre vineyard in Shandong province on the country's northeast coast.[15]

The rationale for this investment is clear. Not only is a trophy wine from a famous château often the currency that closes a deal in China, but it is also the accompaniment to great celebrations, which have been many and frequent in China over recent years. As Cofco's promotional literature explains, "Not only is it an enjoyable drink, but also a symbol of coexistence, fraternity, communication, and shared joy."[16]

Pernod Ricard, Whiskey, and Green Tea

Another French company that is prospering because of the Chinese consumer's newfound taste for Western drinks is Pernod Ricard. In the late 1990s, the Paris-based company suffered a drop in its China business and ordered a rethink of its go-to-market strategy. It conducted a detailed market and competitor assessment, redesigned its sales force, renewed its M&A effort, and established a government relations capability—a key requirement given that many of its local rivals were state-owned corporations.

The results have been striking: a tenfold increase in revenues between 2004 and 2010 and the creation of a business that is now the second-largest in the company's global portfolio, which is expected to surpass the company's U.S. business in 2015. "When Chinese businessmen celebrate, they come together to bond," Con Constandis, Pernod Ricard's managing director, told us while explaining the company's success. "Our products are badges of success. We have the leading scotch in Chivas Regal and the leading cognac in Martell. It's about pure joy and camaraderie."

Constandis says his China business was "on fire," adding that the turning point came when it redesigned its marketing program. "We asked bar operators why they prefer to sell beer," he says. "It was about turnover and margin. We tinkered until we found a formula where we could be ahead. A bottle of Chivas and six teas have more margin than beers. To the Chinese consumer, it's a good taste. Green tea and Chivas became the hottest drink in China. Smooth, easygoing, something to drink all night."

In a typical outlet, prior to the new marketing programs, beer generated thirty times the profit of Chivas. Afterward, the profitability of outlets tripled. Whiskey sales also spurred growth in cognac sales.

Pernod Ricard—whose product line includes Chivas, Ballantine, Martell, Absolut, Beefeater, Kahlua, and a number of local brands—now generates well over $1 billion in annual revenues, roughly half as much as Coca-Cola. "China is now the second-largest market for Pernod Ricard after the U.S.," says Constandis. "We will cross over the U.S. in roughly four years. We can see how the market can grow from twenty-five million consumer targets to two hundred million targets. We've barely gotten started."

Though Chivas Regal has caught the imagination of the Chinese consumers and persuaded them of the merits of Scotch whiskey, many drinkers still prefer *baijiu*—the Chinese brewed spirit. As a result, several multinationals have bought up local distillers to learn how to serve the clientele best. Pernod Ricard has a joint venture with Jiannanchun Group, a local *baijiu* maker.[17] LVMH acquired a 55 percent stake in Wenjun Distillery, one of China's premium *baijiu* purveyors.[18] And in June 2011, Diageo, a U.K. beverage company, received regulatory approval to buy Shui Jing Fang, which bills itself as China's oldest *baijiu* maker.[19]

The Oreo Story: How Kraft Turned America's Favorite Cookie into a Chinese Classic

When Irene Rosenfeld became CEO of Kraft Foods in June 2006, she became the leader of a company organized in two divisions: North America and International. The international business was a low-growth and Europe-heavy counterpart of the core U.S. business. Most of the international business consisted of German coffee, European cheese, and Milka brand chocolate. In addition, there were numerous orphan businesses—small, one-off country positions. Advertising support was in the low single digits and declining. Profits were erratic, as the commodity-driven portfolio lacked pricing power. Consumer market research was a stepchild.

Rosenfeld has three particularly strong leadership skills—curiosity, energy, and instinct. She studied how other multinationals had secured major emerging-market positions, and she vowed to shift her portfolio. She knew that she needed to follow the growth and that the company needed an infusion of talent and international experience. This strategy has worked. In the five years preceding her appointment as chairman and CEO, Kraft Foods International grew at about 5 percent per year. In the five years after her arrival, the international business grew—organically and through acquisition—by 250 percent, and the developing-markets portfolio grew by a whopping 300 percent. Most of that growth was in China and India.

Kraft is now almost as international as Rosenfeld's role model, Procter & Gamble. And it is poised for another phase of growth. In mid-2011, the company decided to create two new companies out of one company: there will be a growth-oriented company consisting of Kraft Foods' European and developing-markets business, plus its North American snacks business; and there will be the North American grocery business—including the beverages, cheese, grocery, and convenience-meals businesses.

The pathway of the Oreo cookie in China is a big element in the story of Kraft's transformation. One of Rosenfeld's first moves as CEO was to recruit a tall, soft-spoken Indian named Sanjay Khosla to lead this charge. Khosla, now sixty, wears wire-frame glasses and loose-knit sweaters and laughs heartily. He has traveled his entire working life, beginning in his early days in the Hindustan Unilever sales force in India selling the full line of Unilever products. He is intensely competitive and, because of his location, works hardest before and after sunrise in the United States—doing phone calls and meetings with his remote lieutenants. He logs close to a million miles a year in travel.

Khosla has trudged into the most remote markets of Asia, hired salespeople, and invented new products and business models. He likes to tell stories about miracles happening when people focus on a brand, a market, a category. He calls it "winning through focus." He pushed the developing markets unit at Kraft to deliver on a five-ten-ten strategy. He used the phrase to divert resources to just five markets, ten categories, and ten brands.

His philosophy of business starts with getting the gross margin right. For Khosla, that means looking at all the elements of cost as well as benchmarking local players. Only when he has the gross margin right will he make incremental marketing investments. He calls it the virtuous circle of growth. "My most important lesson is about sustainable business models," he says. "When people in China or India tell you to wait ten years for profits, they have it wrong. You need the right cost structure, the infrastructure; you need to be able to compete head-on locally."

Khosla, a graduate of the Indian Institute of Technology in Delhi, was living in New Zealand and working for Fonterra, a multinational dairy cooperative, when Rosenfeld called. Rosenfeld's job offer came with assurances that she had a serious appetite for acquisitions to spur growth. Khosla came on board within five months of her appointment. He recruited many people from his network and began his Winning in Kraft International (WIKI) workshops.

He used these to gauge the talent of his local teams, tease out their views, ask about obstacles created by headquarters, and identify opportunities in the market. He vowed change—in particular, the creation of new business models. For him, a winning business model starts with understanding consumers: what they like and dislike about the product, how they consume it, who in the family eats it and how frequently, what the model of brand adoption is, what price points set the retail store on fire and why, and most specifically, what it takes to unlock a rupee or a renminbi.

Khosla looked at China and India with particular glee. Of course, he knew India intimately, but he had also developed several China joint ventures. Despite his low-key personality, Khosla is very strict about three principles: focusing on a small set of tasks, unleashing the team, and paying rigorous attention to delivering to plan. His twenty-plus quarters of sustainable growth have set the bar at Kraft.

His instinct told him that starting an Indian business de novo would take years, cost tens of millions of dollars to develop, and drain talent from his light bench. Likewise, his instinct said that China as structured would never turn a profit—the gross margins were too low, the fixed costs were too high, and the Chinese consumer did not have the same taste characteristics as the U.S. consumer. He did his version of the classic in-home consumer interview in Shanghai, where Kraft China had its headquarters, and he decided that a lot had to change to make the Kraft business come alive in China.

"When I got here, we had less than $100 million in business in China and we were losing money," Khosla explains. "I was told that there was once a dream to make China a $1 billion business, to match the billion-odd people in the country. The trouble was that after five years, we only had a $100 million business. The gross margins were too low, and the cost structure was built for a different scale and a Western world."

Khosla soon realized why: the previous managers had simply transplanted their American go-to-market model—building a large manufacturing facility with "gold plating"; serving only the small, organized trade in Beijing and Shanghai; and relying on a team of expensive, non-Chinese-speaking expats.

To address the problem, Khosla asked his Chinese team to focus on one category—not five. He decided that cookies were core and that Oreo was the key brand, even though it was "on the cusp of being delisted."

As Khosla revamped the Oreo brand in China, Rosenfeld pursued the first major transaction of her tenure as Kraft's CEO. Danone, the French water and yogurt company, had decided to sell its Lefèvre Utile (LU) cookie business, and Rosenfeld realized that inside LU was a China business a little bigger than Kraft's—and much more profitable.

"The neat thing about LU is that it gave us a beachhead in a number of the developing markets where we were not particularly successful," Rosenfeld says. "I am really proud of this fact: the legacy Kraft business, before we bought LU, was about $50 million in China. We sold $100 million there in the month of January 2011." She adds, "It's a real testament to the power of finding the toehold, putting the right managers in place, and then building on that infrastructure. The combination of those two moves leapfrogged us into a whole new position. And that's one of the reasons I'm so confident that we're on a much stronger growth trajectory today than we were a couple years ago."[20]

The LU acquisition also brought talent in the form of Lorna Davis—a tall, blonde South African who was placed in charge of the China business. Today, she is worldwide head of Kraft's biscuit category and still based in Shanghai. She blossomed under Khosla's very particular style of management, which emphasizes "freedom within a framework." He gives his top executives what he calls "blank checks"—virtually unlimited resources within the company's strategic framework. "When you say to someone, 'Spend the money as you see fit within a strategic framework,' they work hard to show results—sales growth, bottom line, cash," he says. "We encourage disruptive new ways of working, and a process that gets to closure."

"We gave Lorna a blank check to grow the business within our strategic framework," says Khosla. "You cannot change 'lick, twist, and dunk' on Oreo. You cannot change the fundamental profile of the cocoa and the ingredients. But you can connect locally." Davis continued the success of LU, which had cleverly customized its products for the Chinese market—to the extent that it was almost seen as a local brand—and which had hustled its products through the many small family-operated outlets and turned a profit.

The first thing that was changed was the recipe, after market testing showed that the American Oreo was too sweet for Chinese consumers. A reduced-sugar Oreo proved an instant success. The team then experimented with the look of the Oreo. No longer just selling the chocolate wafer with a vanilla center, Kraft devised a four-layered crispy wafer filled with vanilla and chocolate cream and covered with chocolate, too. Since then, the company has added other flavors—including peanut butter and green tea ice cream—as well as a hollow, tube-shaped wafer lined with cream. Chinese consumers use the wafer as a straw for drinking milk.

But changing the taste and the look of the Oreo was only one of many challenges. "The fact that it was too sweet was only the beginning," says Khosla. "You need to make it the best. You need to make it local. We realized that we had to compete at low price points and make money immediately."

The Oreo team changed the packaging, shrinking the number of cookies per pack and charging RMB 2 ($0.29) instead of RMB 5 ($0.72). It also made some marketing and operational changes: creating a troop of brand ambassadors to ride through the streets of Beijing on bicycles with wheel covers resembling Oreos and to hand out the cookies to more than three hundred thousand consumers; recruiting Yao Ming, the Chinese basketball star, to appear in commercials explaining the "twist, lick, and dunk" routine; and introducing a proprietary handling process so that the chocolate could arrive in the cold north or hot south and still be good for eating.

The strategy has worked. "Oreo is the number one biscuit in China, up about 60 percent in 2011," says Khosla, "and on track to be ten times bigger than when I started with Kraft."

This same strategy has worked in India, too. When Khosla joined Kraft, the company had little business in India. In his first year, he invited Rosenfeld to accompany him to his native country. They both had their eye on Cadbury, the venerable British firm, with its iconic brands, such as Cadbury Dairy Milk and Trident, and its strong network of distribution channels. The two imagined how they could launch cookies and powdered beverages (such as Tang) if only Kraft owned Cadbury in India.

After a tussle, Kraft eventually acquired Cadbury, and Khosla turned to his new Indian management team and said, "Grow." He gave them virtually unlimited resources to invest in the chocolate business—but again, all within a strategic framework. "We were a $400 million business in 2009 in India," he says. "I just said, 'I want to make it $500 million in 2010, and I'll give you a blank check.' They fell off their chairs. The business proposition was two pages, and it was approved in twenty-four hours. They delivered 27 percent growth in 2010. So Cadbury Dairy Milk, which has been in India for sixty-odd years, was soon growing over 40 percent." Some of that growth was attributable to a massive increase in demand in the Indian market, but some was due to a simple insight: the use of coolers to make the business less seasonal by keeping chocolate from melting in India's oppressive heat.

Khosla has worked hand in hand with his team in Asia to accomplish this growth agenda. Pradeep Pant, one of Khosla's recruits, is the fifty-seven-year-old head of Kraft's Asian business. He joined Kraft Foods five years ago after a career working for multinationals, including Gillette and Fonterra. With a deep, husky voice and an engaging style, he makes direct eye contact and nods to secure agreement from his audience as he speaks. He is strong-willed and decisive with a take-charge attitude.

"How high is high? How big is big? That is our question," Pant says over lunch. "The only thing that will limit our growth is our will and imagination. You need to be a leader who is fearless, willing to take chances, to make things happen. China is not complex. India is not complex. Our focus needs to be on execution."

Pant is thoughtful on the theme of leadership. You cannot fall into the trap of being a division of a multinational waiting for approvals, he says. He likes to make lightning-fast decisions and would prefer to seek pardon if it does not work out. He also believes that many multinationals turn their leadership teams over too fast. "The organization needs to feel settled. The 'oil' needed for success in both India and China is emotional." Today's young executives are "tempted all the time by other companies seeking talent: so, to secure them, you need to earn their loyalty, and to do that you need to really know them, know their hopes, and know their families. You can't learn that in a three-year tour."

If nurturing local teams is essential for success in China and India, so too is creating local products. "We take global ideas from Kraft and we twist them to be local. We've taken the phrase 'glocal' and made it 'think local, act local,'" Pant explains. "We customize to Chinese tastes. We package to Chinese consumers. We understand how you win at the shelves and how you win at home."

"It's not about making thirty-second commercials," he continues. "It's about integrated marketing. It's about engaging the consumer wherever they are. We engage our consumers on multiple levels."

It is these strategies that have helped transform Kraft and Oreo in the world's biggest emerging markets. And there will likely be a second chapter to the story. Khosla believes that Oreo has the potential to eventually be bigger in China (and India) than in the originating market, the United States.

The food and beverage markets in China and India are rapidly growing because of newly affluent consumers' demand for safer, healthier food—and Western-style products. They want wholesome produce, more protein, greater variety, and, for some—especially working women—ready-to-consume products.

Our recipe for success in China and India in the food and beverages categories includes the following practices:

- Doing original research at the point of consumption

- Understanding latent and unspoken needs

- Researching specific tastes, flavors, and forms

- Overinvesting in safety and quality as a differentiator

- Providing international tastes reformulated for local markets

- Using global icons as brand endorsers

- Segmenting the market—by gender, age, income, and lifestyle—and adapting accordingly

- Following the mouths—rural to urban, nonorganized trade to organized trade, at-home consumption to on-the-go consumption, family meals to individuals on their own

EIGHT

House and Home

The "Des Res," Furniture, and the Fridge

The rise of home ownership and how companies can satisfy the needs of house-proud consumers for mortgages, decoration, and household appliances

I T WAS A MOMENT OF great celebration as Jaideep and his wife, Saumya, conducted a *griha pravesh*. After months of preparation, the young couple were giving thanks to the Hindu deities and finally moving into their new home: an apartment on the eleventh floor of a high-rise complex in Whitefield, one of Bangalore's best suburbs.

Surrounded by family and friends, and with a *pandit*, or priest, chanting from the ancient Vedic scripts for the duration of the two-day festival, this housewarming gathering was a blend of old and new. The aroma of marigold tree flowers, scattered throughout the luxury apartment to ward off evil spirits, filled the air. "It was a dream come true," recalls Jaideep, a thirty-two-year-old mechanical engineer.

For his parents, it was even more remarkable, and quite overwhelming. "I wish we could have bought our house when we were in our thirties," says his mother. But when she was newly married, the idea of owning her own home was a far-off prospect. "I still remember the day when we set foot in our own house," says Jaideep's father. "I had already reached fifty."

Three thousand miles away, as Jaideep was celebrating, Zhang, a thirty-three-year-old civil servant, was enjoying the luxurious surroundings of his new apartment in downtown Shanghai. Until then, he and his wife, Zhu Wei, and their one-year-old daughter had lived with his parents, who had saved all their lives to buy a property on the outskirts of the city. Not prepared to wait and anxious to have some independence, Zhang decided to take out a mortgage, something his parents had never considered. "I hugged my wife the moment I stepped into the apartment," says Zhang. "Finally, we had our own place."

In India and in China, the young are not wasting any time getting on to the property ladder. As we will show in this chapter, they are taking out large mortgages, moving into newly built homes fitted with every modern appliance, and spending large portions of their income on decoration and interior design, all in search of the "des res" (desirable residence).

The home has become a haven in China and India. Property—a stamp of achievement—generates the same conversation in China and India that it did in the West in the 1990s.

Home Sweet Home: Dreams of Dependable Power, Indoor Plumbing, and a Big-Screen TV

The rise of homeownership mirrors the rise of China and India. Prior to 1998, few people owned their own homes in China. Then, in that year, property developers were given the go-ahead to begin building a new generation of private homes: everything from *siheyuan* (grand courtyard homes) to gated communities and sky-rise apartments.

India has seen a residential property boom. Building companies have been constructing traditional *bungalows*—handsome mansions, deriving from the Hindi word for "Bengali"—as well as penthouse apartments and so-called integrated townships, where family homes, offices, and shops are built along with hospitals, schools, hotels, and other amenities.

In 1990, there were 227 million houses in China and 145 million in India. By 2010, these numbers had increased to 371 million and 213 million, respectively. The rationale for this growth is threefold. The single biggest reason is urbanization. As discussed in chapter 5, China and India have witnessed a dramatic rise in the number of city dwellers.

Linked to this development is the emergence of the nuclear family—parents and their children—in the two countries. Traditionally, the multigenerational, extended family—or "joint" family, as Indians refer to it—was predominant.

In the past two decades, however, as young people have left the family home and migrated to urban centers in pursuit of jobs, they are moving to the kind of single-family unit more common in the United States and Europe.

This change is influencing the type of housing available in the major cities. In Mumbai, the world's most densely populated city, the preference is for an apartment in a high-rise building, especially units with one or two bedrooms. In 1980, some 82 million Indian households were living in houses or apartments with one to two bedrooms. By 2010, the number had doubled to 163 million. By 2020, the number is expected to grow to more than 189 million.[1]

A third reason for the growth in residential housing is the readiness of today's generation to take out loans to buy their dream house or apartment. Unlike their parents' generation, young people today are not prepared to wait to start climbing the property ladder.

In India, the home loan market grew by an average of about 32 percent per year between 2001 and 2011. In 2001, loans totaled 586 billion rupees ($13 billion).[2] Ten years later, the amount had risen to 9.3 trillion rupees ($200 billion). By 2016, it is expected to grow by an average annual rate of 19 percent to 22 trillion rupees ($480 billion).[3]

It is not just that more people are taking out loans; the growth is also attributable to the growing size of each loan. In 2007, the average loan in urban districts was 1.3 million rupees ($28,000). By 2011, this had risen to 1.8 million ($39,000). It is expected to break the 2 million mark in 2012, rising to 2.5 million rupees ($54,000) in 2013.

Meanwhile, the age at which people feel comfortable taking on such debt has fallen dramatically in the past decade. In 2000, the average age for an Indian taking out a mortgage was forty-three. By 2010, it had fallen to thirty-six. It is expected to fall further, to thirty-four, by 2015. "I have a secure job and I expect my income to grow in the future," one thirty-year-old Mumbai homeowner told us. Taking out a loan with Axis bank, a popular mortgage lender, he adds, "I am confident that I will pay off my debts soon."

But such confidence disturbs the older generation. "I am very scared of my kids' taking such a big loan," one fifty-five-year-old says. "We never know what the future has in store." Another older person, a fifty-eight-year-old located in Bangalore, shares these sentiments: "Taking a loan takes away my independence. I would always be living under the pressure of paying off my debts."

In China, too, the urgency to buy property is such that people lined up overnight outside property developers' offices in advance of a sale of new apartments in 2010—just as shoppers in New York or London will line up outside an Apple store for the latest iPhone or iPad. In one startling case, a property developer sold 150 apartments *in one day* in Nanning, a subtropical city not far from the Vietnamese border.

This urgency is chiefly attributable to an extraordinary spike in prices. According to data from China's National Bureau of Statistics, compiled by the *Financial Times*, Beijing saw property prices rise from RMB 4,557 ($700) per square meter in 2000 to RMB 17,782 ($2,700) per square meter in 2010.[4] In Shanghai, over the same period, prices rose from RMB 3,326 ($500) to RMB 14,400 ($2,200). The coastal capital has some residential districts where the condominiums are even pricier than in Manhattan.

In China, there are fears that real estate is a bubble that could burst, with serious effects on the country's economy. More than 15 percent of the country's investment goes into real estate, and around 12 percent of GDP comes from property-related industries. In 2010, for the first time, China overtook the United States as the world's largest center for construction, investing more than $1 trillion in building projects. Over half of this money was spent on new housing.

The government has taken action, introducing several measures, including these, to dampen prices:

- Increasing the down payment requirements for second homes from 50 percent to 60 percent.

- Imposing restrictions on multiple purchases: local residents that already own one property can purchase only one additional property. Locals with two or more properties and nonlocal residents with one property will not be allowed to purchase any additional property.

- Requiring local governments to set price-growth caps. The target will be in accordance with local income growth, affordability, and economic development.

- Enforcing relevant tax laws (e.g., a tax on properties resold within five years of purchase will be levied on the sales value).

- Allocating land to lower-cost housing: 70 percent of the land supply is dedicated to social housing.[5]

At the more affordable end of the housing market, demand in China and India remains strong, and we expect a significant rise in the amount that Chinese and Indian consumers spend on housing and household goods over the next decade. In 2010, on average, just $147 was spent per person on housing in India.[6] In China, the figure was higher, at $580. By contrast, in the United States the number was $16,880.

We calculate that by 2020, China will see a 234 percent increase in housing expenditure per capita, taking the average expenditure to $1,940, while Indian expenditures will increase almost fourfold to $575. The U.S. figure of $20,760 will still dwarf the Chinese and Indian numbers, but will represent only a 23 percent increase.

As we will show in the final section of this chapter, such growth provides opportunities for all kinds of companies—the house builders and their suppliers, the specialist furnishings businesses, and the makers of household appliances. But first, we will describe the buying decisions of Jaideep, Zhang, and their families.

Two Families in Two Cities: Bangalore and Shanghai

Bangalore, India's third-largest city, is sometimes described as that country's answer to Silicon Valley. Long associated with technical advances—it was the first Asian city to have electricity—it has become home to some of the world's great IT outsourcing companies, including Infosys.

It was to this city that Jaideep returned after a three-year stint in Boston. Married, with a three-year-old son, he set up home in a cramped two-bedroom apartment without any amenities or yard. Purchased as an investment, it no longer suited the needs of a growing family, as Jaideep and Saumya often talked about having a second child.

So they resolved to buy a bigger home. They set their sights on one of the new developments going up on the outskirts of the city. The one that caught their eye had everything they ever wanted: landscaped gardens, children's play areas, a clubhouse, a gym, tennis courts, and a huge shopping complex.

After the first visit, they got excited, imagining their son growing up as part of a community. They went straight to the property developer to book an apartment—even though the building was still under construction.

Then came the tough question: how to pay for it? After much deliberation, they decided not to sell their current apartment, which would have meant letting it go for a low price, but to take out a substantial mortgage.

This raised a second problem: finding a mortgage lender that would give them the money quickly. Time was of the essence. If they delayed more than a month, the property developer would almost certainly have to raise the price to keep pace with the market. They looked at ICICI Bank and Axis Bank, and eventually settled for LIC Housing Finance, part of the mammoth Life Insurance Corporation (LIC), India's largest state-owned life insurance company and the country's single biggest investor. "One of our close friends had taken out a loan with them, and they were very satisfied," says Jaideep. "So we did not think more."

The couple elected to take out a twenty-year loan of 4.8 million rupees ($104,000), at a rate of 8.9 percent. It was then that the hard work began: decorating the house and filling it with beautiful things.

They talked about hiring an interior designer and then thought otherwise. "Ever since my childhood, I had always wanted to design my own house," says Saumya. "I just thought it would be such a great feeling to live in a house that had been designed from corner to corner by me."

The first decisions were about tiles and paint. The property developer was preparing to place standard nonvitrified tiles throughout the apartment. But Saumya resisted this, preferring instead to pay extra for shinier vitrified tiles, which give the home a brighter and more polished look.

For the walls, Jaideep and Saumya toyed with the idea of hiring local painters, but after doing some significant research on the Internet, they came across the "home solutions" service offered by Asian Paints, the country's biggest decorating company. They had already decided on buying Royale Play, a brand of special-effects paint produced by Asian Paints. Reassured by its brand, and hearing positive recommendations from friends, they hired the company's professional painters.

With those decisions behind them, the couple then focused on the two most important rooms in the apartment: the kitchen and the living room. "We searched the Internet for designs," says Saumya, "and we were ready to spend whatever it took to do the kitchen." They also visited some of the big-name home furnishings outlets to get ideas about designs and prices. Saumya's preferred shop is HomeTown, a DIY specialist launched in 2007 by Future Group, the retailer founded by Kishore Biyani, one of India's best-known self-made billionaires. In the end, they opted for a Western-style modular kitchen, which would allow Saumya to shift the units if, at a later stage, she wanted to rearrange the room. But it was not cheap: 350,000 rupees ($7,600).

In the living room, the couple sought the help of a local carpenter, who advised them on the designs for shelves, tables, and other furniture. "This is the place where we were going to spend most of our time," says Saumya, "and so we wanted furniture that was elegant and comfortable."

All this preparation took several months—hence the celebration when they finally crossed the threshold. As they walked into their new home, they entered an altogether more modern world—and the sweet-smelling marigold flowers, which had covered the apartment, were soon replaced by the first of a series of new appliances.

For the kitchen, they bought a Samsung refrigerator—one with double doors and a water dispenser—and, as part of the deal, received a free dishwasher. They also bought an LG washing machine in time for Diwali.

For the living room, they bought a forty-two-inch wide-screen Samsung TV, having also considered Sony's rival product. They set aside their biggest pot of money for a home theater system from Denon, the Japanese electronics firm. It cost them more than 200,000 rupees ($4,300)—nearly two-thirds of the price of the whole kitchen. But rather than compromise on quality, they spread the purchase over four months, and when the wait was over, they celebrated by settling down to watch one of their favorite Bollywood movies.

Zhang's story is remarkably similar—and points to a common aspirational drive among the new generation of consumers. A civil servant, he specializes in youth development and community service. As such, he really knows Shanghai's various districts, having pounded the streets to meet different groups of young people across the city. So when he resolved to move out of his parents' home, he knew exactly where he wanted to live: downtown Shanghai.

But wanting it is one thing, and getting it quite another.

First, Zhang and his wife, Zhu Wei, a thirty-one-year-old civil servant, looked at their finances and discussed some options with his parents. They realized that they wanted to stay together as an extended family, even if they no longer remained in the same house. So they explored the possibility of buying two apartments, relatively close together, so that Zhang's parents could continue to provide child care (the couple have a baby girl) while Zhang and his wife were busy building their careers.

Fortunately, the couple possessed considerable savings, although it was not enough to pay for two apartments, even with the proceeds of the sale of Zhang's parents' home. So they turned to the bank and arranged for a ten-year mortgage, something that had never been available to Zhang's parents.

With their finances in place, they started searching for their dream home, scouring the Internet and making visits to downtown Shanghai. After much research, they focused on the Jingan district, a hip and happening place with swanky shops and a vibrant nightlife, and soon selected Sanhe Garden, a prestigious development produced by Shanghai Sanhe Real Estate Company.

The place has everything they wanted: good facilities, plenty of greenery, and a great community atmosphere. Also, it is just a five-minute walk to Zhang's offices. "I used to hate having to spend over an hour on crowded public transport going to and from work," he says. "I can now spend as much time as possible with my daughter."

The three-bedroom apartment, spread over 100 square meters, was far bigger than his parents' apartment. But it wasn't cheap: RMB 1.7 million ($260,000). And they had to move fast if they were going to buy it. Such is the demand for housing that property prices in Shanghai rarely stay the same for long.

They quickly found a home for his parents a ten-minute walk away, and the total price came to RMB 2.6 million ($390,000). With the sale of his parents' apartment, Zhang raised RMB 1.3 million ($195,000). The remainder came from savings (RMB 800,000, or $120,000) and a mortgage (RMB 600,000, or $90,000).

The monthly mortgage payment of RMB 6,200 ($900) takes a large chunk out of Zhang and Zhu Wei's monthly income. But they are optimistic about the future, and they are confident that their salaries will rise over time. And they kept enough money to pay for decorating their new property and purchasing some vital household appliances. This was a key motivator for moving. As Zhang explains, "I wanted to make my own decisions about what to buy for the house instead of having to always listen to my mom."

The apartment is now full of big-name brands: TVs by Samsung and Philips, air conditioners and a top-loading washing machine by Hitachi, a large refrigerator by Siemens, and a laptop by Hewlett Packard. All told, they have spent RMB 52,000 ($8,000) on household appliances.

At last, after years of feeling embarrassed that he was still living with his parents, Zhang feels that he can hold his head up high. "I can see the admiration in my friends' eyes when I tell them that I have an apartment in downtown Shanghai."

The Commercial Opportunity: From Property Developers to White Goods Manufacturers

In the days of the Raj, the British and the maharajas used to retreat from the hot and humid capitals of Calcutta, Delhi, Bombay, Bangalore, and Madras and head for the hills. They created a network of beautiful hill stations (high-altitude towns) famed for their cool air. Among them were Darjeeling and Simla in the foothills of the Himalayas, and Ooty in the Nilgiri Hills. Nearly seventy years after the end of the empire, the new elite are once again being lured by the magic of the mountains—but this time, the mountains are artificial and located in the middle of the same steamy cities: the super-tall skyscrapers.

One of these, World One, is making its way up to 1,450 feet above the Mumbai skyline. It is expected to reach this vertiginous height—117 floors— by 2014, and would be among the world's tallest residential towers.

At such a height, life becomes very different—at least according to the Lodha Group, the skyscraper's property developer. Preaching the benefits of living in a super-high-rise building, it starts by saying that "it is like living in a hill station": in particular, the temperature drops by as much as 4.5 degrees Celsius. In addition, for every thirty floors, there is a dramatic reduction in air and noise pollution, with the amount of noise falling by 30 percent.[7]

With these kinds of advantages, the property developer is planning to charge $1.5 million or more for the homes, which will be furnished with the finest European brands: interiors designed by Giorgio Armani's design studio Armani/Casa, kitchens by Bulthaup, and bathroom fittings by Antonio Lupi, Dornbracht, Gessi, and Villeroy & Boch.

Competition is stiff. Other Indian companies are erecting similarly ambitious skyscrapers. But Lodha Group, founded by Mangal Prabhat Lodha in 1980, is not resting on its laurels. Toward the end of 2011, it was conducting twenty-seven projects, involving thirty million square feet of prime real estate in Mumbai. The most ambitious was New Cuffe Parade, announced in October 2011—which was India's biggest land deal and which has developed into a multibillion-dollar complex.

These projects serve as symbols of the vaulting ambitions of India's commercial elite—and the consumers who come to buy the apartments. Abhishek Lodha, the thirty-one-year-old son of the group's founder, who joined the family firm after completing engineering degrees at Georgia Institute of Technology in the United States, says, "Every global city is made memorable by its architectural landmarks. Be it the Eiffel Tower in Paris, the Opera House in Sydney, or the Empire State Building in New York, these vibrant forms reflect the passion and culture of the city they are located in." Describing World One, he goes on to say, "In partnership with the globe's finest architects, designers, and engineers, we seek to bring to Mumbai a landmark that will exemplify the spirit of Mumbai—to always soar higher through hard work and passion."

This same sentiment exists in China, where a similar group of property developers has been transforming the country's skyline. China Vanke, the country's biggest real estate company, has seen its fortunes rise dramatically over the past twenty years, with the growing demand for middle-class housing.

The company was founded in the 1980s by Wang Shi, a flamboyant former Red Guard member who—very appropriately, given the skyward trajectory of his company and construction work—has climbed to the top of Mount Everest. In 1990, the company focused on just four tier 1 cities. Fifteen years later, it was covering thirty-four cities, even some tier 4 cities with under one million people, and was selling 2.5 million square meters of property annually. By 2010, the numbers had jumped again: forty-six cities and a staggering 9 million square meters of sold property. Revenues exceeded $15 billion.

"Live in Your Dreams" is a China Vanke slogan. But in China and in India, dreams come at a price. To afford them, the new consumers have turned to banks and specialist mortgage lenders, breaking a generational reluctance to go into debt. In India, Housing Development Finance Corporation (HDFC) has been leading the way, led by Deepak Parekh.

Parekh's uncle founded the company in 1977. Parekh joined the firm a year later, taking a salary cut after a stint with The Chase Manhattan Bank. The Indian company saw its loan book rise from $10 billion in 2005 to

$22 billion in 2010. Yet despite the doubling of its loans, conservatism has been Parekh's watchword. "There are many qualities of a leader," he told us. "One is vision, and in a lending organization, another is conservatism."[8]

Typically, HDFC makes more than 90 percent of its individual loans to salaried householders.[9] Some of its rivals have been forced to give loans to higher-risk customers. Also, most of its focus has been on the major tier 1 and 2 cities, with around 50 percent of its 300-plus branches based in these wealthier metropolises. Loan-to-value ratios average 68 percent, with a thirteen-year term. Cumulative loan write-offs amount to 4 basis points.

"We serve the middle class," says Renu Karnad, managing director of HDFC. "They have the same needs as the middle class around the world. They want a better home, they want modern appliances, and they want space. We estimate that there is a national housing shortage in India of more than twenty-five million units."

Since its launch, HDFC has financed 3.9 million houses. It has grown from eighty-seven outlets in 2001 to offering deposit and loan products in more than twenty-four hundred towns and cities. Today, it has $25 billion in loans outstanding in India. Yet there is room to grow even further. In India, mortgages amount to 9 percent of GDP versus 81 percent in the United States, 88 percent in the United Kingdom, and 48 percent in Germany. HDFC wants to capture the growing power of the Indian consumer.

Just as property developers and mortgage lenders have profited from the property boom sweeping through China and India, so too have the home furnishings and household appliance companies. In India, one company that has been excelling is LG, the South Korean multinational. Its story is one of persistence, and it is a role model for companies wanting to enter the Indian market.

As Lucky Goldstar, it first entered India in the early 1990s, establishing a joint venture with Bestavision, an Indian consumer electronics company. But this failed. It tried again in the mid-1990s, this time with another domestic partner, the CK Birla group. This failed, too.

But LG was not going to be defeated. It knew that India was too big an opportunity. In 1998, it launched an independent venture—something permitted in the wake of the economic reforms—and invested $120 million in a factory in Noida in Uttar Pradesh. This was a significant moment. In 1997, revenues were $34 million. In 1998, they doubled. KR Kim, who masterminded this investment and who has since retired as chief executive of the Indian venture, told us, "The most important difference was our commitment to Indian markets. We were not here to test the waters. We decided to invest for the long term—in products, brands, and manufacturing."

In 2010, LG announced plans for a third factory in the south of the country, after establishing a number one market position in TVs, air conditioners, refrigerators, washing machines, and microwave ovens. Its revenues had broken through the $3 billion barrier.

LG's success is founded on five key pillars.

The first is creating good products at the right price—the very essence of *paisa vasool*. "Companies that succeed in India change the price-value equation," says Kim. "Indian consumers are more complex than those I have encountered elsewhere. They are very smart, and they want a quality brand at a reasonable price. Note that I didn't say 'lowest price.' We have competitors with products that are 10 percent cheaper, and if the lowest price were all that counted, then they would be number one."

For instance, LG created a TV with Goldeneye technology, which automatically adjusted the brightness of the screen to take account of ambient light. Also, the volume was much louder than normal—to take account of the likely noisy surroundings—and its menu was in different local languages. At around 17,000 rupees ($400), it was more expensive than its more basic rivals, but it was still seen to offer good value.

The second pillar is creating region-specific products, recognizing the country's extraordinary diversity. Consumers buying a microwave in the south of India have autocook options for regional rice-based breakfast favorites such as *idli* and *upma*. By contrast, consumers in the east have autocook options for Bengali fish curry and *shukto*, a mixed vegetable dish.[10]

To deliver this quality product at an affordable price, LG has had to create two other key pillars: low-cost manufacturing and strong branding. It achieved the first by establishing two manufacturing hubs—Noida and Pune (with plans for a third in the south)—which cut the freight costs to key distributors. It achieved the second by supporting some major Indian activities—notably the Indian cricket team and the cricket World Cup—and by creating a branded after-sales service that was second to none. With a strong and recognized brand, LG has been able to call the shots with distributors—again, reducing the cost of doing business. Unlike other manufacturers, LG has not had to give credit to dealers as a way of encouraging them to stock their products.

The fifth pillar has been the creation of an extensive distribution network to make sure that the well-made and affordable products reach the consumers who want to buy them. LG's early investment—recognizing India's potential ahead of its rivals—was crucial to its success, but its continued good fortune has rested on finding new consumers across the country. "I have traveled by plane, train, car, and even bullock cart in order to reach every part of India," Kim told us. "I have been to areas where people were scared to go because of security concerns—but we have succeeded there. Other companies focused on the Delhis and Mumbais, but we wanted to be strong all over India."

Besides working with traditional distributors, LG has also experimented with different ways of marketing its electrical goods. In some cases, it has placed its own vans next to *haats*—rural kiosks where products are sold—to carry out demos and pick up orders.

Underpinning LG's success has been an approach to business that we describe in more detail in chapter 14: the accelerator mind-set. As Kim explained to us, "We set ourselves a bold aspiration of being number one in India, and then we went after it with full force. We were focused on revenue and market share in the first three years. Only after that did we shift our focus to profits."

NINE

Luxury

Trading Up in China and India—Fast Cars, Watches, and Catwalk Clothes

How the newly affluent are starting to enjoy their wealth, spending record amounts on the luxuries of *la dolce vita* and providing vast new markets for the prestige brands of Milan, Paris, London, and New York

ALICE SUN, KNOWN AS SUNNY to her friends, takes us for a walk down one of the wide boulevards of Beijing. This ancient metropolis, the stage for the Olympics in 2008, is the place where planners knocked down scores of buildings to create a Hollywood set of a magnificent entranceway for a great city.

Now, it is a permanent celebration of China's success and coming of age. Twenty-four-year-old Alice, who has a degree from Peking University, one of China's most prestigious seats of learning, and who has a well-paid job as an analyst, is an example of the city's new well-to-do generation.

Today, Alice is on her way to buy her first statement pocketbook. But it is no ordinary pocketbook that she has her eye on. It is a Coach bag, her first.

This is a big step for Alice. Although she now makes more money than her father does—who, like her mother, was a teacher—she is deeply conscious of spending her hard-earned cash in a sensible way. When she was growing up, her parents were frugal, saving every last renminbi for a rainy day. They had experienced the pain of the Cultural Revolution, and although the scars from that time have healed, the effects are still visible to their daughter.

"As a university graduate, my father was sent to a farm. He worked long hours. He had little to eat. He lived in a barracks with twelve other men," she explains as we walk toward an exclusive shopping mall. "He would write to my mother. They were sad letters. They were lonely letters, and it took weeks to get them. It was many years before they were allowed to reunite."

Alice was, according to her father, "the gift of life." She says, "So they spoiled me as a child, and they still spoil me now." She had piano lessons, a swimming coach, and a private tutor as she prepared for the *gaokao*, the national college entrance exam. When she scored well, together with her near-flawless grades, she was able to choose her university.

Alice is a striking young woman, with clear skin, jet-black hair cut to her shoulders, and a smile and laugh that she has learned to use to ingratiate herself with others. She is easy to talk to and very conversational.

When we arrive at the Coach store, she knows exactly what she wants. She pays RMB 600 ($90) in cash and makes the transfer of lipstick, makeup, keys, and change purse from her current bag to the Coach bag at the cash register.

She is not alone. Coach's fastest-growing market is China.[1] It has become a land grab for luxury. And, as we will describe in this chapter, Chinese consumers with money, as well as rich Indians, are searching for badges of success, moments of celebration, and joyful expressions of achievement. The beneficiaries are the luxury goods companies from Europe and the United States.

New Luxury: From West to East

Silk, spices, tea, porcelain, ivory—for centuries, China and India were the source of the world's most exquisite things. The Silk Road, a network of trade routes that threaded through the Mongolian steppes, the Himalayan Mountains, and the deserts of Arabia, was developed to convey these exotic products to Europe's richest consumers.

Today, this trade in luxury goods is being reversed, as consumers from the East, especially China, show an extraordinary appetite for *la dolce vita*: bespoke suits and handmade shoes from Italy; watches from Switzerland; wine, jewelry, and perfume from France; sports cars from Germany; schooling in England; and degrees from U.S. Ivy League schools.

In 2010, the global personal luxury market was worth $176 billion, according to our analysis. China accounted for $31 billion of this—17 percent—making it the third-largest market behind Japan (22 percent) and North America (27 percent). However, over the next ten years, the country is set to become the world's biggest personal luxury market.[2]

We calculate that China will have surpassed the United States as the second-largest market by 2015, accounting for $87 billion, or 23 percent, of a $379 billion personal luxury market. And by 2020, it will have assumed the top spot, accounting for $245 billion, or a staggering 40 percent, of a $610 billion personal luxury market.

J.P. Morgan research suggests that the mainland Chinese consumer accounts for a full 22 percent of classically defined luxury goods—9 percent spent locally and 13 percent spent abroad.[3] Using a universe of LVMH, Richemont, Swatch, Gucci, Hermès, Bulgari, and Burberry, the report notes that Asia-Pacific sales for these companies have increased from 10 percent to 36 percent of total sales in the last three years. The sentiment is clearly bullish, driven by more luxury categories, growth among the mass affluent, greater female consumption, and the increasing popularity of purchasing for oneself rather than for others.

The growing number of middle-class and affluent city dwellers will drive this steep increase. "Just 1 percent of consumers are millionaires, and they take 20 percent of our sales," a senior executive for Chanel, the French high-fashion house, told us. "But the middle classes are the key drivers for the future."

There are other factors, too. China is witnessing a surge in the number of credit card users as they embrace the "now" impulse more familiar among consumers in the United States and Europe. In 2005, fewer than 50 million credit cards were issued. By 2010, the number had risen to 221 million. By 2020, the major credit card companies are aiming for triple the number of cards—and increased usage, too.[4]

As described in chapter 6, an increasingly large proportion of women are prepared to spend big on luxury products. Men have traditionally been the bigger spenders in China, accounting for more than two-thirds of the market. But times are changing. Maserati, the Italian sports car brand owned by Fiat, reports that 30 percent of its buyers in China are women, compared with the 2 to 5 percent typical in the United States and Europe.[5]

If China is fast becoming the world's luxury capital, India is expected to see only modest growth in the personal luxury market. On the face of it, this difference is very odd. As noted in chapter 3, India has some of the world's richest people, who are no strangers to ostentatious luxury living. A considerable share of the world's privately owned gold is held by Indians.

This fascination with precious metals and jewelry goes back centuries. In 2011, an astonishing hoard of gold and other treasure was found in the vaults of a Hindu temple in Thiruvananthapuram (formerly Trivandrum), an ancient port on the southern tip of India that was once a vital trading post between India and the Roman Empire. The stash was valued at $22 billion.[6] As another example, on the eve of independence in 1947, many of the world's Rolls-Royces, the world's most expensive cars, were owned by the fabulously wealthy maharajas.

For all this, India accounted for less than 1 percent of the global market for personal luxury goods in 2010: around $1 billion. We expect this to triple in size by 2020. But it will still amount to only around $3 billion, a tiny portion of global luxury spending.[7] "We barely see a luxury market existing at all," says the Chanel executive, speaking of the Indian market.

Why is India, famed for its opulence, so restrained when it comes to luxury goods? There are several reasons. One is that it is just so much poorer: almost a half billion people live below the poverty line, more than twice the number in China. Also, as we have mentioned, India has fewer millionaires and working women. Another reason is that the luxury shopping experience is so limited, with numerous barriers to entry for global retailers. These circumstances force top retailers to sell their products in the sterile surroundings of hotels, airports, and exclusive malls. This does not make for brisk trade. At the Taj hotel in Mumbai, store clerks complain that while hundreds of people pass the stores, few stop to browse and even fewer buy something.

Therefore, it is not surprising that rich Indians choose to buy luxuries when they are traveling in foreign countries. "Shopping for branded goods has become part of my holiday indulgence," one consumer told us. "The experience is so much more pleasurable than shopping in India."

Nor is it surprising that the top brands have resisted the temptation to enter the Indian market as enthusiastically as they did in China. For instance, Chanel has just one store in India, in Delhi, while it has four stores in Beijing, five in Shanghai, one in Hangzhou, one in Guangzhou, four in Macau, and ten in Hong Kong. Likewise, Hugo Boss has two stores in India compared with fourteen in China.

A factor in this decision is that Indian consumers prefer traditional Indian styles, particularly when it comes to clothing, rather than the international styles presented by the luxury goods companies. In 2010, Indians spent some 70 billion rupees ($1.5 billion) on traditional wear for women, up from 45 billion rupees ($1 billion) in 2005. This amounted to 55 percent of the women's apparel market in India.[8]

Other obstacles include steep import duties, few real estate options, and regulatory obstacles. For example, while the government has now allowed 100 percent ownership for single-brand retail, it comes with riders on local small-scale sourcing. As Bertrand Michaud, president of Hermès, the French high-fashion house, in India, puts it, "It's difficult—it's frustrating to do business here."[9]

Over time, Indians are likely to discover a taste for luxury products. And some retailers are already preparing for this day. In 2011, several sports car manufacturers—including Aston Martin (whose cars are featured in James Bond films), Ferrari, Maserati, and Bugatti—announced plans to open showrooms to sell cars worth more than $1 million. In a strange echo of the past, a souped-up Rolls-Royce owned by one of today's maharajas was sold at auction for $1.2 million.

Meanwhile, in July 2011, Hermès opened India's first stand-alone luxury retail store in Mumbai: a 3,000-square-foot shop with an art gallery and a glass elevator. The company followed this up in October by unveiling its first range of Paris-manufactured saris, bowing to the local preference for traditional Indian couture. "If you want to succeed in India," Michaud says, "you have to be part of Indian life."

For the near future, however, China's consumers offer luxury companies the best opportunities.

French Luxury Champion PPR: "China Will Triple for Us in the Next Ten Years"

"China has evolved faster in luxury than any other country in the world," says François-Henri Pinault, the dashing chairman and CEO of PPR. The French luxury producer and retailer, originally called Pinault-Printemps-Redoute, is now a listed company on the blue-chip French stock index CAC 40. "Chinese consumers buy to treat themselves. They buy because they can. It is a way to democratize and individualize. There is much pent-up demand. Chinese consumers want heritage, authenticity, and fashion."

In 1999, when the then thirty-seven-year-old Pinault fought to acquire Gucci, the Italian luxury company, for some $7 billion, he had little sense that China would become Gucci's largest single market. He was on the hunt to reposition the big French conglomerate from the low growth of France and had his sights on the rich American market.

"We were looking to change our portfolio and reduce our reliance on France as the single economy we were dependent on," Pinault told us in his modern, sleek Paris office. "The rapid China market growth was an unexpected development." Today, more than two-thirds of PPR's revenues are outside France. Pinault expects that by 2020, more than 60 percent of his revenues will come from Asia.

The second major bet-the-company purchase of Pinault's exalted career had the same objectives. "When we bought Puma in 2007," he says, "we were trying to shift our portfolio further to businesses with organic growth potential. We wanted a major position in sports culture and sports apparel. We did not understand that cricket is a national addiction in India and that Puma sponsoring the national team could create a brand revolution overnight. Suddenly Puma has become hot in India."

Two big bets equal leading positions in the two economies poised to offer the $10 trillion prize: Pinault expects his company's position in China to triple in revenues over the next decade, and he is hopeful that under the right conditions, India will follow the China growth path.

Pinault, now fifty, believes that "luxury is associated with pleasure, individualism, and unreasonable enjoyment." In both China and India, he says, there is untapped demand. "Luxury goods purchases are about self-expression."

He says he will stake his future on growth in the emerging Asian world. He has announced plans to jettison most of the legacy businesses PPR bought in the 1990s, including its massive direct-mail retail business and most of its remaining French mass-market retail assets. The company founded by his father as a timber and building products company grew to $19 billion in sales in 2010 and $2.3 billion in EBITDA (earnings before interest, taxes, depreciation, and amortization).

By the time the restructuring is done, PPR's luxury division will comprise Gucci, fast-growing Bottega Veneta, fashion houses Yves Saint Laurent and Balenciaga, jeweler Boucheron, watchmaker Girard-Perregaux, footwear producer Sergio Rossi, ready-to-wear producers Alexander McQueen and Stella McCartney, and Italian high-end tailor company Brioni, purchased in 2011. More luxury deals are on Pinault's agenda. PPR's sport and lifestyle division comprises Puma and the action-sport brand Volcom.

Gucci is the jewel in the PPR luxury portfolio, with sales of $3.4 billion and profits of $1 billion in 2010—a full 57 percent of total company profits. Gucci enjoyed 37 percent growth in its China business in 2010. The business has come a long way since the dire days of ownership under the founding family in the 1980s. It is one of the very few luxury brands to have skirted death and recover. After Guccio Gucci founded the brand in 1921, the Gucci family controlled the company through the first seventy years. But by 1991, the firm was in disarray, with sales of $208 million and a loss of $41 million. The company suffered from overexposure, a lack of innovation, and a reputation for shoddy merchandise.

After private-equity investors purchased the brand, designer Tom Ford and Domenico De Sole revived the business with strict quality control, fashion news and excitement, an outpouring of advertising investment, and meticulous control of both distribution and visual merchandising. In *Trading Up*, we described how Ford and De Sole used glamour, the world's most expensive jeans, a retro-plus style, and category expansion to create $1 billion in sales by the time of the acquisition by PPR. Many felt that with their departure after the acquisition, the brand would stumble.

But Pinault has proven his critics wrong. Gucci has prospered under PPR's ownership, more than quadrupling in sales. It has moved beyond a single designer to a collection based on tradition and modernity, artisan craftsmanship, and innovation and fashion authority.

Pinault says the Gucci brand is about passion, emotion, youth, modernism, and world-class fashion. Enter a Gucci store in China, and you find an edgy, pulsating, energetic experience. The store interiors are stunning, and the visual merchandising is distinct. The Chinese consumers still line up at store openings to buy bags, shoes, perfume, accessories, ties, shirts, suits, sweaters, T-shirts, and even the recently introduced children's collection.

The brand is also about sustainability. Pinault has his luxury teams committed to the best labor practices, the use of recycled materials, reduced water consumption, and energy conservation at the store level. He believes that the Chinese will quickly become environmentally sensitive consumers.

He says that Chinese consumers have rocketing taste and believes that the authenticity of a brand requires original sourcing and that "Made in Italy" and "Made in France" will never be replaced. Gucci employs forty-five thousand in Italy, including seven thousand workers in its leather factories in Tuscany.

"The Chinese consumer has a profound belief that they deserve luxury products now," Pinault says. "They had fifty years with so little, and now, many can afford to buy luxury goods. Their growth in demand is rooted in an expression of individualism in the way you dress. It is a way to differentiate yourself from friends and neighbors. Chinese consumers buy to treat themselves. This China market has evolved faster than any other market in the world."

He continues, "China is now the number one market for the Gucci brand, bigger than the U.S. and Japan. If you include Chinese tourists' spending abroad, it's more than 50 percent. Seven years ago, Hong Kong was two-thirds Japanese tourists. It is now 80 percent Chinese."

He says that each of the major brand managers was asked to imagine the world of 2020. "They independently came up with a rough tripling of volume in China."

Pinault says India is its own story. "It is a tough market for us. Our aspirations for the Indian market are very high. But there is less conspicuous consumption and profit is not so rich. There are huge import duties that make prices very high."

"We are lucky to have Puma for India," he says. "Indians are sports enthusiasts. We have the leading position in cricket, and this holds very high promise for us." He describes Puma as starting in sports and ending in fashion. He calls this a key differentiator from the two global sports powers, Nike and Adidas.

Pinault is a dispassionate portfolio manager. He has no fixed allegiances to any business. He knows how to pursue growth and profit. He sees little growth in Western Europe and sees the United States stuck at 2 to 3 percent real growth. He declares, "China, Indonesia, and Brazil are our big growth markets."

Indeed, he thinks that China is France's greatest economic growth opportunity. "Chinese want to experience culture, luxury, art at its source," he says. "I've been telling the French government leaders, 'You want growth, you want spending? Bring the Chinese tourists to France. They will come by the millions over the next ten years. It will revive our economy. When they come, they will spend.'"

China's Luxury Consumers

By definition, relatively few people generate the luxury business. In China, the key consumers are the 700,000 households with assets of more than $1 million. As outlined in chapter 3, they constitute just 0.2 percent of all households in the country, but they control an extraordinary 48 percent of its wealth.[10] These are consumers for whom money is no object, and they spend on every kind of luxury goods and services.

Fast emerging are the consumers in the 1.7 million households with assets of between $250,000 and $1 million—those who constitute 0.4 percent of all households and control 16 percent of China's wealth. These are the people starting to buy luxury watches, leather bags, and catwalk clothes.[11]

These consumers, however different, share three common characteristics. First, as noted in chapter 2, they are vastly more brand conscious than consumers elsewhere. Our research shows that they rank brand name and its visibility far higher than consumers do in Japan, the United States, or Europe. Conspicuous consumption—which is in retreat in the West, where consumers often prefer to have their expensive purchases wrapped in plain, unshowy shopping bags—is alive and well in the shopping malls and major streets of China. This desire to stand out from the crowd, to be seen as different, is part of a broader reaction to the era of colorless collectivism in the years after the Communist Revolution in 1949.

The extravagant gesture can match anything witnessed on Wall Street in the glory days leading up to the Great Recession. "A client once finished two cases of Lafite at one dinner in traditional bottoms-up style," a private banker told us. Considering that a vintage bottle from Château Lafite Rothschild, one of the world's most expensive wines, sells for more than $2,500, that's some gesture.

Chinese officials are having a tough time with the word *luxury*. The *China Daily* reports that officials are looking to end advertising that "promotes hedonism" or the "worship of foreign-made products." Other words that are verboten include *supreme, royal*, and *high-class*.[12]

Second, if rich Chinese like to flaunt their wealth, they also prefer to invest in beautiful things rather than in memorable experiences: right now, they are focused on *owning* rather than *being*. A little-seen element is the boomerang effect in collectibles, ranging from antique automobiles to fine wines to art. In November 2010, Bainbridges, a U.K.-based auction house, sold a sixteen-inch vase from the time of Chinese Emperor Qianlong for $84.5 million. This is a record for a single piece of Chinese artwork. The buyer was a Chinese collector.

This record-breaking sale reflects a major trend. China has moved from 5 percent of the world art market to 23 percent in five years, according to a European Fine Art Fair report.[13] Chinese collectors have an appetite for Chinese art and antiques and are flexing their muscle. Most of the buying is done through agents, and Chinese are very active buyers at both Sotheby's and Christie's.[14]

In 2010, Chinese consumers spent $31 billion on personal luxury goods: specifically, $16 billion on watches and jewelry, $6 billion on apparel and fashion accessories, $5 billion on cosmetics, and $4 billion on leather goods. By contrast, they spent $25 billion on so-called experiential luxury: some $11 billion on travel, hotels, and restaurants; $4 billion each on food and drink, spa and beauty treatments, and personal technology; and $3 billion on home decoration.[15]

The preference for goods rather than services means that the Chinese luxury market is quite different from those of other developed and developing countries. In the United States, personal luxury goods, not including automobiles, account for only 30 percent of the luxury market. In Brazil and Russia, these goods account for 33 percent and 35 percent of their respective markets.

A third general trend is that rich Chinese prefer to purchase their luxury products abroad. If they no longer have to travel along the old Silk Road, they nevertheless travel far and wide in their pursuit of the finer things in life: 58 percent of the money Chinese spend on luxury goods and services is spent outside of mainland China. The biggest beneficiaries are the luxury stores on their doorstep in Hong Kong, Macau, and Taiwan. These three centers account for 33 percent of the money Chinese consumers spend on luxury products. Other foreign countries account for 25 percent.

The luxury consumers go in search of European brands, confirming Paris, Milan, and London as the capitals of global chic. In 2009, Rolex, Omega, Longines, and Cartier held nearly 50 percent of the luxury watch market in China, according to our analysis.[16] Among cosmetics brands, Chanel, Dior, Estée Lauder, and Lancôme are the most sought-after by Chinese consumers. The strong leather products brands include Burberry and Dunhill from London, Gucci and Prada from Milan, and Louis Vuitton from Paris—these brands control 60 percent of the market. Besides Burberry and Dunhill, two Italian brands, Armani and Ermenegildo Zegna, and one German brand, Hugo Boss, dominate the apparel market. And the jewelry market is led by Tiffany & Co. (the New York jewelry house), Cartier, and Bulgari.

As part of our day-to-day work, we talk to thousands of consumers. One of these—a thirty-something named Li—explained to us the central importance of luxury goods in her everyday life.

Li was born in Shanghai in 1979, just as Deng Xiaoping was launching his economic reform program that would signal the opening up of the once-closed Communist state. Her parents, well-educated middle-school teachers, had high ambitions for their daughter. She was sent to a renowned primary school, followed by a middle school that specialized in the teaching of French.

Until 1946, France exerted an extraordinary influence over the part of Shanghai known as "the French Concession." Even today, this collection of streets retains a distinctly Parisian character, with tree-lined boulevards, cafés, and even *boulangeries* serving warm croissants. Li's mother picked the specialist language school with Li's future in mind: there are relatively few French speakers in China today.

After school, Li entered Fudan University, one of China's oldest and most selective universities: it is one of the country's so-called C9 schools, China's "Ivy League." There, she studied finance and business and, at the end, received a job offer from a U.S. professional services company that recruited just four people to its Shanghai office in 2001.

In her first job, when she was earning $4,000 per month, she started thinking about buying luxury products. "It's a good way of compensating for a busy working life," she says. "It's also a good way of standing out from the crowd. It allows me to show my status."

Early on, she bought beauty products. Perhaps not surprisingly, Paris-based brands dominated her choice. L'Oréal and Clarins were her favorites, although she longed to be able to buy the more expensive cosmetics and perfumes produced by Lancôme and Chanel.

In her drive to scale the career ladder, Li seized the once-in-a-lifetime opportunity to go to a U.S. business school, something offered by her U.S.-based employer. She applied to Harvard and Stanford, choosing the West Coast institution for its location in the heart of Silicon Valley.

Returning two years later, armed with an MBA, Li's income doubled to $8,000 per month. Wealthier and willing to pay significantly more for good-quality products, she invested in clothes and jewelry by Chanel and Cartier, which had seemed like a far-off prize for other people when she started her first job. "I did not even dream of them back then," she says.

A $300 dress, a $3,000 leather bag, a $4,500 watch or piece of jewelry—these were now acceptable prices for Li. "I still felt a little guilty," she says, remembering that time. "But I wanted to buy things that reflected my new status. I wanted to signal that I had changed and moved on."

Today, luxury products are not so much a luxury as a necessary part of her life. Married, with a one-year-old son, Li is a principal at her company and enjoys a salary of $15,000 per month. With her husband, she has a household income of $360,000 per year, which puts her in the top-earning 0.6 percent of the population. As a result, she says, "Money is not an issue. I can afford most of the things that I want to buy."

A peek at her wardrobe gives an insight into her buying habits and preferences: dresses from Loewe and Club Monaco, shoes from Salvatore Ferragamo and Stuart Weitzman, a coat from Burberry, and bags from Shanghai Tang, Coach, and Chanel. She also wears Gucci sunglasses, an Omega watch, and jewelry from Cartier's "Love" series.

More often than not, Li buys luxury goods when she is traveling abroad, which she does as part of her international job. This is partly because there is a price premium to pay in China. If the difference is less than 40 percent, then Li will sometimes buy in China for the sheer convenience. Otherwise, she buys abroad.

In addition to price, product variety is a big factor in the choice to buy abroad. She stands a better chance of putting her hands on hard-to-get products when she is in Europe or the United States. "Some of the best jewelry is often out of stock," she says. "When I wanted to buy the Cartier 'Love' series, it was even out of stock at the IFC mall." This was a real surprise, as the mall at the city's International Financial Centre is the new epicenter of Chinese luxury shopping. In the end, she had to ask a friend, who happened to be visiting Paris, to bring back her chosen rings.

If Li's luxury spending has focused on products, she is starting to think about spending on having a good time—again, so-called experiential luxury. "Time," she says, "is now my biggest concern." From 7 a.m., when she gets up to check her baby, till 11 p.m., when she finally finishes her last e-mail for work, her day is mapped out for her. She expects to devote more of her money on activities that allow her to buy back some of that time: already, she does yoga, and she indulges herself with a beauty treatment twice a month at the Banyan Tree Spa in Shanghai. She also wants to introduce her son to new experiences that will enrich his life.

Such a transition, with a growing emphasis on luxury services as well as luxury goods, characterizes the journey taken by many Chinese consumers. The growing desire of Chinese consumers to travel abroad will open some significant opportunities for luxury goods companies. We estimate that Chinese travelers will make fifty-three million trips in 2020—up from sixteen million in 2010—and spend some $120 billion.[17] Some companies are already taking advantage of this. Burberry, the British luxury brand, has estimated that Chinese consumers can account for one-third of all the sales made in its U.K. stores.[18]

But the biggest opportunities lie in China itself. As you will now see, there are some luxury companies prospering in this vast country.

LVMH: The Luxury Giant

As described in chapter 7, if there is one company that is perfectly positioned to profit from China's newfound passion for luxury goods, it is LVMH, the Paris-based company whose acronymic name masks some of the world's most famous luxury brands: Louis Vuitton, the fashion accessories label; Moët & Chandon, the manufacturer of the finest champagne; and Hennessy, the last word in cognac.

As the world's largest luxury goods company, LVMH boasts some fifty brands. Watch brands include TAG Heuer, Zenith, Hublot, Dior, and Bulgari, acquired in 2011; fashion brands include Marc Jacobs, Fendi, Pucci,

Givenchy, Kenzo, Donna Karan, and Loewe; perfume and cosmetic brands include Dior and Guerlain; and wine and spirit brands include Moët & Chandon, Dom Perignon, Veuve Clicquot, and Krug.

There was a time when the prospect of China's surpassing Japan as LVMH's third-largest market, behind the United States and France, seemed outlandish. Even in 2006, China accounted for only 3 percent of global sales, far behind Japan's 13 percent. But by 2010, China accounted for 8 percent of global sales, only a whisker behind Japan's 9 percent. In dollar terms, sales in China have rocketed from $569 million in 2006 to just over $2 billion in 2010.[19]

In an interview, Bernaud Arnault, CEO of LVMH, told us he believes that China is one of the great opportunities of our time: "It is clear that China represents a great opportunity for LVMH over the next decade: the size of the country, the rapid increase of their wealth, their education, their appreciation of quality brands with a heritage, and their culture of offering the best to their colleagues, family, and friends are all factors that will contribute to this growth. If we execute our individual brand strategies correctly and continue to provide the same quality of product and service that we provide around the world, there is no reason why China should not become one of the largest markets for LVMH."

He says getting there early has created advantages. "Being a pioneer in China with our strongest brands has enabled LVMH to establish a good knowledge of how to work efficiently within the country; Hennessy cognac was first shipped to China in the mid-nineteenth century, Louis Vuitton's first store opened in Beijing in 1992, Dior in 1997." He continued, "It has been important to ensure that we maintain the same quality standards in products, service, and stores to which customers are accustomed around the world; local and international training programs, high-quality stores, and excellent products have been key. Equally in the long-term interests of the individual brands, we have been patient and have needed to wait for the right opportunities. Finally, working together with local communities to ensure that their longer-term needs and interests are taken into account has been an important factor in our success."

Arnault believes that India needs to resolve obstacles and other issues to get to a strong growth position. "India's full potential will be realized once some of the obstacles of doing business in the country become more relaxed. It has great potential: a large population; a strong, well-educated middle class; and a good appreciation of luxury. The potential is there. It just needs to be unleashed!"

He is not particularly worried about reliance on China. "While it is always preferable to have your eggs in more than one basket, it is inevitable that some countries will grow faster than others. We have a good geographic balance in revenue and a diversity in our businesses at present, and while the opportunity in China seems more imminent, there are other places like India or Latin America whose growth potential is enormous once they become more accessible."

Drilling down further into the numbers, it is possible to see that in some luxury categories, China has surpassed Japan *and* France to become the second-largest market for LVMH. In wines and spirits, as discussed earlier, China's consumers account for 25 percent of the company's global sales, behind U.S. consumers' 45 percent. In fashion and leather goods, the Chinese account for 21 percent, just behind Japan at 22 percent but ahead of the United States at 18 percent.[20]

The key success has been Louis Vuitton, which is now firmly established as the number one brand among Chinese millionaires. Rivals, and companies in other sectors, should study how this brand has achieved such stellar performance.

Officially, Louis Vuitton launched its retail operation in 1992, when Yves Carcelle, CEO of Louis Vuitton, opened its first store in Beijing's ultra-exclusive Peninsula Palace Hotel, just a short walk from the capital's historic Forbidden City. Since then, he has opened ninety-two Louis Vuitton stores in twenty-nine cities in China and has brought the global revenues of Louis Vuitton from €600 million in 1990, when he joined, to €6 billion in 2011.

But, in fact, the connection with China goes much further back—to 1907, when the company sponsored the Peking-to-Paris motor race, with competitors driving the nine thousand miles in cars outfitted with Louis Vuitton's distinctive trunks. By then, the company was already more than fifty years old, having established itself as the favored luggage manufacturer of Europe's aristocracy.

This colorful heritage has endeared Louis Vuitton to its Chinese customers. "I like Louis Vuitton, especially the bags, because of its quality and long history," one wealthy housewife told us. "It is the biggest brand that nearly every Chinese wants to own."

Far from resting on its laurels, the company has been careful to nurture its brand since its formal arrival in China in the 1990s. It has consistently been the biggest spender on advertising, especially in glossy magazines. In the first quarter of 2009, it spent around $10 million, with 75 percent going toward magazine advertisements.[21] By contrast, Gucci, its nearest competitor in advertising expenditure, spent around $6 million, with 67 percent allocated for magazines.

Louis Vuitton has also sought to preserve its global image, knowing that by buying its products, consumers are trying to buy into an exotic, international, rich way of life. This includes some local marketing, too. In 2011, Louis Vuitton staged an exhibition at the National Museum of China, where the company presented some of its most treasured, handsome, and historic trunks and bags. Called *Voyages*, the exhibit sought to underscore Louis Vuitton's long connection with China and its deep roots in the business of handcrafted luggage—a characteristic that consumers most identify with the brand. The company has also created some podcast travel guides to Beijing, Shanghai, and Hong Kong. The guides are narrated by famous Chinese actresses, including Gong Li, Shu Qi, and Joan Chen.

In 2003, Louis Vuitton had just two stores—the one in Beijing and another in Shenzhen. The following year, it opened six, including one in its first tier 2 city: Xi'an, the start of the fabled Silk Road. By 2008, the company had opened twenty-six stores, including one in Sanya, a tier 3 city on the southern island of Hainan. This last store was an important addition. As one Louis Vuitton executive told us, "The Sanya store is meant to represent our travel spirit—so we have almost the full collection of bags there."

By 2010, Louis Vuitton had opened thirty-five stores: five in the top three cities (Beijing, Shanghai, and Guangzhou), sixteen in tier 1 cities, seven in tier 2 cities (including two in Shenyang), and the one in the tier 3 city of Sanya.

In opening these stores, Louis Vuitton benefited from its well-known brand when it came to securing the best places in new shopping malls and to negotiating the rent. "Louis Vuitton always gets the best locations at the cheapest price," says the store manager of one rival in Shanghai. "For example, they have been able to open a much bigger store than ours in Plaza 66." This shopping complex, located beneath two skyscrapers designed by New York architects, is one of the epicenters of luxury in the city—and Louis Vuitton's store is situated in the most advantageous position.

From the beginning, Louis Vuitton's executives understood that its potential customers were widely dispersed. (As described earlier, the 700,000 households with assets of more than $1 million are located in some 650 cities.) Today, the executives follow a four-step process to get a handle on their customer base.

First, they track their existing customers, collecting information such as the customers' address and occupation. This helps the executives determine where next to open a new store. "For example," says a manager at Louis Vuitton's store in Shanghai's Plaza 66, "we saw a lot of customers from Wenzhou, and now we have a store there." The store at Wenzhou, a tier 1 city with nine million inhabitants, was opened in 2006.

In order to select a city—the second step of the process—Louis Vuitton carries out a thorough program of research. Typically, a team of ten to fifteen people visits a potential location up to ten times, assessing the spending power of local customers, the quality of the property, and the strategic value of the city.

The third step, setting up the store, requires a careful choice of property management partner and heavy investment in the outfitting of the store. The fourth step is to constantly adapt the product range in the store to ensure that customers get what they want, when they want it.

A new store, however well planned, will fail without the right sales staff. Sean Connery and Angelina Jolie may be "the face of Louis Vuitton" in the global advertising campaigns, but the sales executive in the local store is the all-important "face" when it comes to buying a leather bag.

As a result, Louis Vuitton invests heavily in the selection and training of its frontline employees. It advertises locally, through newspapers and Web sites, and conducts several rounds of screening. Typically, only six people are recruited out of sixty applicants, and the six are then sent on a ten-day training program in Shanghai, where they learn about the company's history and basic sales techniques. As a reward and incentive to others, Louis Vuitton sends the best-performing sales executives, around thirty to forty each year, to Paris for a twelve-day program that includes a visit to the flagship store and factory as well as further tutoring on Louis Vuitton's brand and advanced sales techniques.

These strategies have helped Louis Vuitton's China operation increase from 1 percent of the company's global sales in 2003 to around 20 percent in 2010. They have also helped LVMH see profits jump, despite the gloomy forecasts for the global economy. In the first half of 2011, the conglomerate's overall net profit rose 25 percent to $1.9 billion, on sales that were up by 13 percent to $13.7 billion. Asia, excluding Japan, saw sales growth of 26 percent, suggesting that China's business remained buoyant.[22]

Louis Vuitton remains at the heart of LVMH's strategy. In July 2011, it opened its biggest store in mainland China, in the Taikoo Hui mall in Guangzhou, the country's third-largest city, with nearly thirteen million inhabitants. And the company is currently refurbishing its Shanghai flagship in Plaza 66, which will have a library and room for art exhibitions.

Its largest Chinese store is on Hong Kong's Canton Road, located in the Tsim Sha Tsui (TST), on the Kowloon Peninsula in Victoria Harbour. On any given day, thousands of Chinese tourists are in and out with packages from Louis Vuitton, Chanel, Dior, Ferragamo, Gucci, and Hermès. In fact, the Hong Kong store is Louis Vuitton's largest outside of Paris—18,000-plus square feet spread over four levels. Its street-level facade, designed by the Japanese architect Kumiko Inui, is a massive LED screen, which creates a dramatic nighttime effect. The store is open until 10 p.m. seven days a week. Inside, you can find vintage Louis Vuitton trunks hanging in the luggage department, a jewelry and watch salon, and two private VIP rooms. It is a breathtaking store with a heavy emphasis on gold and silver and beautiful bamboo floors. Many products sold are limited editions marked for the Canton store. According to competitors, the single store also has stunning sales—more than $250 million, a remarkable $14,000 per square foot.

If LVMH, with its many brands, is capitalizing on the newfound passion for luxury goods in China and India, so too are some category-specific companies. Another example is L'Oréal China, under its head, Paolo Gasparrini. He has had fifteen years of experience in China, and he was part of the company's start-up. The company now has thirty thousand workers, and it has built an R&D center in Pudong. "China is a country for skin care and facial products," he says. "Chinese consumers don't want to copy the beauty products of the United States or the European Union. You need to understand and be humble in this market. Prepare for fast change."

Another sector taking this advice and earning its piece of the prize is premium cars: Audi, owned by Volkswagen; Mercedes, owned by Daimler; and BMW.

The Glamour of the Sports Car

The roads may be full of potholes and filled with slow-moving traffic, but the market for fast cars is growing at an astonishing speed. In China, sales of prestige autos rose from 24,000 in 2000 to an extraordinary 576,000 in 2010. In India, sales jumped from 30,000 in 2006 to 58,000 in 2010. We expect these numbers to continue to grow dramatically over the next five years. At a time when the luxury market in the West is stalling, this is an extraordinary lifeline for the manufacturers of fast cars.

The BMW 3 Series is targeted at young lawyers, bankers, and fund managers—professionals aged twenty-five to forty-five. Costing between $45,000 and $60,000, it is meant to appeal to their functional needs (a fast car with rear-wheel drive, an engine that does not burn up gasoline, and a convenient system for quick and affordable repairs) and their emotional needs (a sporty and status-enhancing design and a roaring sound).

The BMW 5 and 7 Series are targeted at the owners of small and medium-size companies—entrepreneurs between forty and fifty years old. Priced between $80,000 and $200,000, these large cars satisfy several functional needs of these executives: the vehicles are safe to drive, with a state-of-the-art braking system; comfortable, with ample room in the backseat for important business partners; and suitable not only for business travel but also for family occasions.

They also satisfy some of the typical emotional needs of the targeted customers: the cars convey a sense of superiority and a sense of "forever young." Indeed, to underscore the grandiose, BMW has modified the 5 Series for its Chinese customers, making it marginally longer and wider than the 5 Series cars available in the rest of the world.

One of BMW's well-trained dealers greeted Zhai Wenqin when she walked into a Shanghai showroom. She is a classic target luxury car customer: in her early thirties, well educated, a foreign exchange trader with a household income of around $250,000 per year, and married with a one-year-old daughter.

Her best friend had a Mini Cooper, the British marque bought by BMW in 1994 and revitalized with a fresh, bubbly design and a soft-top roof, and Wenqin initially thought she would like to buy one, too. "The Mini looks so cute and fashionable," she says. "I saw lots of trendy women driving them. I could just imagine driving it, with my hair blowing in the wind."

But when she took a Mini Cooper for a test drive, she was not impressed. "It was just not roomy enough. My mother is quite a large lady, and I couldn't see how she and my daughter could both squeeze in the back." Also, there were no other functional benefits to outweigh its overly petite size.

Disappointed, she walked along to the BMW showroom. She test-drove a BMW 318. It was larger than the Mini Cooper. In Wenqin's book, that was the first tick in the box. Also, it was zippy. "I drove to around a hundred twenty kilometers per hour during the test drive. It felt really good overtaking all the other cars. It gave me the feeling that I could drive as fast as those Formula One racers."

Importantly, her husband, who drives a Toyota Camry, liked the BMW, too. So, after further reflection, Wenqin paid $50,000 for a white BMW 318—a comparable price to the Mini Cooper but, as she puts it, "better value for the money."

The Luxury Sector: Some Success Factors

PPR, LVMH, and BMW are showing how companies can capitalize on the luxury boom that is under way in China and which should take off in India in the next ten years. More than one hundred million Chinese and ten million Indians will enter the premium markets, demanding world-class clothing, food, wine, cars, travel, and accessories. In their own way, they will recreate the U.S. market for trading up—a market that we witnessed from 1995 to 2005. Companies with the potential to make products that serve these premium markets will prosper if they enter now, achieve broad and comprehensive distribution, and learn to customize to Chinese and Indian tastes and preferences. It is not too late to make the necessary investment, first in China and then in India, to achieve your share of this $1 trillion prize within the $10 trillion.

TEN

Digital Life

Netizens, E-Shoppers, and the New Internet Giants

How a vast new generation of digital consumers uses the Internet and mobile devices, creating an unprecedented level of connectivity and commercial opportunity for businesses ready to make the right moves

MEET JING. SHE IS ONE of a new generation of netizens who live their lives in the all-too-real virtual world of the Internet. Jing, twenty-eight and single, lives in Beijing. She is a young professional with a master's degree and a monthly income of around $1,200.

Jing spends almost all day connected to the Internet. "All my needs can be met in the digital world—products, information, everything," she says. E-commerce and m-commerce—business conducted over a mobile device— already account for 60 percent of Jing's monthly spending. "I love online shopping! I purchase almost every amusement service or activity online, such as movies, meals, books, et cetera. It's so convenient, and you can find so many bargains!"

She has a Lenovo smartphone, which is the first thing she looks at when she wakes up, checking the news before she leaves for work. On the way to work, she reads and posts on Sina Weibo (the Chinese equivalent of Twitter). When she gets to her office, she switches on her Lenovo laptop, reads and replies to her e-mails, and searches online reports for her work using Google and IBISWorld.

During lunch, she searches the latest bargains at Taobao, the online shopping mall often likened to eBay and Amazon.com. If she is unsure about the quality, she buys from the brands' official Web sites instead. After lunch, Jing is busy at work, using the Baidu search engine and Yahoo! Finance to collect data for a client report. As the workday draws to a close, she logs on to Tuan800 to find movie and dinner deals.

After work, she usually chats with friends on MSN, Microsoft's Internet service, and then goes home to watch a program—not on TV but on Sohu HDTV. She watches the latest episode of *The Big Bang Theory* or *Desperate Housewives* for an hour or two. Before putting the light out at night, she spends a few minutes to download a new app onto her iPad. There is hardly a moment in the day when she is not connected.

It is a breathless, round-the-clock experience. It is life lived to the full—but online.

And Jing is not a rarity. There are many people like her in China and India. As we will discuss in this chapter, they are willing participants in the consumer online revolution.

Netizens and the Rise of a National Conversation

For centuries, China and India have been diverse, disparate, and disconnected countries. Now, however, they are on the verge of a new era, thanks to the arrival of digital technology. For the first time, the two populations are engaging in something new: a national conversation. It is already having a profound impact.

In July 2011, one of China's much-touted bullet trains crashed in Wenzhou in the east of the country, killing forty passengers—and the sense of public outrage was so great that it forced Wen Jiabao, the premier, out of his sick-bed to go and visit the site of the accident. But whereas people had, in the past, reacted to such calamities by taking to the streets, this time, they chose a different means of expression: the Internet.

Sina Weibo, China's answer to Twitter (which is banned on the mainland), was overwhelmed by the vociferous opinions of angry citizen microbloggers tapping away on their mobile keyboards, laptops, and the computers installed in hundreds of Internet cafés across the country. The train crash became a topic of discussion for many of its 250 million registered users, who, on average, make ninety million posts every day.

Such is the prevalence of the new social media that people of all classes and all parts of the country are contributing to the *weibos*, or microblogging sites. When Wang Gongquan, one of China's most famous investors, decided to leave his wife for his mistress, he made the announcement to family, friends, and thousands of strangers in a message on Sina Weibo. Within twenty-four hours, his post had been republished sixty thousand times. His friend, Pan Shiyi, a fellow billionaire and chairman of Soho China, one of the country's major property developers, went on the site to urge him to "get in touch with me as soon as possible."[1]

In India, too, Twitter and other social media channels have become common tools of communication for a wide range of people. In 2011, during spirited anticorruption protests led by Anna Hazare, thousands of people turned to Twitter, Facebook, and other sites to register their support—especially during his hunger strike.

One of those was Anand Mahindra, one of the country's top business leaders and managing director of Mahindra Group, who commented on Twitter, "Democracy means no voice, however small, must go unheard. The anti-corruption sentiment is not a whisper—it's a scream. Grave error to ignore it."[2]

So powerful was the online protest that Hazare—a septuagenarian—has since started Twitter and Facebook accounts. "My voice has already reached the people through print and electronic media," he wrote, in an official letter released from Ralegan Siddhi, his village in the western state of Maharashtra, "and now, I shall try to get comfortable with Twitter and Facebook, too."[3]

These stories indicate the extraordinary grip that the Internet has on the world's two most populous nations. China has more Internet users than any other country. In 2011, there were 525 million, more than twice as many as the 245 million in the United States. India had 121 million, more than the 88 million in Japan.

If these are large numbers, they are only a hint of what might be. China's half-billion Internet users amount to a penetration rate of 39 percent of the population (figure 10-1). In 2009, they numbered 384 million, or 29 percent

FIGURE 10-1

Internet penetration in China and India

China is closing the Internet penetration gap with the United States, but India still lags considerably.

Internet users as a percentage of the total population

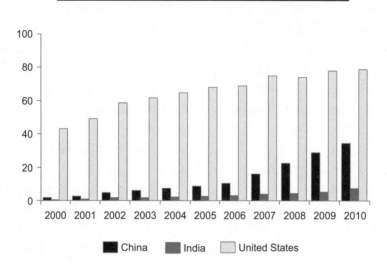

Source: International Telecommunication Union (ITU), ICT Data and Statistics, http://www.itu.int/ITU-D/ict/statistics/; ITU, *The World in 2011: ICT Facts and Figures*, www.itu.int/ITU-D/ict/facts/2011/material/ICTFactsFigures 2011.pdf; BCG analysis.

of the population. And three years before that, there were 138 million Internet users. By 2015, we expect the number to rise to over 700 million, or more than 50 percent of the population. That would still leave it trailing the penetration rate in the United States, whose 265 million users will amount to 83 percent of the population. In India, the 121 million users in 2011 represented a big increase from the 31 million recorded in 2006. But they still constituted only 10 percent of the country's population.[4] By 2015, we expect the number to reach more than 200 million, or 15 percent of the population.

Right now, consumers in China and India access the Internet in different ways. In China, the PC is much more prevalent than in India. Our research shows that there were 267 million PCs in China in 2009—covering 20 percent of the population. In India, by contrast, there were just 55 million, covering a mere 4 percent of the population.

The other major access point is the mobile phone. Here, the gap is smaller between the two countries, which are the two largest mobile phone markets in the world. In 2011, there were 950 million mobile phones in China, accounting for 70 percent of the population.[5] In India, the numbers were 893 million and 70 percent, respectively. By 2015, our research suggests that 92 percent of the Chinese population—1.27 billion people—will have mobile phones. India will not be far behind, with 953 million mobile phones, equivalent to 75 percent of the population.

A fast-emerging third way of accessing the Internet is the tablet. In a BCG survey in 2010, some 23 percent of Chinese respondents said they owned a tablet, compared with 16 percent in the United States. A further 24 percent said they were "extremely familiar" with them, compared with a further 18 percent in the United States. Certainly Apple's iPad has been especially successful in China, driving the company's revenues to record levels. In the first three quarters of its 2011 fiscal year, revenues in greater China, which includes Hong Kong and Taiwan, amounted to $8.8 billion, six times the previous year's revenues. Its four stores in China—two in Beijing and two in Shanghai—recorded the highest traffic and most revenue of any stores in the world, including even the iconic flagship store on Fifth Avenue in Manhattan.[6]

In India, the iPad has not enjoyed quite the same success. It has some committed fans. In one of his daily tweets, Anand Mahindra noted that he was traveling in Europe and "'seeing' the ball-by-ball progress of the one-day international [cricket match between India and South Africa] on my iPad." His verdict? "Amazing device. No wonder laptops are reeling from the punch!" The Indian government is expecting that the market for tablets will take off and, in October 2011, agreed to buy one hundred thousand ultra-cheap tablets from DataWind, a U.K.-based company.

Over the next five years, it plans to buy ten million of these devices for schools in order to boost computer literacy. In doing so, it may also boost the appetite for tablets. DataWind's Aakash, or "sky" in Hindi, retails at $60, a fraction of the cost of the iPad ($500) and the Kindle Fire ($199).[7]

Mobile phones and tablets allow anybody anywhere to access the Internet. But the telecom infrastructure—in particular, the availability of broadband—is critical. When it comes to infrastructure, China and India lag the major developed economies—as reflected in BCG's e-Intensity Index, which measures how the Internet is being used in different economies.[8] In principle, children with an Aakash tablet should be able to reach for the sky. Without Wi-Fi, however, they are holding the equivalent of a car without gas.

Only 15 percent of India's population has access to a broadband connection, and only 8 percent have access to a third-generation mobile network, which offers faster speeds for downloading mobile Internet. Only a few cafés, shopping malls, and modern offices based in the more affluent cities offer Wi-Fi hotspots. China is in a different league: an extraordinary 80 percent of the country's population has access to broadband, and 95 percent to a 3G mobile network.

In India, plans are slowly in process to begin to address the issue. In 2010, the government held a controversial auction of the 3G spectrum, and Tata Docomo, a joint venture between Tata and NTT Docomo, a Japan-based mobile operator, became the first company to launch 3G services in the country.

The way consumers in China use the Internet reflects its accessibility. In 2011, Chinese consumers spent a total of 1.9 billion hours on the Internet—every day. This was nearly three times as many hours spent by American consumers: 637 million hours. The difference reflects the size of the populations—but it is nevertheless striking that on average, Chinese Internet users spent more time on the Internet than did U.S. Internet users: 3.6 hours and 2.6 hours, respectively.

The prevalence of the Internet in China means that consumers have taken to using a much wider range of digital services. In some cases, Chinese consumers are more avid users of Internet services than American consumers are. For instance, in 2010, 79 percent of Chinese Internet consumers used instant messaging—compared with just 21 percent of U.S. consumers. They were also bigger consumers of online music (79 percent versus 61 percent), gaming (64 percent versus 46 percent), e-books (40 percent versus 7 percent), and Weibo/Twitter (40 percent versus 13 percent).

Indian consumers also have a bigger appetite for instant messaging, online music, and gaming than American consumers do—but where Indians overtake even Chinese consumers is with their use of e-mail and job searches. Almost all Indian digital consumers (95 percent) use e-mail—compared with 52 percent of China's consumers—and nearly three-quarters (73 percent) go to job-hunting sites such as Naukri.com, Monster.com, and the job portal run by the *Times of India*.

Where Indians are also different from Chinese is in their preference for international sites—something attributable to their familiarity with English and with their freedom to surf the Web without state intervention. In 2009, only two of the top ten Web sites—as measured by usage—were Indian: Rediff, a news, entertainment, and shopping portal, and the *Times of India* site. The most popular were Google's Indian site and Google.com, followed by Yahoo!.

In China, by contrast, only two of the top ten Web sites were *not* Chinese: Google Hong Kong and Google.com. The most popular was Baidu, the search engine company (and the world's third-largest Internet company), followed by QQ, an instant messaging service from Tencent (the world's fifth-largest Internet company).

Among digital consumers, the ones to watch are the teenagers—the big consumers of tomorrow. By way of example, we look at two young digital natives: Swapnil and Jianhong.

Swapnil is a middle-class teenage boy. He lives with his parents and sister in Lucknow, the capital of the northern state of Uttar Pradesh. It is a very tech-connected household, and Swapnil himself possesses a $600 computer, a $150 mobile phone, and a $250 digital camera.

His parents give him $40 in pocket money every month, and he spends a quarter of this on phone calls and texts. "My mobile is always by my side," he says. "It's like my best friend." Like many Indians, he has two SIM (subscriber identity module) cards, so that he can take advantage of different operator rates.

During a typical day, Swapnil texts friends about schoolwork and after-school activities, uses his pen-mounted jump drive to save class presentations, and invariably sets his computer to download movies and songs from peer-to-peer file-sharing sites while he is taking lessons. Back home, he will typically click on to cricinfo.com—the most popular of the cricket news Web sites—and then check his e-mail and chat with friends on an instant-messaging platform. Before going to bed, he will also find time to chat on Facebook, do some online research for his homework, and send the last of the two hundred text messages he typically sends every day.

Four years younger, Jianhong lives with his parents in an apartment in Guilin, a tier 3 city in a mountainous region in the far south of the country. Like most children of his generation, he is an only child and is showered with digital gifts. He owns a $220 Nokia mobile phone and an MP3 player, and he spends a third of the $30 in pocket money that he gets every month on his digital pastimes: roughly $3 each on instant messaging—he uses QQ—online games, and his mobile phone.

His parents also usually send him to school with RMB 10 ($1.50) for snacks. But, as he says in a confiding whisper, "I always use it to pay for an online game such as *Dungeon Fighter*."

E-Shopping in China: The Rise of the World's New E-Commerce Superpower

The Chinese say they love to shop. For cars, motorbikes, shoes, mobile phones, and several other types of goods, they are the biggest shoppers in the world. By 2015, we expect them to have overtaken U.S. consumers as the biggest e-shoppers in the world.[9]

Already home to the world's largest population of Internet users, China boasted 145 million online shoppers in 2010—second only to the United States, with 170 million e-shoppers. But there is plenty of room for growth: only 23 percent of the urban population is engaged in online shopping, and e-commerce represents just 3.3 percent of total retail sales.

We calculate that by 2015, there will be 356 million e-shoppers in China. The United States, meanwhile, will have 199 million. By then, some 44 percent of China's urban population will be shopping online. And how much will the e-shopping market be worth? A cool RMB 2.3 trillion ($364 billion)—up from RMB 461 billion in 2010.[10]

This striking increase is attributable to a number of factors. The biggest, of course, is rising incomes. Another is the affordability and availability of the Internet, thanks to the government's efforts to modernize the country's telecommunications infrastructure. A third is the growing trust that people have in the online channel. According to our China research, word-of-mouth recommendations from friends and relations are the most trusted sources of consumer information. But the second-most-trusted source is online blogs and product reviews, followed by social networking sites. The Web sites of manufacturers and TV advertisements rank fourth and fifth as trustworthy sources, respectively.

A fourth factor is the limited scale of real—as opposed to virtual—shops. By 2015, as we have described, about 365 cities will have 100,000 or more middle- and upper-class consumers, yet the country's largest retailers have stores in only about 260 of these cities, and Wal-Mart has stores in fewer than 120 (as of 2010). Because of the lack of development of organized trade, China's top retailers account for only about 13 percent of overall urban retail sales (as of 2010). By contrast, the Internet has almost unlimited reach.

A fifth factor explaining China's rise as an e-commerce superpower is the low cost of delivery. Not only do land-based retailers pay high rent, but they also incur the extra costs of the intermediaries and wholesalers needed for distribution. Shipping by mail costs an average of $1 in China, compared with $6 in the United States.

But if the growth trajectory is clear, the challenge of building an online business is altogether more complex. It requires a real understanding of the unique characteristics of the Chinese e-commerce market.

For a start, there are huge logistical challenges. Although mailing is relatively inexpensive, the quality of the delivery infrastructure remains dire. Consumers worry about receiving damaged goods, and a large number— 45 percent—fear that their purchases will be switched for fakes during delivery. For this reason, online vendors are increasingly reliant on small specialist courier services that have traditionally delivered newspapers to individuals. Indeed, in 2010, online goods accounted for 60 percent of the revenues of the package delivery business.

Another defining characteristic of the Chinese is the way they go about shopping online—which is quite different from Americans and Japanese. Only 19 percent of e-shoppers in China go to official brand or manufacturer Web sites—compared with up to 60 percent in Japan, the United States, and Europe. Instead, and perhaps perplexingly, they trust the views of anonymous reviewers more than the claims of the product manufacturers. More than 70 percent of Chinese e-shoppers said they had read or posted a product review—twice the percentage of American consumers.

Chinese e-shoppers search differently, as well. The top search engine is Baidu.com—the country's answer to Google. But Taobao blocks searches to Baidu for anyone buying through its channel, and this has forced the Chinese to find other ways to find products online than through a classic search engine.

This last point highlights perhaps the most important characteristic of the Chinese e-commerce market: the dominance of Taobao. Part of the Alibaba Group (which also owns the popular business-to-business site Alibaba.com), Taobao has virtually defined the e-commerce landscape in China. In 2010 it accounted for 79 percent of China's online transaction value. Other e-commerce markets are far more fragmented: in Japan, for instance, the leading player, Rakuten, has just a 30 percent share of online transactions, while Amazon.com has only a 14 percent share in the United States.

Unlike eBay, most of the products sold on taobao.com are new. The Web site boasts more than eight hundred million online products, selling them at a rate of forty-eight thousand per minute. In 2010, it sold more than China's top five brick-and-mortar retailers combined, which makes it the biggest retailer in China. The sellers are usually suppliers that have not succeeded with other retail channels, or distributors selling excess inventory.

Taobao benefits from high consumer loyalty, or "stickiness," due to its bargain pricing (online shoppers claim to be able to find items that cost 25 percent less on Taobao than through other channels), its convenience, and its enormous pool of merchants. Also, shoppers are reassured by Taobao's customer service. It has the largest call center in the world, as well as an innovative instant-messaging tool called Taobao *wangwang*, which allows buyers and sellers to communicate in real time. Two other distinguishing features are its seller-credibility rating system—which allows buyers to rate and post feedback about vendors, creates a high level of trust regarding the products sold, generates word of mouth for the site, and makes the shopping experience on Taobao appealingly social and interactive—and its escrow service for payments, Alipay.

The challenge for rivals—and other retailers—is that Taobao is not standing still. A relative latecomer to China's consumer-to-consumer market—only launching in 2003—it successfully captured more than 60 percent market share within two years, thanks to its "free" strategy: it does not charge any registration or transaction fees. From there, it took off further because of a network effect: its large merchant pool made for high consumer traffic, which, in turn, attracted still more merchants, generating even more consumer traffic.

Then, in 2009, in an effort to diversify from its original no-fee model, Alibaba launched Taobao Mall, or Tmall, and it is now strategically shifting resources to this new platform. The site mimics an offline mall, with different product categories offered on different virtual "floors," storewide sales, and a loyalty points program. Consumers tell us that Tmall is more discerning than the original Taobao and offers better customer service and reliability. Participating merchants must be authenticated by the site and pay both registration and transaction fees. Many branded suppliers have already set up official stores on Tmall, either directly or through distributors.

The model is proving successful. There are now about 150,000 merchants and 200,000 brands on Tmall, selling to 180 million customers. It benefits from synergy with the main marketplace site: searches on Taobao automatically return Tmall shops, and the majority of Tmall users say they know about and trust the site because of Taobao. While consumer perceptions of Tmall may not be as favorable as for other business-to-consumer companies in terms of delivery, fulfillment services, and reliability, they are quickly catching up and are already a vast improvement over perceptions of Taobao in these areas.

In June 2011, in another step toward diversification, Alibaba restructured Taobao into three separate companies: Taobao Marketplace, Tmall, and eTao (a service for searching across different Chinese shopping Web sites).

Going forward, we see five major trends in the rapidly growing e-commerce market in China:

- So-called super-heavy spenders are on the rise. They not only spend more money than other consumers, but also buy more branded and high-end or premium products.

- The different demographics of the super-heavy spenders translate to different attitudes, preferences, and emotional needs. Fulfilling the emotional needs of super-heavy spenders will be key to future success in China's e-commerce landscape.

- There will be a clear shift in consumer demand from low-priced but non-guaranteed items sold by sometimes dubious or unknown vendors to high-quality service and products purchased from trustworthy sources.

- The future trend is multistop online shopping. Consumers frequently visit more than one type of Web site for different category needs, and their desire for multiple options will only increase going forward. Companies need to actively manage their online presence and engage consumers via a diversity of online options in order to win.

- The offline, in-store experience remains a key factor that influences consumers' purchase decisions.

Digital India: A Subprize of $100 Billion

Roti, kapda, aur makaan. This has long been the rallying cry of the ordinary people of India: food, clothing, and shelter. But, in the last decade, they have expanded the list to include cell phones: *roti, kapda, makaan, aur mobile.*

Less than twenty years ago, not even one in a hundred Indians had a phone service. Now, as we have shown, the country has become the world's second-biggest consumer of mobile phones, and by 2015, nearly one billion people—three-quarters of the population—will have such a device. As a result, the mobile phone will become the engine of India's digital transformation.

Today, according to our calculations, the market for digital products and services is about $65 billion a year. By 2015, we expect this to break the $100 billion mark.[11] Nevertheless, things will become intensely competitive, embracing not just the telecommunications companies such as Bharti Airtel but also technology companies with a strong consumer presence—device manufacturers such as Nokia and Apple and Web giants such as Google and Facebook. Companies such as Bharti Airtel and Nokia are already launching new kinds of products and services that take them in an altogether new direction.

India's traditional telecom market is worth about $32 billion. But when other related businesses are accounted for, the digital market is double this size. It is in these other businesses—digital devices, video, software, and applications—where the real commercial opportunity lies over the next ten years.

The core of the telecom industry's business is access to mobile networks. Access generates about $31 billion of annual revenue. Devices and services—which contribute $22 billion and $12 billion, respectively—have traditionally been seen as supplementary to the access business. But with access reaching a new plateau, the next wave of growth will come from four types of newly created services: educational, financial, and other consumer-facing services delivered on handsets and on the "wide screens" of personal computers, laptops, and tablets; corporate network and managed services enabled by cloud computing; machine-to-machine applications; and mobile advertising, marketing, and commerce.

Three factors will make this new wave of growth possible. The first is the rollout of 3G and wireless broadband networks. Initially, these fast networks will be limited to the top one hundred to two hundred cities, but smaller cities will eventually be beneficiaries, too. Second, technological and product development in devices and user interfaces, such as touch screens and voice recognition and even gesture recognition, will encourage consumer adoption. Third, prices will fall. The average price of smartphones will likely drop to less than $100 by 2015 from more than $250 today, while the price of advanced-feature phones will fall to around $60.

With the right networks, products, and prices in place, and with continued widespread penetration of mobile connectivity, operators will need to start offering the right services. Young Indian consumers, in particular, are increasingly digitally savvy and want to enjoy the convenience and entertainment value of mobile communications—in particular, social networking, video, and instant messaging.

A bigger opportunity may be the provision of services that help consumers improve their employment and earning prospects and that fill gaps in health care, financial services, and education. We expect that by 2015, the access business will be worth $44 billion, while the services business will have risen threefold to $36 billion and the devices business will have increased by more than 60 percent to $36 billion.

Bharti Airtel and Nokia have been rapidly expanding into services and devices. Both companies are identifying the sweet spot of improving the lives and livelihoods of consumers.

Sunil Bharti Mittal, founder of Bharti Enterprises, one of India's biggest conglomerates, has long been a prominent participant in the country's digital transformation. Yet he started out manufacturing parts for bicycles in the mid-1970s in Ludhiana in the Punjab. Working sixteen- to eighteen-hour days, he tried his hand at various businesses—with varying degrees of success. Eventually, having moved to New Delhi, he launched Airtel after winning a contract from Siemens, the German engineering company, to manufacture its push-button phones for the Indian market. This was his breakthrough— and he knows he was fortunate. "I believe there are miles to go—always," he once said. "Everybody nurtures dreams, but few manage to realize them."[12]

Today, Bharti Airtel is the world's fifth-largest mobile operator, measured by the number of subscribers. In 2006, it was just thirty-second in the world. Beyond being India's biggest cell phone company, it also has expanded into nineteen countries and is the leading provider in twelve of them. In 2010, the company generated revenues of $8.8 billion. The secrets of its success—and its founder's, as he now has an $8.3 billion fortune—are innovative business models relating to operations and distribution.[13]

In 2004, Airtel developed what is known as its "minute factory" model. Under the model, Airtel took the radical step of outsourcing significant parts of its network—long considered the crown jewel among telecom operators—to Ericsson and other companies. In this sense, its factory was *minute*, as in "small." More significantly, outsourcing allowed Airtel to flexibly increase and manage its network capacity, essentially building minutes—as in "time"—with the increased demand, just as a factory line accelerates in line with demand.

This model has delivered many benefits. First, as an early champion of outsourcing, Airtel won great terms from vendors, thereby enjoying lower operating costs than those its rivals faced. Second, the model allowed the company to build its network in a fast and market-responsive way: by lowering its capital expenditure, the company had the cash to buy more spectrum, or airwave capacity. Third, the model enabled Mittal and his managers to devote more time to the development of new customer products.

One of these new products relates to the burgeoning mobile money market. Most Indians do not have a bank account—they are, to use the jargon, the "unbanked." There are just 240 million individuals with bank accounts, 20 million credit cards, 88,000 bank branches, and 70,000 ATMs.[14] The government, which wants to address this issue, thinks the mobile phone industry can help—because 42 percent of those who do not have a bank account *do have* a mobile phone. We estimate that by 2015, as much as $350 billion in payment and banking transactions could flow through mobile phones, compared with about $235 billion of total credit- and debit-card transactions today.

Various mobile phone companies have formed alliances with banks. In January 2011, Bharti Airtel took its first step to develop services for the unbanked and to enable financial inclusion and economic empowerment for people across India. The company will do this through strategic partnerships with leading banks in India. Together with the State Bank of India (SBI), it announced the formation of a joint venture to develop services for the unbanked. As Mittal put it, "The services offered by the joint venture will enable financial inclusion and economic empowerment for people across India. This will be a complete game changer, leveraging SBI's expertise in the banking sector along with Airtel's 150-million-strong customer base and an ecosystem of more than 1.5 million retailers and distributors across India."[15]

Another company sensing new opportunities is Nokia, which has teamed up with Union Bank of India to offer mobile banking. The Finnish giant entered the Indian market in 1995 with a modest $10 million investment. By 2001, it had set up R&D facilities in Bangalore and Hyderabad. It saw its first major growth spurt in 2003 after launching its first phone for the Indian consumer. By 2008, it was selling more than one hundred thousand handsets annually and generating more than $4 billion of revenue, according to various industry estimates.

Its key success has been customizing products and services for the Indian market. Its 1100 phone, which became India's most popular phone within two years of launch, had a number of features designed to appeal to consumers: a torchlight to help vision during the frequent power blackouts; a menu of options in Hindi and other languages; a dust-resistant silicon key mat to improve durability in dusty environments; and an antislip outer coating to aid grip on hot and humid days.

Nokia's services vary, too. In 2009, it launched its Nokia Life Tools service, aimed at rural and semi-urban communities. This provides subscribers with the latest information on the weather, crop prices, and other essential, time-sensitive aspects of farming. The service also offers useful farming tips to help subscribers boost their productivity and profits. Bharat Kumar Patel, the cotton farmer introduced in chapter 4, uses the service to determine which of the four nearby *mandis*—or marketplaces—he should go to in order to sell his cotton for the best price. In 2010, this service was broadened to offer health care services.

China and India have boldly entered the digital era—and it is allowing them to catch up to and, in some cases, leapfrog the United States and Europe. Over the next ten years, if China and India construct the right infrastructure, they will be the dominant consumers of digital technology. This presents companies with an extraordinary window of opportunity—not only specialist technology companies but also retail and other companies that have struggled to reach the consumer.

To succeed, companies require a customized digital strategy, which means addressing consumers' online and offline shopping habits. But if companies squander this opportunity, the risks are serious. Companies without an active, targeted online strategy might not only miss out on a key opportunity for growth, but also allow their brand identity to develop online without their input. Moreover, other companies, better adapted to the times, could race ahead and take their place.

ELEVEN

Education

The Escalator to Higher-Paying Jobs

How innovation and investment in education are driving the race to produce
knowledge workers, spurring growth, and creating the next generation of
newly affluent consumers in China and India

WHILE VISITING THE INDIAN INSTITUTE of Technology in Delhi, we
met Shriram, a young man who ranked 19 out of 485,000 on the
entrance exam. We call him Mr. Number 19. He is a handsome young
man—tall, slender, with short black hair and a carefully trimmed goatee—
who "thinks in English" and could easily pass as an American teenager. He
has a quick smile and a soft laugh. We met him outside on the IIT campus on
a hot late-summer day and asked him what motivated him, why he works so
hard, and where he wants to go.

"All my life I wanted to be here," he says. "I knew that if I could go to
IIT, major in engineering, work and study hard, my life would be perfect.
I would marry a beautiful girl, start a company, help my country advance,
and deliver on my family's hopes and dreams. It is from hard work that I will
be able to achieve all I hope for. IIT is the pinnacle. I am surrounded by the
best minds of India. It is here that I am learning to solve problems, get away
from rote learning."

China and India have intense national testing programs to find the best
and the brightest students for their elite universities. The competitions, the
preparation, and the national anxiety about the outcomes make the SAT and
ACT testing programs in the United States seem like the junior league.

The stakes are high for all participants. The "chosen ones"—who rank near the top on the tests—get their choice of university, which acts as a booster rocket to their careers, their longevity, and their life experience.

In 2011, the Indian Institutes of Technology accepted only 9,618 of 468,000 applicants.[1] There are now sixteen campuses scattered across the country.[2] But the campuses lack the prestigious buildings and extensive grounds of the elite Western universities, and the faculty is not the draw—there are no Nobel laureates at any of the institutions.

So a reasonable question to ask is, what's the attraction? "We come here for each other," says Shriram. "When you put the best of the best together and you give them a chance for hands-on problem solving, amazing things happen. We learn from each other. My classmates are my education. We compete academically, athletically, but we are all in this together. Our predecessors are our heroes. They set the bar high on what we can achieve. IIT has a huge influence on our country."

Shriram can tell you the date and time when he logged on to the IIT Web site to see the results of the IIT Joint Entrance Exam (JEE). This is because the exam—and the preparation for it—dominated his teenage years. Born in 1989, he was singled out as academically bright at an early age, with a keen aptitude for mathematics and science. He had started taking part in interschool math competitions by the time he was eleven years old and did extremely well. He says, "I liked winning and to do better than others. It must have been around class eighth term [eighth grade] that I decided that I would take the IIT entrance exam."

He enrolled at Vidyamandir Classes, a private IIT coaching institute that prepares students with aggressive drilling in the major testing areas—physics, chemistry, and math. The students study and memorize the answers to thousands of test questions. For two years, Shriram followed a demanding schedule. "It was a hundred and four weeks of constant preparation—more like a marathon," he says. "I studied regularly for those two years without fail." In an average week, he attended the coaching class for three hours, three times a week. He then spent six to seven hours per day reading and solving the assigned problems and preparing for the mock tests. At the same time, he continued to attend his regular school five days a week. Shriram estimates that he studied for about eighty to ninety hours every week.

When he finally arrived at the IIT in Delhi, he found a class filled with academic superstars. The faculty takes pride in setting high expectations and establishing the reality of competition from the very first week. On the first math exam, his freshman class received an average grade of 30 percent. Shriram soon bounced back, putting in his trademark ninety hours a week of studying. He sacrificed sleep so that he could earn top grades and have an active extracurricular life. The IIT in Delhi offers thirteen cultural clubs (ranging from music to photography to joining a quiz team) and a plethora of opportunities for people to pursue these interests, whether cocurricular or extracurricular. "I never wanted to be only a nerd," says Shriram, a leader on IIT's debating team.

"A lot of my learning has been outside classrooms and labs," Shriram adds. This is consistent with what many "IITians" say about their experience. Nandan Nilekani, one of the founders of Infosys, talks about the time that he organized the IIT Bombay cultural festival as his earliest management experience.

Today, Shriram is a confident young man. He is animated and chatty, laughing heartily in his responses to our questions. He is comfortable with his accomplishments and believes his work ethic, his natural gifts, and the opportunity in a resilient India will give him a life of success: "I will work as hard as necessary, put in as many hours as anyone. I will make the most of my gifts. I am ambitious. I care about my country and family. I will make both proud. I was stamped very, very smart. It will carry me a long way."

It is striking that he has a clearly defined blueprint of his life, both personal and professional. "My life will be good," he says. "By virtue of my rank on the test, I have my choice of major. I will get a good job at a good salary. I will learn business and engineering. And then I will apply my skills in my own company. It will grow. In ten to fifteen years' time, I will be married with a kid or two. It will not be an arranged marriage. But I will marry an Indian girl. We will live a good life. We will live in India and help to make our country stronger, more secure economically. The future is bright indeed."

Beyond Mr. Number 19: The Battle to Be Best—and BCG's E4 Education Index

Not everyone can be a Shriram, a Mr. Number 19.

There are nearly forty million other university students in China and India.[3] Most attend institutions that do not have an international reputation and that churn out students at prodigious rates. It is not surprising that many companies tell us that these graduates need a year of additional on-the-job training before they can achieve a moderate level of productivity.

The primary schools are worse, and the educational experience can be grim. In both countries, lessons take place in crowded classrooms with unmotivated teachers and classmates who would rather be elsewhere. In India, the student-to-teacher ratio is 40-to-1. In China, it is a more manageable 18-to-1.

But there is a recognition that the system needs to change. The governments of both China and India have made educational reform a core building block of their five-year plans. They realize that they need to transform their populations from day laborers into knowledge workers. They need to create a skilled workforce for the knowledge economy of the future if they are to continue on the path of growth. They understand that there is a straightforward equation: education equals innovation, greater productivity, and higher-paying work. This is why there is a looming war for engineers, innovators, educators, and entrepreneurs. The winners lock in real wage increases, increased longevity for all citizens, global leadership in business, and social and political stability. Also, they create a new generation of newly affluent consumers.

To determine how much needs to be done, we have developed the BCG E4 Index, a rough measure of the relative global competitiveness of a country's educational system. The four Es are enrollment (the number of students going through the educational system); expenditure (the level of investment in education by government and private households); engineers (the number of qualified engineers entering the workforce, driving economic development through research and innovation), and elite institutions (the number of top global higher-education institutions).

We have weighted the four components equally on a 1,000-point scale. The United States and the United Kingdom are ranked one and two, driven by their dominance in globally ranked universities, raw spending, and engineering graduation rates (figure 11-1). China ranks third, largely on enrollment. Germany is fourth, based on top universities, engineering graduates, and spending. India is fifth, driven almost entirely by enrollment rates.

Let's take each of the four components in turn, starting with expenditure. China spends $300 billion on public education. Next to defense, it

FIGURE 11-1

BCG's E4 Index of education strength

Despite China's and India's strong scores for enrollment, the United States and the United Kingdom remain on top for education.

Country	Rank	Total points	Enrollment points	Expenditure points[a]	Engineering grads points	Elite university points
U.S.	1	237	25	73	48	91
U.K.	2	125	4	26	46	48
China	3	115	86	17	4	8
Germany	4	104	5	25	37	38
India	5	104	90	4	3	6
France	6	87	4	24	41	18
Canada	7	85	2	25	39	18
Japan	8	72	7	31	19	16
Brazil	9	38	17	16	2	3
Russia	10	32	9	10	10	3

Sources: United Nations Educational, Scientific and Cultural Organization; U.S. Census Bureau; Oppenheimer & Co Research; Organisation for Economic Co-operation and Development; Duke University; *U.S.News & World Report*; BCG analysis.

a. Sum of points for total expenditure and per-student expenditure.

is the biggest category of government investment. Families contribute an additional $180 billion in private expenditure. India's government spends much less: $110 billion. Families contribute $70 billion. In the United States, with one-fourth as many students, spending totals $980 billion, or twice as much as China and five times as much as India (figure 11-2).

Enrollment is key here. The United States has just sixty-seven million students. China and India, offering nine years of free education, have nearly a

FIGURE 11-2

Data used in the E4 calculation

Country	Total enrollment (millions)	Est. total education expenditure (US$B, PPP)	Est. total expenditure/ student (US$, PPP)	Annual employable[a] engineering grads/thousand population	Number of top 400 global universities[b]
U.S.	67	980	14,600	741	87
U.K.	12	150	12,400	710	46
China	235	480	2,000	55	8
Germany	14	145	10,700	566	36
India	244	180	700	49	6
France	12	130	10,600	622	17
Canada	6	85	13,600	603	17
Japan	19	215	11,500	290	15
Brazil	47	210	4,500	31	3
Russia	25	105	4,200	152	3

Sources: United Nations Educational, Scientific and Cultural Organization; U.S. Census Bureau; Oppenheimer & Co. Research; Organisation for Economic Co-operation and Development; Duke University; U.S.News & World Report; BCG analysis.
a. Quality adjusted based on MNC employer willingness to hire graduates.
b. Per U.S.News & World Report (2010).

quarter of a billion students each. This represents a significant achievement. Since 1950, China has trained nearly half a billion people, including four hundred million through high school and sixty million through college. In doing so, it has improved literacy from 20 percent of the population to very close to that of the United States and above the global average of 84 percent (figure 11-3).[4] India has trend-line growth in literacy to match the United States in about twenty years.

With new investments, and expanding populations, the number of students is set to rise over the coming decade in both China and India. The best of these students will progress into the higher education system. The two countries are expected to turn out nearly 140 million postsecondary

FIGURE 11-3

Key facts: population, education, and investment by country, 2010

Country	GDP growth (%)	Δ Working pop.[a] (millions)	Employment rate (%)	Relative wage rate[b]	Productivity of labor[c] ($)	Literacy rate (%)	Enrollment (millions)	Combined GER[d] (%)	Scientists in R&D (per million pop.)	Quality of edu. system[e]	Gross fixed capital formation ($B)	R&D investment ($B)	Total edu. expend[f] ($B)
China	9.5	54.4	93.9	20.6	12,130	93	235	68.7	1,071	62.6	2,040	39	480
India	8.1	81.2	89.2	11	8,760	66	244	61	137	72.7	430	8	180
Russia	4.2	6.8	92.1	16.7	28,660	100	25	81.9	3,305	44.6	368	15	105
Brazil	4.1	25.6	93	20.6	20,470	91	47	87.2	629	26.6	307	19	210
U.S.	2.8	3	90.3	100	94,340	100	67	92.4	4,663	82	2,414	293	980
U.K.	2.7	1.5	92.2	81.6	69,410	100	12	89.2	2,881	80.6	446	29	150
Canada	2.4	2.3	92	90.3	70,050	100	6	99.3	4,157	97.1	340	20	85
France	2.1	1.2	90.6	86.7	75,920	100	12	95.4	3,440	79.9	627	36	130
Japan	1.9	-2	95.1	84.3	62,720	100	19	86.6	5,573	75.5	1,134	108	215
Germany	1.7	1.2	92.9	73.1	67,700	100	14	88.1	3,453	87.8	702	55	145

Sources: United Nations Educational, Scientific and Cultural Organization; International Monetary Fund, World Economic Outlook; United Nations Development Programme; National Center for Education Statistics (U.S.); National Bureau of Statistics of China; Oppenheimer & Co., "Stay in School: A Secular Growth Story for China Education," white paper, New York, December 17, 2009; U.S. Census Bureau; Edelweiss Research, "Indian Education: A Leap Forward," October 7, 2009; Economist Intelligence Unit; BCG analysis.

a. Change from 2000 to 2010.
b. Indexed average monthly wages (U.S. = 100).
c. GDP per worker at purchasing power parity (PPP).
d. Primary, secondary, and postsecondary; gross enrollment ratio (GER) is the number of students enrolled, divided by the number of people in the target age population.
e. Based on survey rankings from World Economic Forum, "The Global Competitiveness Report 2010–2011," converted to 100-point scale.
f. Public and private, PPP adjusted.

graduates from 2011 through 2020, more than four times as many as the United States (figure 11-4).

The largest group of students is composed of engineers and scientists, the third element in the BCG E4 Index. In China, the government's policy is to invest in indigenous technology to drive economic advancement, technology advantage, and job creation. It says it produces 644,000 bachelor and sub-baccalaureate degrees a year in engineering, computer science, and

FIGURE 11-4

Postsecondary degree graduates by country, 2011–2020

By 2020, the projected annual number of graduates in China and India will significantly outpace that in the United States.

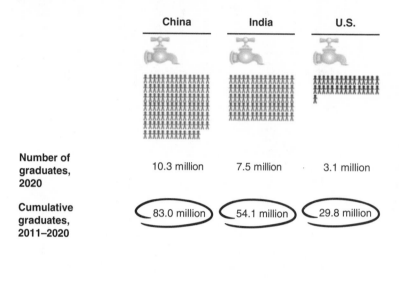

	China	India	U.S.
Number of graduates, 2020	10.3 million	7.5 million	3.1 million
Cumulative graduates, 2011–2020	83.0 million	54.1 million	29.8 million

= 100,000 graduates

Sources: UNESCO; T. Jing, "The Popularization of China's Higher Education and Its Influence on University Mathematics Education," *Educational Studies in Mathematics* 66 (September 2007); S.Kunjabihari Singh, "The Higher Education System Under Review," *E-Pao!* Web page, November 23, 2010, www.e-pao.net/epPageExtractor.asp?src=education.The_Higher_Education_System_Under_Review.html; Nasscom Strategic Review 2010; National Bureau of Statistics of China; U.S. Census Bureau; World Bank, World Development Indicators; BCG analysis.

information technology, which is nearly three times as many as the United States and India.

But these numbers do not tell the whole story. The United States remains more engineer-intensive, with 981 engineering degrees per million citizens, compared with 553 in China and 197 in India. Also, there is the issue of quality. As we have noted, companies are skeptical of the standard of the graduates coming out of China's and India's universities. The World Economic Forum estimates that immediately "employable" engineers account for 81 percent of U.S. graduates—compared with only 10 percent of Chinese graduates and 25 percent of Indian graduates.

This is something that Chinese and Indian academics—many of whom were educated abroad—understand. "Chinese students can swarm a problem," a dean at a major Chinese university told us. "But when it comes to original thought and invention, we stumble. We are trying hard to make that up. We are trying to make technical education the grounding from which we solve problems."

But there is a long way to go. When it comes to elite education—the fourth E in the BCG E4 Index—China and India are far behind the United States.

Certainly, for the best students, access to the top universities in China and India sets them on the path to success—as we have shown with Mr. Number 19. The tough national entrance exams create magic carpet rides for the lucky few. We calculate that the winners will earn a return of at least thirty times their education investment. These young graduates from the elite institutions get the best jobs, earn the highest salaries, move into modern apartments, buy cars and luxury goods, eat higher-quality food, enjoy access to the best health care and investment services, and influence the future of their countries in profound ways.

Yet, even among the best students, many choose to study abroad, traveling to the United States and the United Kingdom in search of world-class education. The U.S. educational system, institutional capability, and faculties remain the envy of the world. It has the most elite institutions, a hundred-year advantage in research and education, and an unparalleled level of investment. According to *U.S. News & World Report*, the United States holds eighty-seven of the top four hundred global university rankings.[5] The United Kingdom has forty-six, along with the second-highest ratio of engineers per million citizens. China has only eight of the top four hundred universities (not including universities in Hong Kong), and India trails with just six.

Some of the top entrepreneurs profiled in *The $10 Trillion Prize* studied in the United States, including Adi Godrej, Frank Ning, Ratan Tata, and Anand Mahindra. Many thousands of people are following in their footsteps. According to the most recent data, U.S. universities have 103,000 students from India and 156,000 students from China.[6] In the United Kingdom, there are 75,000 Chinese students and 19,000 Indians.[7] Also, according to the U.S. National Academy of Sciences, some 52 percent of the country's PhDs under the age of forty-five are foreign-born.[8]

FIGURE 11-5

Enrollment measures by level of schooling

China and India still lag behind the United States on key education metrics.

Enrollment	China	India	U.S.
Primary school (%)	99	92	99
Middle school (%)	92	77	99
High school (%)	62	47	89
College/ university (%)	23	14	56
Graduate school (number of students)	1,280K	1,585K	3,750K

Sources: National Bureau of Statistics of China; U.S. Census Bureau; World Bank, World Development Indicators; BCG analysis.
Note: All data are from 2008, except that India's college enrollment is 2007 data; college enrollment in the United States is the number of college students aged 18–22 divided by the population of 18–22-year-olds reported by the U.S. Census Bureau in 2009.

The United States remains dominant in graduate school enrollment, thanks to its tradition of peer review and active participation in PhD programs. It has nearly four million graduate students, compared with less than half that number in either China or India (figure 11-5). And in terms of the percentage of the student-age population enrolled in school at various levels, there is a significant drop at the high school level in China and India relative to the United States—and a dramatic drop at the university level.

But if China and India are far behind, they are starting to introduce measures to close the gap. Indeed, as we will now show, China's determination to divert resources to fund education and its ability to import talent bode particularly well for its future.

China's Education Challenge: Peking University and the Rise of China's Ivy League

Most rank Peking University as China's top school. It is located in the Haidian District of Beijing and was founded in 1898. The modern campus is spread over 680 acres and has beautiful ponds, scenic walkways, an interesting mix of old and new architecture, and stunning investment in research facilities, modern classrooms, and infrastructure.

The university has an enrollment of thirty thousand students, with a faculty of twenty-nine hundred. It costs under $2,000 per year to attend, with approximately 20 percent of students receiving financial aid. There are 110 undergraduate programs, 278 master's programs, 229 PhD programs, an eight-year MD program, and 36 postdoctoral research centers.[9] The top programs are basic and applied sciences (especially math and chemistry), social science, and management.

Peking University has played a central role in China's history. Chairman Mao once worked in the university library and began studying Marxism under the influence of two Peking University professors—and it was a central hub of the student demonstrations that began in the 1980s and that led to the Tiananmen Square massacre in 1989.

Now, the university is part of the effort to create a Chinese Ivy League. In 2009, the government formed the C9 League, meant to be the Ivy League of China.[10] Peking was among these elite institutions. It is a very distinct policy choice to improve the economic and social future through educational advancements at a handful of institutions. In China, there is a saying that "compared to education and learning, everything else is secondary." Also, the goal of a *xiaokang* (well-off) society, which is something China's leaders espouse, can only be delivered through an educated, motivated workforce. The government has declared education as the key to twenty-first-century success in world trade, income growth, and innovation.

Before this, Peking University had received major funding under Project 211, which identified one hundred key universities and provided them with funding for facilities totaling $2.8 billion; it had also received an extraordinary $360 million under Project 985, which first identified the top nine universities.[11] Through these sources of funding, Peking University has received nearly $500 million in invested physical plant.

Given this level of support, it is not surprising that the university attracts the best and hardest-working students. As one student told us during a campus visit, "Good luck finding a place in the library. You can't find a seat even at three in the morning."

Lea Chung, a twenty-one-year-old student at Peking University, told us of her ambitions. She has always been a math whiz kid, one of the few women with a math major. She hopes to find a job in investment banking or consulting. "My future is bright," she told us during a visit. "I expect my starting salary will be four or five times my father's salary. I hope to have a beautiful apartment, a husband, two children, and a house in the country. It will be a very good life. No one will hand it to me. I will have to earn it, but I am used to working very, very hard. That is part of my character."

She continues, "I had a typical Chinese mother. She pushed me hard as a child. I worked at least twelve hours a day on school. I wouldn't say I never played. But play was less important than study. I worked to be ranked first in my class. Both my parents put pressure on me, but even more came from within."

The challenge for China is that not all universities are like Peking. More than 80 percent of the graduates are coming out of secondary universities—and the students, as mentioned earlier, do not impress employers. There are some 6.1 million new graduates each year, compared with 850,000 ten years ago. In 2011, The Mycos Institute, a human resources consulting firm, surveyed 227,000 graduates who earned diplomas in 2010 and found an 83.5 percent six-month employment rate.[12] Many of these newly employed live in what the Chinese call "ant tribes"—cramped squalor in cheap buildings in urban centers. They are waiting for good jobs to become available. For many graduates of secondary universities, it is going to be a long wait.

But China is determined to reform its education system. It claims to have more than 25 million students in more than 2,200 colleges and universities—the world's largest higher-education system. The five-year plan for 2011 to 2015 focuses on supporting emerging industries—including energy conservation and environmental protection, information technology, biology, advanced manufacturing, new energy, and new material science—and providing a pool of talent to build them.[13]

Beyond this, China wants to develop its primary and high schools. The number of schools is staggering: more than 115,000 kindergartens, nearly 500,000 primary schools, 65,000 junior secondary schools, and 3,000 branch vocational schools. In our visits to some of these institutions, we noticed the striking level of discipline in the classroom. Teachers expect to be paid respect in class. There is no slouching, and students wear neat uniforms and are attentive to teachers. Leng Hui, a Chinese educator, has translated a few extraordinary and emotional idiomatic phrases used by parents and teachers to push students: "Diligence is the path to the book mountain and pain is the boat for the knowledge ocean" and "If you work hard enough, you can grind an iron rod into a needle." As one Shanghai student told us, "You are literally never good enough in school. Perfection is the goal." The Chinese "Tiger mother" popularized in the American press is alive and well in China. She drills into her children a sense of honor in excelling, a long workday, and a sense of responsibility to achieve.

The schooling is quite different from the schooling of young Americans. In primary school, up to 75 percent of the curriculum is Chinese language and math. The emphasis is on memorization: math tables and all of the characters in the alphabet have to be learned by third or fourth grade. In secondary school, the *gaokao*, the national college entrance exam, dictates what is taught. Three topic areas dominate: Chinese, math, and English. Ten million students take the *gaokao* each year. It is considered a national event and a personal ordeal. The top scorers become national celebrities, and the student's success reflects on his or her parents, family, teachers, and the community.

In Shanghai on exam day, the number of subway trains is increased to get students to the exam site. Police and security guards mobilize throughout the country to ensure physical safety and arrest those suspected of cheating. The result is college selection based on academic merit, memorization, fact recall, and processing speed.

Some high schools focus solely on college admissions rates. The one-child policy continues to focus parents on their only child's achievement and educational attainment. It is not surprising that the test puts enormous pressure on students.

There is an upside to this system. Objective test results improve the standard of teaching, and the national test has been a key tool for rural students to gain access to urban institutions and national careers. But some of the best students still dream of going to a U.S. university.

In an effort to reverse this brain drain, China is not only improving its education system but also wooing the émigrés. Between 1972 and 2009, some 1.4 million Chinese students emigrated. Of these, around 400,000—the *haiwai guilai*, which means "returned from overseas"—have been lured back with lucrative packages, large relocation bonuses, and sponsored jobs. The relocation bonuses are as high as $150,000, and their overseas experience is highly prized.[14]

India's Education Challenge: Building on the Success of the IITs

IIT Bombay is the best-ranked engineering university in India. *U.S.News & World Report* ranked it thirtieth in the magazine's top one hundred global universities for civil engineering.[15] The school was established in 1958 with an initial enrollment of one hundred students. Four other IITs rank in the top global one hundred.

As we heard from Mr. Number 19, the IIT facilities do not match the standards of some in the United States and China. IIT Bombay runs on a budget of about $26 million, and we estimate that the value of the physical campus is well under $100 million, excluding real estate. Classrooms are basic, housing is primitive, and students consider the food service very poor. Students talk about the living quarters being more like prison cell blocks than dormitories. The faculty is paid substantially less than industry wages.

Despite this, IIT Bombay and the other IITs turn out some brilliant students. R. Gopalakrishnan, executive director of Tata, summarized the strengths of the IITs in a fiftieth-anniversary celebration speech. The strengths included objective problem-solving, collective discipline, "self-driven," competitive spirit, humility, merit, and "measuring progress by the ratio of current creature comforts to those had at the campus."[16]

This success is attributable to the tough entrance test: the JEE. It is a six-hour-long test of math, physics, and chemistry. Under new rules, the JEE can only be taken twice. Prior to this national test, high school students take the national board exam at the end of grade 10. It is a significant moment in a student's life. As one Delhi high school student lamented, "This score follows you for the rest of your life."

The Joint Entrance Exam takes a toll on students. One student we met at IIT Delhi describes the stress: "I had two curricula in grades eleven and twelve: what we studied in school and what I prepared for my exam. I didn't even go to classes every day after I'd fulfilled my mandatory attendance requirement in grade eleven."

Another student we interviewed in India took the IIT exam and told us, "I ranked nine hundredth out of 485,000 students on the IIT exam. There were three thousand to four thousand seats available [before the recent expansions]. Keep in mind, you're not applying to all those slots; you're applying to the slots that are available to people who are not from disadvantaged groups and not women. Nine hundredth, and I still couldn't get into the major of my choice."

If you ask IIT students what they want from life, as we did in a group session, they are ambitious and clear in their dreams:

"I want to run my own company."

"I want to become a millionaire."

"I want to take my skill and create jobs for my country."

Sandipan Deb, in his book *IITians*, estimates that up to 40 percent of IIT alumni have settled permanently outside India. Three IIT graduates are on the *Forbes* 400 list: Bharat Desai, founder of Syntel; Romesh Wadhwani, chairman of Symphony Technology Group; and Vinod Khosla, founder of Sun Microsystems and Khosla Ventures. These were the role models of recent IIT classes.

Sanjay Khosla, the Kraft Foods executive who joined Unilever's training program right out of IIT Delhi, remembers his school days very fondly: "We were all in it together. The facilities were modest, but the excitement about our futures was breathtaking. It was a chance to make a difference, change the world."

Long term, however, the underfunding is a serious issue. In an interview, a senior dean at IIT Delhi told us he deals daily with shortages of equipment, poor pay for teachers, and a quota system that puts unqualified students in the classroom with no remedial assistance. "We are underfunded, we have too few PhDs on faculty, and we have a fifth of our enrollment taken by quota with no remedial programs," he lamented in his hot, open office.

As we spoke, students milled in and out of the office. A poorly maintained room air conditioner blasted warm air into the room. Rotary dial phones rang continuously during the conversation with no assistant available to answer. At IIT, the students create their own intellectual 'music' in the form of interaction, challenge, culture. "Our facilities need investment. We have no big endowments, we have few alumni who contribute, and we have many needs," the dean said.

Despite all this underfunding, the IITs are the best institutions in India, with 1 to 2 percent admission rates. When you drop one level down, however, the colleges have very poor infrastructure and even more limited funding. For instance, the University of Delhi has to cope with nearly a quarter of a million students spread across two campuses. Meanwhile, the public grade schools are worse: 16 percent of public schools lack drinking water, 37 percent lack modern toilets, and 86 percent do not have a computer. It is not surprising that India performs poorly in international rankings. The UN Human Development Programme has ranked it 134 out of 182 countries on education. According to the Indian government's own planning commission, dropout rates across education levels are high: 29 percent for grades 1 through 5, 50 percent for grades 6 through 8, and 62 percent for grades 9 through 12.[17] About eight million primary-school-age children from "marginalized social groups" remain out of school. Literacy rates for women average twenty points lower than for men. It means that India has the largest illiterate population of any country in the world, estimated at three hundred million.[18]

One of the problems is the relative weakness of India's central government. The central government accounts for only 15 percent of total expenditure on education. The twenty-eight states that account for the balance have highly varying wealth and infrastructure. But private education is significant: there are nearly two hundred thousand private schools and seventeen thousand private colleges in India. And there is hope that private entrepreneurs will help drive change.

Educomp is one private company that is attempting to change the status quo in India. It has invented SmartClass, a set of digital instruction materials designed to meet the specific objectives of the different Indian states. The content, produced in eleven regional languages, consists of thousands of animated multimedia modules. It is consistent, entertaining, affordable, and completely repeatable. Parents pay a modest fee every month for their public school students to enjoy a better education. "What we offer is content customized to the student," says Shantanu Prakash, the CEO. "We make the educational experience fail-safe. The student can learn a language, study chemistry, understand math in a way that is predictable and reproducible."

The company was started in 2005 and has grown to $175 million in revenue, earned at a rate of approximately $1 per month per student. It now has a partnership and exclusive license with the Discovery Channel. In addition, it provides online tutoring services. This is an alternative or supplement to physical classes and includes lectures, tests, and homework support delivered via the Internet. One of the most popular options in a country where math is often thought of as a sport is "maths guru."

Other Indian companies attempting to solve the problem of unmotivated, poorly paid teachers include NIIT and Everonn. Meanwhile, The World Bank and private investors are pouring billions into education in India. These efforts will complement the government's bold plans to expand the Central University, the Indian Institutes of Technology, the National Institute of Technology, community colleges, and degree colleges in educationally backward districts. With three hundred million young Indians poised to enter the labor force between now and 2025, there is no time to lose.

Advantage Harvard

The elite Western schools have a compelling set of advantages. Harvard University, established in 1636, has twenty-one thousand students, an operating budget of $3.9 billion, an endowment in excess of $30 billion, and grounds spreading over eight million square feet. Its research facilities are second to none—the libraries have more than sixteen million volumes—and it has twenty-eight hundred faculty members, five times the number at IIT Bombay and about the same as at Peking University. And Harvard is investing in facilities. Between 2000 and 2009, the physical plant at Harvard grew by 43 percent.[19] The university attracts the country's best students, who pay huge fees: the cost of tuition, room, and board is twenty-five times the cost at Peking University and roughly fifty times the cost at IIT. A Harvard undergraduate education has a $200,000-plus all-in price tag.

In the *Times Higher Education Supplement*'s *(THES)* World University Rankings, the United States takes all top five spots, with Harvard at number one. The United States has seven of the top ten universities, twenty-seven of the top fifty, and seventy-two of the top two hundred. Of course, the merits of rankings can be debated. The critics say that the "shutter speed" of the rankings is slow and there is much change in the middle section of the list.

Even so, the *THES* rankings are a measure of academic achievement seen through the eyes of teaching and research staff. The newspaper's survey is sent by invitation only and translated into eight languages, including simplified Chinese. In 2011, there were 13,388 responses from 131 counties.[20] The top three categories, worth 92.5 percent of the rank, are teaching, research, and research influence. The ranking features scores for reputation, PhD awards, admissions rate, income per faculty member, research volume, productivity, research income, and the internationalization of the student body.

For now, the United States is still far ahead. The BCG E4 Index underscores this, too. More broadly, the developed world, with its 500-year-old-plus educational traditions and vast investment in graduate research programs and facilities, still commands an enormous intellectual leadership advantage.

✦❦✦

Over the coming decade, incremental investment in education will provide fundamental growth and advantage in all three countries. The United States needs to raise graduation rates, spur the growth of entry-level jobs, and divert resources to focus on math and sciences. China needs to develop elite graduate programs, recruit excellent faculty, and use its wealth to create the best of Stanford, Massachusetts Institute of Technology, California Institute of Technology, and the London School of Economics. India needs to invest in primary education to fundamentally break the generational poverty for its poorest citizens—and create incentives, such as high-paying jobs and access to venture funding, to keep its best and brightest in India.

From what we have seen, China, more than any other emerging economy, is committing the resources, the culture, and the political energy to close the gap. We predict that China will change the future with ambitious plans to create facilities, faculties, and world-class education. By contrast, India will proceed more slowly. It is at an inflection point. The country needs to up the ante in the form of funding, facilities, and faculty if it is to compete.

PART III

The Lessons for Business Leaders

TWELVE

Paisa Vasool

How to Captivate the Newly Affluent in China and India

How an innovative business strategy, first developed in India's market
stalls and street bazaars, is starting to spread from East to West as
companies search for ways to deliver value for money in an era of austerity.
It is an idea driven by the consumer's search for value and exposure to
higher-quality goods—and a global consumer view that there is a need to
acquire the best goods at lower prices.

W HEN INDIAN CONSUMERS experience the perfect mix of quality and
value, they will often say "paisa vasool." It is the highest praise.
Around the world, consumers are budget squeezed, skeptical of suppliers
and merchandisers, and worried about their future. *Paisa vasool* can become
the watchword to creating greater value, more features for less money, and
consumers who become your advocate.

For more than a thousand years, there has been a vigorous exchange of
ideas and technology between the East and the West. Until the 1500s, China
led the way, with an extraordinary catalog of inventions. Since then, the
West has been at the forefront of innovation, and the East has been scram-
bling to catch up.

But the newly affluent consumers in China and India are changing the
direction of the stream of ideas once more—particularly in business. To some
degree, the East-West flow began again in the 1950s, when Japan became

a manufacturing hub for consumer electronic equipment and automobiles. Japanese companies learned from the West, grew, and then gained market share. Over time, U.S. and European multinationals picked up new thinking from Japanese companies—notably *kaizen*, or continuous improvement, which sparked the rise of lean manufacturing.

Now, across China and India companies are, through intense rivalry, redefining the nature of competition and introducing an altogether sharper, harder-edged, cutthroat approach to business. In Shanghai and Mumbai, Delhi and Beijing, it is not the MBA that counts but the MO—the modus operandi—forged in the heat of commercial battle. As Ratan Tata, chairman of the Tata Group, puts it, companies in the emerging markets are "almost working in a war-like situation" as they battle for commercial supremacy.[1]

In pursuing their goals and dreams, these companies and their leaders are not content with business as usual. Yes, they have listened to and learned from their rivals in the West, but the Eastern firms are cherry-picking the best ideas and then developing their own, without feeling weighed down by legacy thinking. How else can one explain their remarkably rapid rise, when some of them did not exist twenty years ago? Or the astonishingly quick completion of mammoth infrastructure projects like the world's longest sea bridge—a breathtaking twenty-six-mile, six-lane highway connecting the booming northern port of Qingdao and the industrial suburb of Huangdao— in just four years?

Ambition, drive, determination, ingenuity—these characteristics are not, of course, unique to Chinese and Indian business leaders. But in the daily battle to survive, the leaders have elevated these traits to a new level, and U.S. and European companies must learn to do likewise—or lose. There is still time to develop these attributes and hone the skills—but this time is measured in months and years rather than a decade or more. Take a look at Broad company's YouTube video, which we mentioned in chapter 3, to get a sense of the speed of the challenge to conventional time frames. In the video, the company uses time-action photography to demonstrate the construction of a fifteen-story hotel using prefabricated parts in six days.[2]

The best companies are repackaging the knowledge and know-how developed in China and India, allowing it to spread throughout the rest of the company to stimulate growth in their domestic and other emerging markets. In chapter 14, we discuss this fast-forward approach to business. Here, however, we focus on another strategic export from the East.

Besides being ultracompetitive, the most successful companies are ultrasensitive to the requirements of the newly affluent consumers: high quality and a low price. The companies have cleverly developed strategies to cater to these apparently paradoxical demands. Much has been written about *jugaad*—the concept of doing more with less. This is attracting great interest in an era of scarce resources and heightened concern about climate change and sustainability.

We give greater focus to another powerful concept that promises to have a profound impact on global business—*paisa vasool*. *Paisa vasool* is an Indian expression that is used to categorize a purchase or service as fully satisfying—high quality, great value, a complete package that delivers value for money (figure 12-1). We first heard it used on the streets of Delhi at an outdoor market. Since then, we have seen it continuously applied in both China and

FIGURE 12-1

Paisa vasool

Sharp value assessors and tough negotiators want it all
(technical, functional, and emotional components at bargain prices).

Image: Shutterstock.

India. It is part of a natural frugality that many Indians and Chinese have. They grew up with little, often heard stories from their parents about deprivation, and, as a result, try to stretch their incomes as far as possible. They are also quick to complain and discredit a supplier for poor value, low quality, or misrepresentation.

The Indian and Chinese consumer wants the complete range of product benefits packaged at a price point that sizzles with value. As Pawan Goenka, president of Mahindra & Mahindra's autos and agricultural business, told us, "The Indian consumer will not be like any consumer. They want Western technologies and features and Indian cost." Goenka knows. He was the leader of a project to build India's first SUV—a product that costs half as much as its competitors and delivers a full range of benefits. This SUV is now a key export item for Mahindra.

How *Paisa Vasool* Comes to Life in the Market

If you travel in India, you quickly discover that the majority of consumer goods are exchanged in street markets and bazaars, which cover almost all categories of goods. You are warned not to pay the asking price, because buyer and seller lose face if the exchange of goods takes place at the first bid. From an early age, children learn that they offer only what they can afford and only what they think the goods will sell for. Children are urged to "spend money wisely, learn to bargain, never be embarrassed about offering a lower price."

In a typical Mumbai bazaar, you can buy three polo shirts for $10 or half a dozen pairs of socks for less than $5. In the same market, you can buy an electric fan, a pair of "Pumo" sneakers—clearly designed to pass off as the more famous Puma brand—pineapple slices, "secret" medicines for almost any ailment, and a wide range of personal care products. Here, *paisa vasool*— where goods with appropriate features and benefits offer great value—is alive and well.

Sometimes, next to the market, there is a modern mall with an array of luxury stores. The stores are clean, quiet, and pristine in appearance. At one of these, we inquired about a pair of Nike running shoes—they were $150. We asked if the shopkeeper had sold any that day, and the answer was a slow shake of the head, no.

If *paisa vasool* is an Indian phrase, the underlying concept is nevertheless flourishing in China, too. Western-style chain stores may be much more prevalent in China than in India—we estimate that "organized trade," the regional and national chain stores, will account for nearly half of consumer transactions in 2013 in China—yet Chinese consumers continue to use the simple stalls of local merchants for fresh vegetables, meat, local delicacies, inexpensive clothing, shoes, medicines, and home decorative goods.

Companies that have found ways to build a *paisa vasool* approach into their strategy are among the most successful in China and India. One way to translate *paisa vasool* is low entry pricing. This will vary by category. In China and India, it puts most foods and personal care products under RMB 6 or 10 rupees (less than $1). This is the loose change that millions of the new consumers carry in their pockets when they go to market stalls and other traditional retailers. Yet, added together, it can create fortunes.

In India, for instance, Godrej has a powdered hair dye packaged in three-gram containers and sold for 7 rupees ($0.15). The company sells this in 1.1 million retail outlets, which translates into a 65 percent share of the hair dye market. Likewise, in China, Coca-Cola has come up with the "RMB 1 Coke" in some of the smaller, lower-tier cities. This has made the company the largest beverage manufacturer in China, with a 25 percent share of the market.

On the face of it, such a strategy sounds so easy: repackaging products into small, low-priced units and making them affordable for millions of customers. But it is much more complicated than it seems. It requires a combination strategy: one that provides the right manufacturing assets, a retail network with broad distribution, innovation in ingredients, creative packaging that delivers gross margins, and the ability to move fast.

We have taken the concept back to Western markets with substantial success. As we explain later in this chapter, *paisa vasool* will become an even more important frame of reference as many Western consumers caught in the global war for high-paying jobs experience real income declines. They too will want more for less and more features for the same price.

We have created a checklist to help companies devise the right strategy (see the sidebar "BCG's *Paisa Vasool* Checklist"). Follow these recommendations and answer these questions, and your company can develop the art of manufacturing *paisa vasool* products.

Make Entry-Level-Priced Products Your Mantra

It is necessary to develop a three-step combination strategy.

Step 1: Consumer Product Offering

In the lab, engineers need to design a simplified portfolio that provides features at what we call the "magic" price point. This is the "design to price point" approach.

- Do we understand the needs and desired product attributes for each consumer segment?
- Have we removed all costs that consumers do not value?
- Are we providing tested, superior value?
- Do our products have an affordable price point?
- Do we have a set of high-velocity stock-keeping units (SKUs) that earn a disproportionate share of category profitability?
- Have we provided our retail partners a visually stunning way of displaying the goods?
- Do we have pathways for consumers to trade up?
- Do we scream value and defined benefits at the point of sale?

Step 2: The Supply Chain

In the production process, companies need to develop capital-light, low-cost, localized sources for their products. There is no room for frills in the supply chain.

- Have we leveraged local suppliers when searching for raw materials?
- Are we lowering transport costs using distributed manufacturing?
- Are we lowering labor costs by outsourcing the manufacturing process?
- Are we driving 5 percent or more productivity improvements at the product level every year?
- Have we stripped out all unnecessary packaging materials, concentrated raw materials, and provided innovation in resealability?

Step 3: The Go-to-Market Approach

In taking their products to the consumer, companies need to find distribution channels in rural and other remote markets, use in-store branding, and achieve a dominant store position.

- Do we have a target list of engaged, loyal distributors that will muscle up our physical count of distribution?
- Do we track and police distribution, share of shelf, and velocity?
- Have we optimized the frequency of store visits by our promotional team to help the retailer drive visibility, consumer frequency, new usage, and trial?
- Are we reaching even the most remote markets?

Aravind Eye Care: *Paisa Vasool* in Action

Vaidheyan, a fifty-two-year-old farm laborer from Muthupettai village in the interior of Tamil Nadu, is a typical patient of Aravind Eye Care, a company attempting to bring cataract surgery to the 7.5 million needy in India. Married with two children, he earns about 25 rupees a day—less than $1. As he told us, "I was not able to see people at a distance. I was not able to see people visiting my farmland."

One day, he visited an Aravind-sponsored eye camp that came to his village. He was given a battery of tests, and then he was prescribed surgery at the main hospital in Madurai. After a free ten-minute operation, Vaidheyan regained his sight. It was one of more than three hundred thousand surgeries that are carried out each year under the auspices of Aravind Eye Care.

The company is the brainchild of G. Venkataswamy, an ophthalmologist who founded the company at the age of fifty-eight, after retiring from India's government medical service. India has the largest proportion of cataract blind in the world. There is only one ophthalmologist for every 120,000 people in rural India.

Dr. V, as he was known before his death in 2006, opened the first Aravind Eye Care Hospital, with only eleven beds, in the mid-1970s. Today, there are six major hospitals and forty-eight eye care centers that conduct research, manufacture supplies such as the intraocular lens, operate an international eye bank, and run an institute to transfer best practices to other eye hospitals in developing countries worldwide.

To provide high-quality eye care in large numbers and make it affordable and accessible, Dr. V devised a three-pronged strategy:

1. Adopt highly standardized processes to optimize the doctor's time. The time spent by the surgeon per operation is significantly lower at Aravind Eye Care Hospital than at other institutions (twelve to twenty-two minutes, versus fifty-five minutes at a private medical college).

2. Introduce an assembly-line approach to surgery to enhance the productivity of surgeons. Surgeries at the Aravind hospitals are carried out by surgeons in blocks of two or three hours, with as little as one minute between consecutive surgeries. The routine tasks are carried out by well-trained, low-cost staff who constitute almost 60 percent of the total workforce. The productivity of Aravind surgeons is six times greater than that of their peers in India: a surgeon at Aravind does 2,000 surgeries a year, compared with a national average of about 350. This also results in significantly lowering the cost.

3. Provide low-cost manufacturing of expensive consumables. Cataract surgery shifted to intraocular-lens-based (IOL) surgery in the late 1980s; the lenses then had to be imported and generally cost between $100 and $4,200. Aravind established Aurolab, an independent entity, to make intraocular lenses at one-tenth the cost per lens. The facility soon expanded to other eye care products, making them at the same level of quality as their Western counterparts but at a fraction of the cost—a relevant consideration in developing economies.

Dr. V found a way to cut costs—and he also found a way to guarantee quality. Aravind hospitals have a lower incidence of complications during surgery than surgeries done through the U.K. National Health System. Not surprisingly, the company, with an EBIT (earnings before interest and taxes) margin of 46 percent in 2010 on revenues of about $30 million, thinks that it can take the lessons to the West and reduce the cost of health care—applying innovation, industrialization, and the in-sourcing of material components.

Taking *Paisa Vasool* to the Rest of the World

Low-priced goods with deep, rich features will become the fastest-growing parts of all markets as consumers everywhere struggle to make ends meet. *Paisa vasool* might be an Indian concept, but it will soon be demanded in New York, London, and Paris as well as in rural India and China.

Our research suggests that consumers in the United States and Europe are feeling even more cautious about the future than they were during the depths of the financial crisis. In our annual survey of twenty-four thousand consumers from around the globe, more than 90 percent of respondents said they would maintain or reduce—but not increase—their spending in 2012. It is as if the true tragedy of the crisis—and the likelihood that there is not going to be a sharp recovery anytime soon—is finally dawning on consumers and affecting their spending patterns.

Moreover, "value for money" is the characteristic that has seen the sharpest increase over the past two years—in the United States, nearly 60 percent of respondents to our 2011 survey reported that it was more important than in 2009. By contrast, "luxury" and "status" saw a sharp decline in the rank of important factors for shoppers. These hard-up consumers, many of whom are traditionally classified as middle class, have become the "squeezed middle": they still have the taste for Italian coffee and organic products, but these consumers no longer have the disposable income to devote to luxury as often as they did in the halcyon days. And then there are the traditional poor, who still exist in surprising numbers, even in the West. The United States has thirty-eight million people living below the U.S. poverty line—12 percent of the population. Likewise, Japan has twenty million, and Germany nine million living below their national poverty lines.

Beyond the battles in the backyard, the next big battlegrounds will be in Africa, Latin America, and parts of Southeast Asia. Here, a *paisa vasool* approach will be a necessity—and, potentially, a very profitable one. A third of the world's population—2.6 billion people—lives in cities located in the emerging markets. By 2030, this number will have risen by 1.3 billion—a 50 percent increase—whereas cities in developed markets will add only another 100 million new residents. This massive increase will transform the competitive landscape—and the companies that prosper will tap into larger profit pools, generate more innovation, and grow faster than their rivals. As with China and India, it will be important to segment the markets. When advising companies, we divide emerging-market cities into the four categories we described in chapter 5: megacities, cluster capitals, specialist hubs, and horizon towns.

Besides an increase in the number of cities, there will be an increase in the number of newly affluent consumers. According to our calculations, some 42 million households in the cities of Russia, Indonesia, Brazil, Turkey, Mexico, and South Africa will move into the middle class by 2015—taking the total in these countries from 85 million in 2010 to 127 million. Consequently, their spending habits will change, with products previously regarded as unaffordable becoming necessities.

This rising population of affluent consumers in other emerging markets will demand—and be ready to pay for—bigger houses, better infrastructure, and new products and amenities that are familiar to consumers in the United States and Europe. Companies that have competed in China and India will be well prepared to meet these new demands.

They will also be well prepared to meet the threat presented by a host of new rivals. Not only will companies face competition from Chinese and Indian companies that are fast developing their global footprint, but they will also face tough new *global challengers* headquartered in these countries and run by executives who have grown up with *paisa vasool* concepts. We have identified one hundred such companies from rapidly developing economies that are reshaping global industries, and while more than half (fifty-three) are from China and India, others are from Brazil (thirteen), Mexico (seven), and Russia (six), as well as from Argentina, Chile, Egypt, Hungary, Indonesia, Malaysia, Saudi Arabia, South Africa, Thailand, Turkey, and the United Arab Emirates.[3] (We will return to these global challengers in chapter 14.)

Africa, rich in natural resources, is a target for many of these companies— especially those from China. To a large degree, the continent mirrors the diversity of its countries: it has 20 percent of the world's land and 15 percent of its population, but only 4 percent of its GDP. The 450 million people in Africa have very different life experiences and expectations—depending on where they live. Five countries (Algeria, Egypt, Morocco, Nigeria, and South Africa) account for 60 percent of the continent's GDP, and GDP per capita ranges from $330 in the Democratic Republic of the Congo to almost $15,000 in Botswana.[4]

In 2010, Bharti Airtel, India's largest telecom company, acquired the African business of Zain, a Kuwait-based telecom company. This catapulted the Indian company to a number one position in six countries. In 2011, Godrej made its biggest global acquisition in Africa, buying a majority stake in Darling Group, a pan-African hair care company based in South Africa.

Meanwhile, Chinese companies have been engaged in a hectic land grab in Africa—activity supported by the Chinese government, which has been doing everything possible to woo the continent's political leaders. In November 2007, virtually every African leader was invited to a China-Africa summit in Beijing. But what has been dubbed China's "scramble for Africa" began in the early 1960s, when Zambia became the first African country to establish diplomatic ties with China. In the mid-1970s, Mao Tse-tung gifted Zambia with the Tanzania-Zambia railway, connecting the landlocked country with the Tanzanian port of Dar es Salaam, in China's single biggest foreign-aid project.

Today, copper-rich Zambia has three hundred Chinese companies and benefits from foreign direct investment amounting to around $2 billion. Nevertheless, although China is now Africa's biggest trading partner, some Chinese companies, especially those in the mining industries, have been accused of exploiting African workers.[5]

Of course, not all Chinese companies are entering Africa for its natural resources. Some, such as Huawei, see nearly half a billion consumers. The information communications and technology company has been building its business from nothing over the past fifteen years. As one executive told us, "When I first came to Africa, no one knew anything about Huawei, or even China. Facing twenty-five countries, with a population of four hundred and fifty million, I started everything from scratch. I traveled frequently, visiting different African countries. In 1998, I stayed in Kenya for two months, without speaking any Chinese. I can't count how many flights I've taken, using up three passports within two years."

In 2011, Huawei introduced its $100 IDEOS smartphone to Nigeria, one of the continent's richest countries. The company seeks to tap into African consumers' appetite for connectivity in a land with poor infrastructure—and to do so in an affordable way.

Paisa vasool may not be second nature today—but it describes a strategy that is starting to spread far beyond the borders of India. For the most part, the newly affluent consumers in China and India grew up with little and bargained for what they did buy in local bazaars and street markets, and now they are taking this approach to the shops on a day-to-day basis. In the wake of the global economic downturn, consumers in other emerging markets—as well as in the United States and Europe—are also bargain hunting, which means that companies must provide a unique value proposition: products that square the circle by being affordable and high-quality. Done right, this strategy can simultaneously deliver gains in market share in China, India, and the rest of the world.

THIRTEEN

The Boomerang Effect
The Global Impact of the Race for Resources

How demand growth in China and India will give rise to supply-constrained commodities and wild swings in global demand—and what actions companies should take to protect themselves and profit from the volatility

T HE NEWLY AFFLUENT CONSUMERS in China and India are creating an unparalleled opportunity for growth, which has the potential to lift the global economy out of the gloom that settled during the depths of the Great Recession. At the same time, they are creating unexpected challenges for the global economy—what we call the *boomerang effect*.

We have demonstrated throughout the book the reasons why demand will rise rapidly over the next few years in China and India. The boomerang effect is about the consequences of that rise in demand—the second-order outcomes. As consumers in China and India change their diets, demand personal vehicles, build bigger homes with modern amenities, and live in high-rise towers, they will generate staggering increases in the demand for corn, fertilizer, copper, cotton, steel, cement, oil, gas, electricity, and many other commodities. For markets that are supply constrained, prices will swing wildly as a function of month-by-month imports, inventory fluctuations, and new production capacity.

The upsurge in consumer demand will have the same impact on specific markets that Apple has had in music. Great fortunes will be made and lost.

The growth in demand will drive innovation, force consolidation, increase input costs, and spur the creation of substitute products. It will be a time of heady market growth and market shaping. There will be new pockets of local wealth spurring surprising growth in luxury markets—and there will also be pressure on global real incomes as middle-class consumers struggle to compete to buy the same goods they wanted before but now at world market prices.

The boomerang effect started in the 1990s, when foreign direct investment began flowing to China and India—in effect, the propelling of an economic boomerang from the West to the East. At first, when the boomerang—a twenty-year cumulative investment of nearly $1 trillion in China and $200 billion in India—returned to the West, it delivered huge profits for companies that sold inexpensively made products for high prices. The West enjoyed low-cost goods produced with low-cost labor. At the same time, the jobs fueled growth in consumption in China and India. Over time, real incomes—particularly in China—increased at a rapid rate. They are set to continue that growth trend, and much of that real income will go to the purchase of capital goods.

But the flight of the boomerang is now changing. As Chinese and Indian consumers alter their spending habits—buying more food, moving into high-rise apartments, purchasing their first automobiles, acquiring modern household goods—they are sparking a race for resources. Put together, the individual spending habits of millions of people mean that, as countries, China and India have become mammoth importers.

China is now one of the largest consumers of the top ten consumer durable goods. It is the top consumer of bicycles, motorbikes, automobiles, shoes, mobile phones, and many categories of luxury goods, and the second-largest consumer of home appliances, consumer electronics, jewelry, and the Internet. India is also becoming significant in a variety of categories. It is, for instance, the world's second-largest consumer of soaps, motorbikes, and mobile handsets.[1]

By 2020, China will be consuming 54 percent of the world's coal (up from 47 percent in 2010), 53 percent of the world's aluminum (up from 42 percent), 48 percent of the world's iron ore (up from 38 percent), and 39 percent of the world's copper (up from 30 percent) (figure 13-1). Meanwhile, India will be consuming 14 percent of the world's coal (up from 10 percent), 12 percent of

FIGURE 13-1

Changes in China's consumption, 2010 to 2020

Product	2010 Consumption	% of global	2020 Consumption	% of global	Increase in total annual consumption
Food					
Total calories	4,256B/day	20	4,856B/day	19	219 trillion
Meat	98B kg/year	30	134B kg/year	32	36B kg
Fruit	94B kg/year	17	139B kg/year	21	45B kg
Vegetables	474B kg/year	44	716B kg/year	52	242B kg
Fish	37B kg/year	28	43B kg/year	30	6B kg
Energy					
Total	2,348M TOE/yr	22	4,170M TOE/yr	28	1,822M TOE
Coal	3,271M Mt/year	47	5,721M MT/year	54	2,450M Mt
Natural gas	101B m³/year	4	327B m³/year	9	226B m³
Petroleum	10,199K barrels/day	13	18,457K barrels/day	18	3.01B barrels
Refined products	10,618K barrels/day	14	19,165K barrels/day	18	3.12B barrels
Mining					
Iron ore	705M Mt/year	38	969M Mt/year	48	264M Mt
Steel	471M Mt/year	34	641M Mt/year	38	170M Mt
Aluminum	17M Mt/year	42	32M Mt/year	53	15M Mt
Copper	6M Mt/year	30	12M Mt/year	39	6M Mt
Zinc	4M Mt/year	30	6M Mt/year	40	2M Mt
Nickel	350M kg/year	21	700M kg/year	32	350M kg

Source: Economist Intelligence Unit; U.S. Census Bureau International Data Base; BCG, "Mining Market Overview," June 2009; UN Conference on Trade and Development, "Joint India/OECD/IISI Workshop on Steel," May 2006; BCG, "China Steel/IO Demand Outlook Tier 1," January 2009; *Bloomberg Businessweek*, "China 2010 Aluminum Consumption Better Than Expected," January 2011; BCG analysis.
Abbreviations: B, billion; K, thousand; kg, kilogram; m³, cubic meters; M, million; Mt, metric tons; TOE, tons of oil equivalent.

the world's copper (up from 5 percent), and 7 percent of the world's iron ore (up from 4 percent) (figure 13-2). These natural resources for new housing, roads, railways, and power lines will support the future growth of China and India.

The dramatic growth in China and India is, in turn, leading to rising global commodity prices for everything from corn, copper, and coal to aluminum, cement, oil, iron ore, and every kind of food and beverage.

The modern apartment is a natural resources storehouse. According to estimates by Bloomberg, the modern Chinese apartment has 41 kilograms of copper, including 13 kilograms of wiring, 20 kilograms for the air conditioner, and 4.6 kilograms for the stove.[2] Let's now look at the impact on a couple of other categories: iron ore and food.

FIGURE 13-2

Changes in India's consumption, 2010 to 2020

Product	2010 Consumption	% of global	2020 Consumption	% of global	Increase in total annual consumption
Food					
Total calories	3,022B/day	15	3,908B/day	16	323 trillion
Meat	7B kg/year	2	11B kg/year	3	4B kg
Fruit	46B kg/year	8	66B kg/year	10	20B kg
Vegetables	85B kg/year	8	118B kg/year	8	33B kg
Fish	6B kg/year	5	10B kg/year	7	4B kg
Energy					
Total	532M TOE/yr	5	1,092M TOE/yr	7	560M TOE
Coal	687M Mt/year	10	1,526M Mt/year	14	839M Mt
Natural gas	49B m³/year	2	104B m³/year	3	55B m³
Petroleum	3,175K barrels/day	4	6,059K barrels/day	6	1.05B barrels
Refined products	3,190K barrels/day	4	5,777K barrels/day	5	0.94B barrels
Mining					
Iron ore	79M Mt/year	4	149M Mt/year	7	70M Mt
Steel	50M Mt/year	4	90M Mt/year	5	40M Mt
Aluminum	1M Mt/year	4	3M Mt/year	5	2M Mt
Copper	1M Mt/year	5	4M Mt/year	12	3M Mt
Zinc	0.5M Mt/year	4	0.8M Mt/year	5	0.3M Mt
Nickel	70M kg/year	4	140M kg/year	6	70M kg

Source: Economist Intelligence Unit; U.S. Census Bureau International Data Base; BCG, "Mining Market Overview," June 2009; UN Conference on Trade and Development, "Joint India/OECD/IISI Workshop on Steel," May 2006; BCG, "China Steel/IO Demand Outlook Tier 1," January 2009; *Bloomberg Businessweek*, "China 2010 Aluminum Consumption Better Than Expected," January 2011; BCG analysis.
Abbreviations: B, billion; K, thousand; kg, kilogram; m³, cubic meters; M, million; Mt, metric tons; TOE, tons of oil equivalent.

Iron Ore: The Ups and Downs of an Essential Component of Modern Middle-Class Life

In a consumer book about consumer needs, why are we writing about iron ore? The answer is simple: the growing demand for iron ore and steel is a profound second-order outcome of China's and India's rising middle class. In this sense, iron ore is a consumer business—driven by the demand for better housing, cars, appliances, dependable utilities, transportation, hospitals, and schools. When turned into steel, it is a core component of a middle-class life.

The demand for steel is set to rise dramatically in China and India. There are four primary end-use markets for steel—cars, appliances, construction, and infrastructure—and all of these markets are growing as a result of rapid economic growth in the two countries. This growth will continue to pressure suppliers, which in turn will continue to drive a rapid consolidation of supply, with indigenous Chinese and Indian suppliers playing a major role in consolidation. Demand growth will precede capacity additions, threatening inflation and shortages. This will drive up the price of end-use products in both China and India—as well as in the developed economies.

As we have described, China, in particular, has embarked on a building spree of epic proportions, driven primarily by a government that is putting top priority on infrastructure and housing: an estimated seventy-five million units of affordable housing are needed immediately.[3] This situation has been a bonanza for iron ore producers—real prices have increased substantially since the 1990s. There are roughly a billion metric tons traded every year, and China accounts for 62 percent of the world's traded volume.[4] In the period from 2000 to 2010, global demand increased at a 6.1 percent compound annual rate.[5] International trade doubled.

As the market has grown, the major miners—notably Vale, BHP Billiton, and Rio Tinto—have invested in significant new capacity with lower cost structures. There is a staggering 685 million tons of new capacity planned by 2015—a dramatic increase in the world supply if it comes to be.[6] The Quantum mine in Australia is rated at 110 million tons. The Carajás Serra Sul mine in Brazil is rated at 90 million metric tons. Rio Tinto's Simandou mine in Africa is a 95-million-metric-ton facility.[7]

Of course, not all new projects and expansions will come on stream as forecast. Some capacity is described as conceptual and prefeasible. Nevertheless, the iron ore producers are now running a big risk: if China's construction and infrastructure projects do not continue over the next decade, the producers will be left with expensive spare capacity. And in all likelihood, there will be volatility in demand. This volatility will affect most of the core industrial commodities—iron ore, copper, cement, aluminum, nickel, precious metals, and lumber.

Soft periods in real estate development can drive calamities in the iron ore markets. As a result, bonanza can quickly turn into depression. In the world of commodities, it is so easy to be dead wrong. In early 2011, investors were beating the drum for investment in commodity producers, only to dump these shares in a vicious stock market sell-off during August and September of that year. It was a salutary lesson.

Pork, Chicken, and Pecans: New Diet, New Prices

The race for resources, as well as for goods and services, is a direct conse-quence of the Chinese and Indian consumers' new purchasing power and their changing needs, requirements, and appetites—sometimes quite lit-erally. We estimate that the Chinese will spend nearly $1.4 trillion a year on food in 2020, up from $650 billion in 2010, principally because they are starting to buy greater amounts of more expensive foods such as fresh veg-etables, dairy products, and meat—once considered a luxury. In 2010, pork and chicken accounted for 19 percent of the average Chinese citizen's diet. By 2020, we expect this figure will have risen to 28 percent. Put another way, in 2020, the Chinese will be consuming 215 billion more servings of pork and 185 billion more servings of chicken than they were in 2010.[8]

This taste for meat will drive up the demand for corn, soybeans, and amino acids needed to feed pigs and chickens. We calculate that China will need an additional 166 million metric tons of corn, equivalent to 20 percent of global corn production in 2010. The incremental consumption, which could drive up the price of corn from $186 per metric ton in 2010 to as much as $292 per metric ton in 2020, will lead to a supply-demand imbalance and volatile pricing that will affect many finished food products.[9]

"One item that really highlights China's appetite in world agricultural markets is their sharp rise and dominance in world soybean trade," says Dan Basse, president of AgResource, an agricultural forecasting agency in Chicago. "Twenty years ago, China imported limited tonnages of soybeans. Today, China takes an estimated fifty-six million metric tons—representing 62 percent of all traded global soybeans. Soybeans are the world's third-most important crop by value and reflect what can occur when Chinese political leaders accept their role as a food importer—and break from their traditional self-sufficiency model."[10]

Pecans provide another good illustration of the boomerang effect. Five years ago, Chinese imports of U.S. pecans were close to zero. But as the middle class has grown in China, the appetite for healthy food, including pecans, has boomed. In 2009, the pecan became a favorite alternative to the local hickory nut during the Chinese New Year celebration. Indeed, in 2011, pecans were in such demand that they were practically unstockable in Chinese grocers—even when priced at $5 or more per pound, five times the average hourly wage of a factory worker. Worldwide, the price of pecans doubled between 2009 and 2011.[11]

In theory, China could grow its own pecans, but time and resources—money, water, and land—are formidable obstacles. It takes ten years to raise a pecan tree through to full commercial production. During that time, it needs plenty of water, a scarcity in much of China. It would also have to compete for land with other crops.

So the United States, the world's biggest producer of pecans, will remain the dominant supplier for the foreseeable future. This is great news for American pecan farmers—some of whom own trees that are a thousand years old and one hundred feet tall, with trunks that are six feet wide. But the Chinese consumer's newfound passion for pecans is a problem for other pecan consumers and for producers of pecan pies, fruitcakes, and ice cream. No one wants to spend $30 on a Christmas fruitcake or $10 for a half gallon of vanilla pecan ice cream.

The Boomerang Effect: What It Means for You

Over the course of this decade, it will become evident how the growth in demand from Chinese and Indian consumers translates into higher prices on all kinds of goods and greater demand for commodities—and the resulting supply squeeze on energy, water, and food. These supply shortages will ultimately trickle down into higher prices for cars, motors, appliances, jeans, T-shirts, and even leather shoes.

Such whipsaw inflation (up, down, up, up) and S-curve consumption (subsistence consumption at $1,000 per capita income followed by a disproportionate jump to $4,000 and $12,000 per capita) in the East is the most significant boomerang effect. It will present companies in the West with new challenges—not only in China and India but also in their own backyard.

In the United States, the lowest 40 percent of households earn $40,000 or less and, on average, spend roughly $3,000 per year on food. This population is already facing a squeeze on jobs, with unemployment among men lacking a high school education running above 20 percent. If, let's say, they faced a 10 percent increase in food costs (and that is a conservative estimate, given the possibility of a 50 percent increase in average corn prices over the next ten years), they would have to allocate an additional $300 per year to food: anywhere from half a week's to a full week's pay.[12] Suddenly, all kinds of companies will have to face consumers who, no longer able to afford their products, will start to scrimp, save, and bargain hunt.

Another boomerang effect will be the competition for jobs. There will be a rushing stream of college graduates from both China's and India's educational systems—83 million people will earn their degree over the decade in China and 54 million will do so in India, while about 30 million will graduate in the United States, and even fewer in Europe. There will also be a massive flow of young workers, twenty to thirty years old—who currently number 204 million in China and 218 million in India, versus 43 million in the United States—with an undeniable "want more now" attitude (figure 13-3).

FIGURE 13-3

Size of the young working-age population by country, 2010 and 2020

By 2020, India's young working-age population—the twenty- to thirty-year-old age group—will have overtaken China's.

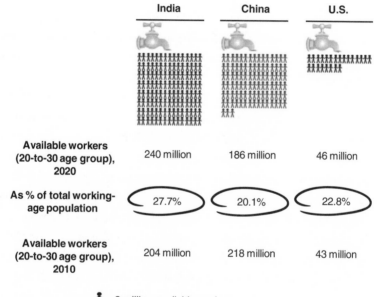

	India	China	U.S.
Available workers (20-to-30 age group), 2020	240 million	186 million	46 million
As % of total working-age population	27.7%	20.1%	22.8%
Available workers (20-to-30 age group), 2010	204 million	218 million	43 million

𝝙 = 2 million available workers

Sources: Economist Intelligence Unit, Market Indicators and Forecasts; United Nations, Department of Economic and Social Affairs, Population Division, Population Estimates and Projections; U.S. Census Bureau International Data Base; BCG analysis.
Note: The total working-age population consists of those in the 15–59 age group: U.S. = 202 million, China = 924 million, India = 868 million.

They will earn increasingly better incomes and, as a result, consume more goods and services.

A third boomerang effect of the rise of newly affluent consumers is the emergence of new companies with international ambitions. We see the once-local domestic companies that served big multinational companies with cheap labor now becoming powerful rivals. Chinese and Indian companies are approaching leadership positions in several global industries. Petro-China is one of the world's most valuable companies, measured by market capitalization. China Mobile is the world's most valuable telecom company, and China's ICBC bank is the most valuable financial institution.[13]

Enriched by newly affluent local consumers and vibrant local markets, these companies are competing for talent. They are also competing for M&A opportunities, leading an extraordinary global land grab for natural resource companies, branded white-goods manufacturers, and technology innovators, among others. And they are taking the fight to Africa, Latin America, and even to Europe and the United States.

Among the companies that have acquired substantial subsidiaries, often household names, in North America and Europe are Birla, Infosys, Mahindra, and Tata—all Indian companies—and the Aluminum Corporation of China, Lenovo, China Petrochemical, China National Chemical Corporation, Geely Holding Group, and China HuaNeng Group—all Chinese companies.

To recap, the boomerang effect can be a threat or an opportunity. Rapid growth in China and India market demand will fuel indigenous competitors. Global pressure on supply will lead to rising commodity prices in supply-constrained sectors. Indigenous Chinese and Indian companies will expand to global markets, particularly emerging markets in Africa and South America. The companies that cater to the emerging consumers in China and India will focus on low-cost, high-feature designs. There will be a loss of market share for companies that come to the party late. A few multinational corporations committed to victory will adapt and win.

To prosper, companies will need to master new skills, including alternative sourcing, product size flexibility, fast-response pricing, and improved commodity hedging. We will see a "winner takes globe" strategy based on leadership in China and India. Halfhearted attempts at participation will translate into cash traps—investments without return. We believe that ignorance permits others to gather strength and return to your home market.

Now is the time to get ahead of the boomerang effect. Companies that respond will need to take several actions:

1. Go on a shopping spree, paying full price for leadership positions in China and India.

2. Fully integrate your acquisitions, paying careful attention to cultural integration, and listening and responding to your new employees.

3. Take the lessons of affordability and low price to heart and to the lab.

4. Drive distribution reach and breadth.

5. Invest in the creation of brand.

FOURTEEN

Fast Forward

Doing Business and the Accelerator Mind-Set

Why the Chinese and Indian approach to business—ambitious, aggressive, audacious, adaptive—could be one of their most enduring exports. They really do not take "no" for an answer.

ADI GODREJ, WHOM WE INTRODUCED in chapter 3, has a big vision. With a $7.3 billion family fortune, he is one of India's wealthiest entrepreneurs—but he dreams of an even bigger, more diverse set of businesses.[1]

Sitting in his white-marble-floored office in Godrej Park, a sprawling, chaotic 3,500-acre business park in Mumbai where manufacturing takes place near mangrove forests, Godrej talks animatedly about his ten-by-ten vision: growing tenfold in ten years. He is no stranger to the ways in which the United States and Europe do business. Born into a powerful industrial family—his grandfather, a lawyer-turned-locksmith, founded the company in 1897—he studied at the Massachusetts Institute of Technology before joining the family firm. He says the potential for organic growth in India is unprecedented, and for Godrej Group, a conglomerate with interests in real estate, consumer goods, and appliances, there is the very real prospect of growing from $3 billion to $30 billion in ten years.

Sipping a Diet Coke, Godrej explains that the company has already enjoyed annual growth of 17 percent for the past forty years. "We have had much success, and I am proud of what we have accomplished," he says. "But there is much to do—many, many more opportunities to conquer." His plan for ten-by-ten growth is offered with humility and earnest commitment.

Tough-minded, courageous, unflappable, determined—these qualities are typical of the people transforming the face of business in India and China. As we explain in this chapter, such people are running companies that are poised to become household names around the globe.

The Accelerator Mind-Set

It does not take long to realize that many top executives in China and India have developed a distinctive way of working, a distinctive way of defining goals, and a distinctive mentality—ambitious, audacious, aggressive if necessary, and adaptive.

It's fast-forward. We call it the *accelerator mind-set*, and it is characteristic of people who are relentless in their pursuit of success.

Strategy is as they see it: a big-picture vision, colossal dreams, and no limits on opportunity. They do not feel beholden to anything, least of all the textbook business rules and the constraints of commonly held business logic. They start with a clean slate, focus on a specific opportunity, scale up or refocus as needed, learn by doing, and drive relentlessly forward.

In China and India, strategy is not about perfection. The successful entrepreneur has little fear of mistakes, believing that any errors can be fixed with time or made palatable by the rising tide of demand. Of course, not every entrepreneur is successful or a model of best business practices: sometimes, entrepreneurs cut corners, adopt modes of behavior that the West would dismiss as unethical and corrupt, or use political influence to achieve their goals. But whatever they do, they emphasize *execution*—getting things done.

Godrej is just one of many top corporate leaders we met who dream big and bold, who show every confidence that optimism can triumph over obstacles. One told us, "We will grow to $100 billion." Another said: "Up and down, yes; but in the end, up, up, up!" A third said, quite plainly, "Our strategy and our investments are limited only by our dreams."

Dhirubhai Ambani, the founder of Reliance Industries, India's biggest company, was the classic example of a business leader with an accelerator mind-set. His rags-to-riches story is almost a parable of how to persevere and prosper.

"Our dreams have to be bigger, our ambitions higher, our commitment deeper, and our efforts greater," he once said. "Only when you dream it can you do it." But dreams alone would not suffice. "Pursue your goals, even in the face of difficulties," he advised, "and convert your adversities into opportunities."[2]

Today's Chinese and Indian entrepreneurs pulled themselves up by their bootstraps, driven to succeed by their ambition and guided by an extraordinary adaptability that evolved over the course of surviving a tough, uncompromising, Darwinian environment. "People come here expecting a red carpet, but one should know the ground rules," one CEO told us. "If you come to India knowing that life in India is a struggle, that makes all the difference."

These comments are echoed by Ratan Tata, the scion of the Tata dynasty, who was critical of the British managers he encountered when buying Corus, formerly British Steel, in 2007 and Jaguar Land Rover in 2008. "It's a work ethic issue," he said in an interview with the *Times*. "Friday after 3:30 p.m., you can't find anyone in their office."

He went on to note that the same pattern of complacency could be observed across the Atlantic. "In the U.S., a Hispanic will happily work more hours than an American. A Korean in a plant is quite happy to come in and work overtime to get something done. The same is true of the Chinese and the Indians. The American will go home and his leisure hours are more important. He may quit a job because it is too hard. So I think there is a certain comfort level that comes from a country that has had good times."[3]

Note that the accelerator mind-set is not unique to corporate executives. It is evident in people at all levels of society. The poor, hungry, and driven— the "PhDs," whose only qualification is a bountiful supply of energy and enterprise—dream about success, achievement, hope, material wealth, and a better life. It is their version of the American dream, and they are prepared to work hard for it: the ninety-hour study weeks for teenagers; the fifty hours of weekly practice for an eight-year-old aspiring concert pianist; the sixteen-hour days, seven days a week, put in by the engineers who are developing electronics products that will have twice the functionality of their Western competitors and sell at half the price.

Liu Jiren: From Steel Worker to Global IT Captain

It's exactly 7 a.m. in Dalian, China, at the Howard Johnson Hotel, a five-star hotel. Across the breakfast table is a slender, handsome man of fifty-five with a warm, kind smile and a hearty laugh. He speaks flawless English and has more energy than almost anyone we've ever met. He is telling a story from his youth: "I was born in a time of revolution and deprivation."

Liu Jiren—founder, chairman, and CEO of Neusoft Corporation, China's largest IT solution and service company—is a prime example of a business leader with an accelerator mind-set. He has had an extraordinary journey. He started out as a seventeen-year-old steel worker, eventually going to college and completing a PhD before establishing a business with a current market capitalization of $1.6 billion.

Born in 1955 in Dandong, a tier 4 city in Liaoning, a province in China's northeast, Liu grew up dirt-poor. When he finished high school, he had only three employment choices—farmer, soldier, or factory worker. He entered a steel mill in Benxi, and the assignment he received was risky: if the steam pipes erupted, he was to go in with a team of much older men and seal them up. "It was dangerous work," he recalls. His coworkers had burned faces, scars, and wounds from prior encounters with danger. His pay was RMB 41 ($6) a month—three times that of other factory workers because of the danger. The hours were another form of compensation. "My job provided lots of downtime between emergencies," he says. "I had time to draw party posters, learn mechanical watch repair, and learn to print photographs."

It was a tough existence. "We lived eight to a dorm room, we didn't have enough good food, and I was lonely for my family," he says. "But I only served a year." He was one of three hundred thousand workers at the plant, but soon his natural industriousness caught the attention of the senior managers, who gave him experience across the company divisions.

At twenty-one, he was accepted as one of only two applicants from the factory to attend Northeastern University of China in Shenyang, and his life took off to untold riches, unimaginable influence, and more. "Because of my hobbies," he says, "I got to know more people and had many friends. This helped me to win in the university application competition." He studied automation control, a precursor major to software engineering. He threw himself into school, working from 6 a.m. to nearly midnight seven days a week.

He was the top student, secured a place in a master's program, and worked as a teaching assistant in computer science before studying for his PhD. He became a favorite student of Li Huatian, a Harvard-educated Chinese professor at Northeastern University of China who helped Liu get a job at the U.S. National Bureau of Standards. "I was in Washington looking out at the Potomac River," he says. "I sighed to myself, 'Someday I will build a software park in China with advanced equipment and research funds.'"

Liu returned and set up a research lab at Northeastern University of China, whose Web site is neu.edu.cn—hence his company's name. Neusoft went public in 1996 with sales of $7.5 million and profits of less than $2 million. Sales have increased by nearly a hundredfold since then, with profits running at about 10 percent of sales.

"We are not China's IBM or Microsoft," he says. "We have our own business model." In our tour of its facilities, Liu proudly showed off the various subsidiaries and businesses. They provide IT solutions for multiple industries, including telecom, energy, finance, social security, health care, manufacturing, transportation, and education. Neusoft's embedded software is in a large number of digital home products, mobile terminals, automobiles, and IT products that have global presence.

But Liu is most proud of his decision to invest in the setting up of three IT university campuses in China. They are private colleges with roughly $60 million invested. The largest campus of Neusoft University is located in Dalian, and it now has more than fourteen thousand students and offers thirty-four majors, including computer science, software engineering, IT management, digital arts, English, and Japanese.

Students operate according to a mantra of CDIO: conceive, design, implement, operate. When we visited, the students gladly repeated "C-D-I-O" as their methodology. At SOVO (Student Office, Venture Office), each student is required to participate in a venture experience. The students are very informal and friendly—they look like Berkeley students, with their dyed long hair, blue jeans, T-shirts, and messenger bags. They have practical skills, and the university is one of the major talent sources for Neusoft.

At Neusoft University in Dalian, students enjoy a wide variety of arts, technology, and entrepreneurial studies. The students dream up Internet start-ups, gaming companies, multimedia ventures, and other businesses. It is a chance to see new ideas come to life.

The campus has the look and feel of an American college—the Babson College of China. On the day that we visited, the students at SOVO had prepared a mass immersion program in their ideas and businesses. Each student wanted to talk about his or her business concept, how it was created, what problem it solves, and how it will change the world. It is a stark contrast to China's other universities.

"I am creating a gaming company," one student says proudly. "If you are a farmer in a rural district, you have time at night to be online. They will be playing my games. It is about creating wealth for me, but it is also about creating distinctly Chinese games." This young man is wearing Levi's and a black T-shirt. His shoulder-length hair has a dyed streak of red hair down the side.

It is no accident that the company's largest global development center and its university are located in Dalian—a city of six million in the southern tip of China's northeast region. About one hundred years ago, a group of Russian engineers came to Dalian. Today, the Dalian Economic and Technological Development Zone is also home to Intel's billion-dollar chip-manufacturing facility—the largest single foreign enterprise investment in China. When complete, the Intel plant will employ fifteen hundred.

Dalian offers significant tax exemptions to new businesses—no tax for two years, 50 percent reductions for the next three years—and other financial incentives. By clustering software and other IT, the region develops skills and capability—Dalian is one of China's responses to Silicon Valley. Venture funds, secure private-data protection, physical resources, and a strong orientation to export markets support the growth.

Liu's dream of a software park is now complete. There are more than six thousand software engineers working in the Neusoft Dalian Park. "I will be remembered for starting the university," he says. "It is my dream to give back to my country. It is my dream to have a legacy of students with the ability to innovate, create new businesses, and compete on a world scale."

The Global Challengers

If anything demonstrates the impact of the accelerator mind-set, it is the astonishing rise of a set of what we call the global challenger companies: public and private businesses that are based in China, India, and other emerging markets and that are shaking up the established economic order. In 2000, there were eight Chinese companies and one Indian company in the *Fortune* 500. By 2010, those numbers had risen to forty-six and eight, respectively. In the latest edition of BCG's 100 Global Challengers report, there were thirty-three from China and twenty from India: in other words, over half of the global challengers were from these two countries.[4]

We started tracking these companies more than five years ago, when the idea of a new generation of multinational companies emerging from China and India seemed far-fetched. Although Lenovo Group, a Chinese technology company, had just bought IBM's PC business, this was a rare success. Since then, however, a host of companies have ventured abroad, acquiring major Western brands and establishing themselves as serious rivals to the traditional multinational companies from the United States and Europe.

Take Tata, for example. This major conglomerate has six different businesses in the BCG 100 Global Challengers: chemicals, communications, consultancy services, global beverages, motors, and steel. Over the past decade, it has completed cross-border acquisitions worth more than $17.5 billion. Among others, Tata Steel bought Corus, formerly British Steel; Tata Motors bought Jaguar and Land Rover, among the biggest names in the prestige car industry; and Tata Global Beverages bought Tetley Tea, the world's second-biggest manufacturer and distributor of tea. As a result, Tata now earns about three-fifths of its revenue abroad and employs more British workers than any other manufacturer does.[5]

Tata and the other global challengers have benefited from a series of natural advantages as they have grown to compete with the established multinational companies. For a start, the challengers have typically enjoyed privileged access to high-growth local markets and resources, rarely facing threats from muscled global competitors that were confronted by protectionist state legislation. Second, they have not been encumbered by outmoded business practices and technologies, which had become a burden for their rivals operating in slow-growth markets. Third, the challengers have had access to vast pools of cheap labor.

But the vital ingredient, and the one that will endure as global competitors gain access to their domestic markets and as the gap between workers' wages in the East and West gets smaller, is a defining accelerator mind-set. An accelerator mind-set is not unique to Chinese and Indian entrepreneurs, of course. But we continue to be surprised by the sheer abundance of people with this characteristic. Time and again, we encounter people who display an extraordinary inventiveness, an enormous capacity for industry, and an exceptional willpower: they really do not take no for an answer.

A Chinese Challenger: Huawei Technologies

Ren Zhengfei, founder and CEO of Huawei Technologies, has used the accelerator mind-set to achieve extraordinary leadership in telephone equipment and computers. Huawei is a $32 billion company that few have heard of. It is a global leader in mobile broadband, optical transmission, and core telecommunications network equipment. The February 2010 issue of *Fast Company* ranked Huawei the fifth most innovative company in the world, just behind Facebook, Amazon, Apple, and Google.

In less than twenty-five years, the company has grown from a start-up to the world's second-largest telecom equipment company, behind Ericsson. Approximately two-thirds of sales are outside of China. Sales tripled from 2006 to 2010. Profit margins were 12.8 percent and return on equity was 42.9 percent, according to the company's 2010 annual report. Huawei is a research and service company, outsourcing the production of most of its hardware. According to our translation, the two Chinese symbols that form the name Huawei mean "splendid achievement."

Ren founded the company in 1987, with a capital investment of less than $5,000, as a sales agency for a Hong Kong producer of PBX (private branch exchange) switches used in telecommunication stations.

Technology at Huawei is highly advanced. When we visited in 2011, an on-campus conversation required a technology interpreter, not a Chinese interpreter. The company participates in all forms of radio access networks, software development for mobile office and home applications, power supply, fiber and copper infrastructure, systems integration, mobile devices, handsets, terminals, and telepresence. Everything is an abbreviation for a technology or standard.

Industry insiders attribute Huawei's success to its "wolf spirit." The company says it is driven and inspired to work as a team, to pursue multiple growth opportunities simultaneously, and to fearlessly focus on low-cost innovation. The coup de grâce maneuver is to pursue market share in developed markets with a sustained and vigorous attack.

Today, Ren holds just under 2 percent of the company and his net worth is estimated at about $1 billion. He is ranked among China's top two hundred wealthiest people.

Headquartered in Shenzhen, the industrial center on mainland China just over the border from Hong Kong, Huawei boasts an impressive set of buildings on a thousand-acre park with some five million square feet of space for offices, R&D facilities, and manufacturing. Workers, among the best-paid in China, arrive for their staggered work shifts by public transportation, snaking along broad boulevards that have a feel of Paris or Washington, D.C.

His senior managers say Ren's tough-minded approach in business was forged by his tumultuous youth and his early career as a military engineer. One of seven children, he was born in the remote mountainous province of Guizhou in 1944, during the Second World War. Both his parents were educators. He attended Chongqing University, a leading engineering institution. From there, he joined the People's Liberation Army's engineering corps, ultimately rising to deputy director, which was a professional role equivalent to a deputy regimental chief but without military rank. He retired from the army in 1983 when the Chinese government disbanded the engineering corps.

Ren developed a fascination for all things new: during his ten-year military career, he registered two telecom-related patents. He also developed a focus on strategy, studying the guerilla tactics devised by Mao to build support for his revolutionary movement and applying those tactics to Huawei's strategy and daily operations. For example, a guerrilla war focuses on winning the countryside and then attacking the cities. Huawei started in rural markets and expanded to cities later; the company also globalized from developing countries to developed countries. Another critical element is performance assessment and self-criticism. Huawei holds organized monthly meetings to improve operations and add to core competence. In addition, there is a heavy emphasis on combining theory and practice. Senior managers at Huawei are regularly rotated upward and downward. Finally, the company emphasizes the dialectic, encouraging active debate of major shifts in the world markets, changes in technology, and threats from new competitors. There is a sense within Huawei that you can never be too optimistic and that crisis planning is critical.

As Huawei has grown, it has expanded into international markets, serving British Telecom (BT), Vodafone, France Telecom-Orange, T-Mobile, and Bell Canada, as well as companies in many emerging markets, including Brazil,

Nigeria, Russia, Turkey, Vietnam, and the Philippines. At the same time, it has gradually imported Western management systems into its process development, corporate governance, finance, information technology, human resources, and quality control functions.

On average, Huawei's employees are university-educated, in their late twenties, and paid a starting salary of around RMB 130,000 ($20,000). They are also entitled to medical insurance, a housing allowance, and a stake in the company, which is wholly employee owned. But they work hard for their privileges. According to one estimate, Huawei's R&D staff work, on average, 2,750 hours per year, compared with around 1,300 to 1,400 hours in Europe: in other words, twice as many hours. Of course, many Chinese work longer hours than their Western counterparts, but in the case of Huawei, the high level of employee ownership promotes a strong work ethic. Huawei has created large numbers of middle-class jobs in China, and it is driving up productivity.

If this hunger to succeed has helped Huawei, so too has its focus on innovation. When the company was founded, China's economy was dominated by bloated and inefficient state-owned enterprises and sweatshop factories churning out cheap, and cheaply made, me-too commodity goods.

Against this backdrop, Ren's decision to build a high-quality and high-performance company is extraordinary. "Every year, I am willing to invest several billion U.S. dollars in innovation," he says, "even if the results of R&D will not come up for several years." Typically, Huawei reinvests 10 percent of its revenues in R&D. Some forty-three thousand of the company's one-hundred-thirty thousand employees are engaged in R&D in seventeen specialist centers around the world. Originally just based in China, Huawei established R&D facilities first in India in 1999 and then, a year later, in Sweden, on the doorstep of Ericsson, its most powerful rival. By 2001, it had also set up four R&D centers in the United States.

With such a strong focus on research, Huawei had become the world's largest patent applicant by 2009, filing 6,770 new patents and taking its total to a remarkable 42,543. But all the innovation in the world would be useless without an overarching strategy for winning market share—and here, Huawei really excels. Stressing value, service, and fast response, Huawei targets its rivals' weak spots, strikes with unrestrained ferocity, and does not let go.

It first won new business by building its presence in rural China, which had been largely ignored by the bigger, state-owned businesses and the multinational companies. Here, it could compete on price. It then marched into the urban centers, where it competed on price *and* quality of product and service. Huawei's tactic is to swarm a market, much as a wolf pack overruns and overpowers its prey with overwhelming force. With more than one hundred branch offices, technical experts can offer personal service—24/7. "I remember when our server went down at midnight, I called Huawei's service center," recalls an official from China Mobile, the world's largest mobile phone operator. "After just one hour, a technical expert arrived onsite and helped us solve our problem. They were so responsive!"

It took eight years to move from the rural districts to the urban centers and establish a national profile, amid strong competition from many foreign players in the local Chinese market at the time. Then, in the mid-1990s, Huawei started going global. First, the company moved into other emerging markets, where it undercut its rivals' prices by as much as 40 percent. Then, it ventured into developed markets, where its technical prowess and persistence have triumphed. In 1997, it established a joint venture in Russia, building on Boris Yeltsin's state visit to China the year before. By 2005, Huawei had broken into the established markets of Western Europe, with Vodafone and British Telecom making it their largest supplier.

In our visit to Huawei, company leaders beamed about the future based on their growth vision of digital technology, video interaction, mobile devices replacing PCs, the broadband revolution, and the emergence of cloud computing. Huawei has a strong presence in each of these markets. They are making a major investment in mobile handsets and believe they will be one of the remaining smartphone suppliers as that industry undergoes technology shift, changing consumer needs, and the growth of the cell phone as fashion accessory and status symbol.

The next frontier for Huawei is the United States, where it has struggled in part because of Ren's past as an engineer in China's army and allegations of a national security threat. In an open letter published March 1, 2011, the company quotes President Barack Obama's inaugural speech about "hope over fear, unity of purpose over conflict and discord."[6] It adds that it is seeking cooperation with American firms and a growing footprint in the United States. "Ren is just one of the many CEOs around the world who have served in the military," according to the widely published letter. Huawei counts more than one thousand U.S. employees and says it is spending $62 million in R&D in the United States. The company says it paid Western companies $222 million in licensing fees in 2010, of which $175 million went to U.S. firms.

Ren, and the firm as a whole, is going on a charm offensive. It is positioning itself as one of China's most socially responsible companies, saying that it is eager to change, eager to grow, eager to learn. It will take all of Ren's determination—one of the hallmarks of the accelerator mind-set—to succeed. But the company is willing to make sustained investments in foreign markets. It uses a low-cost, high-work-ethic labor force to deliver high customization, strong customer service, and superior value to its customers.

An Indian Challenger: Mahindra & Mahindra

Anand Mahindra is a very different kind of entrepreneur from Ren Zhengfei. A dapper and cosmopolitan global leader, he is the original Harvard Boy—graduating magna cum laude in 1977 after winning a full scholarship. As an undergraduate, he studied filmmaking. He earned an MBA from Harvard Business School in 1981. He runs the publicly listed company started by his family, Mahindra & Mahindra (M&M).

During his time as head of the company, its market value has increased from $1 billion to more than $14 billion. Today, it is a strong player in the automotive business (both cars and parts), farm equipment (the largest unit count of tractors worldwide), IT, financial services, hospitality, and other industries.

The company was founded in 1945 by Mahindra's grandfather as an assembler and distributor of Jeeps. Anand Mahindra joined its steel division in 1981. A decade later, he moved to the parent company. He then rose rapidly, introducing modern management, recruiting professional managers, encouraging innovation, and offering private-equity capital to his team for investment in new ventures. He became managing director in 1997. A demanding, emotionally engaging leader and a global deal-maker, Mahindra acquired a Korean automotive company, an electric car manufacturer, multiple European auto components manufacturers, IT companies, and aerospace interests.

He says his group is a federation of companies, not a conglomerate. "We are very happy with our constellation of businesses," he says. "We have a rhythm—our strategic planning process, our annual conferences, our capital allocation system, how we inculcate values, and our governance practices. We have a private-equity model for growth now. We bring in outside investors, and it gives us focus on value creation. For us, it's about shareholders and their money. At end of day, I make it my job to deliver returns. We don't choose or favor one business over the other. They each have to earn their way."

Mahindra focuses his management on strategic principles—segment leadership, globalization, innovation, and a ruthless focus on financial returns. He has recently embarked on a company rebranding called Rise.

"Rise has three building blocks," he says. "First, accept no limits; second, alternative thinking; third, driving positive change. We are not simply focused on quantitative objectives such as market share. It is about giving back, improving life. In the agriculture group, for instance, it is about creating a second green revolution. We will rise by enabling other people to rise."

And M&M has certainly risen. "If you had looked at us ten years ago, and if I had said that we would grow from $1 billion to $14 billion, no one would have believed it," he says. "Yet that is what we have accomplished. In ten years' time, we want to be one of the fifty most admired brands in the world on the basis of metrics that are both quantitative and qualitative."

Mahindra says that India has become more challenging for businesses lately. He calls it "political factionalism and policy paralysis." And yet he is optimistic about the Indian economy in the long term "as long as the neighborhood—China, Pakistan, Korea—remains safe enough to not worry about survival. We will have hiccups, small pauses, but there is inevitability about the consumer economy," he says.

Because of his experience and knowledge of the Indian economy, he sees many opportunities for investment in his native land: "If I had an incremental billion dollars, I would, of course, continue to invest in India. We also would intend to continue to invest in China. But why should I look away from India? I know India well. We have scale and size. In fact, I believe that when you invest in an Indian company that is going global, you are, in fact, investing in the world." In China, M&M has become the second-largest tractor company. Mahindra's target is to become number one in China. "Life is too short to be number two," he says.

The company's successes include the first Indian SUV—the Scorpio. From a standing start, M&M created a rival to Toyota and Land Rover. It is a textbook lesson in fast-forward business development, consumer-centric product design, and frugal innovation. Much of the credit for the Scorpio goes to Pawan Goenka, an IIT Kanpur and Cornell graduate. Mahindra recruited Goenka to the company in 1993 from General Motors. Goenka told us that the Scorpio was created with a design team one-third the size of a GM or Ford team and with engineers hired at one-tenth the cost of U.S. engineers. The company used deep consumer market research to drive the project according to nuanced consumer need. M&M worked with suppliers from other emerging markets, notably Korea, to keep costs low. And it built its factory for about $120 million, around 40 percent of the estimated costs for other global manufacturers.

In India, M&M's tractors command 42 percent of the market, ahead of TAFE, a Chennai-based company, and Escorts Group, based in the northern Indian city of Faridabad. Now, entering the U.S. market, M&M is looking for ways to serve the needs of U.S. farmers and to compete with local tractor businesses such as Deere & Company. As Goenka, now president of M&M's automotive and farm equipment business, told us, "We make more tractors than John Deere. We truly want to be multinational."

Mahindra is aiming for high visibility—and the company's billboards, which flank the Interstate 80 highway traversing Indiana, do so with a humor designed to appeal to Americans. It turns out that many of M&M's customers are women—hobby farmers who leave hectic city living and take up the good life by buying plots of land that can be plowed with small tractors. One billboard on the U.S. interstate shows a blonde woman driving a tractor and carries the caption: "Deere John, I have found someone new." In some states in the southern United States, M&M's share of the tractor market has reached 20 percent.[7]

Adi Godrej, Ratan Tata, Liu Jiren, Ren Zhengfei, and Anand Mahindra are examples of entrepreneurs with an accelerator mind-set. They give the impression that there is no time to lose. Doing business in China and India requires not only the best products and processes but also the best people—and global ambition. As these business leaders and their companies go global, they will take this mind-set with them. We think that it could be their most enduring export.

FIFTEEN

The BCG Playbook

Practical Strategies for Winning Over New Consumers in China and India

How to move from your current position to take advantage of the growth in China and India, and what expectations you should have about priorities, timing of returns, and staying power

I N *THE $10 TRILLION PRIZE*, we have tried to highlight the ambitions and anxieties, the aspirations and appetites of the billion-plus newly afflu-ent Chinese and Indian consumers. We have tried to show how they live today and how they hope to live in the future. We have sketched their back-grounds, their living environments, their spending habits, their dietary pref-erences, their health concerns, and the goals that they have for their children.

The Chinese and Indian consumers are the most optimistic in the world. The Chinese, in particular, are bullish about the future. They like to trade up, shop online, and buy the best brands in the world. They are a marketer's dream: millions of consumers ready to buy, without major debts, supported by parents and grandparents with a memory of want.

Indians, too, are confident about the future. The emerging middle class is a bonanza for the world's branded companies. These consumers empha-size family, home, health, and education. They are looking for durability and quality, brand names and authenticity. But they are not easy to con-vince. They are discerning and demanding, with the refined bargain-hunting skills acquired during the years of haggling in dusty street bazaars. India is the homeland of *paisa vasool*—the Hindi expression for the perfect mix of features and affordability.

It is a magnificent opportunity.

We have tried to establish the size of this consumer opportunity: $10 trillion of annual consumer spending in 2020.

As we write this book, there are signs that China may hit a speed bump in 2012 and 2013. The government's massive stimulus package in the wake of the global economic crisis in 2008 has boosted consumer sentiment and confidence. Now, real estate prices, interest rate movements, decelerating global demand, and wage inflation are conspiring to slow growth in China— at least in the short term.

Yet, for all this, we remain confident about China's and India's long-term prospects. This is why it is imperative to understand how Chinese and Indian consumers think, shop, buy, and dream. Without this, the $10 trillion prize will be a distant prospect.

We have tried to explain how very different Chinese and Indian consumers are from consumers in the United States and Europe. Unlike consumers in the West, they do not have any long-standing or legacy brand loyalty. They want the very best value in everything they buy. They want respect, innovation, things that will save them time, and more for less. For all their success, these newly affluent consumers are not fully secure in their call on a better life. So they are willing to work very long hours for higher incomes.

Together, these consumers are creating a vast new opportunity—but one that has significant consequences for the rest of the world. There is a boomerang effect, and we have tried to quantify the amount of commodities, water, and energy that this change in lifestyle will demand. We describe how it will pressure supply for some commodities, causing inflation, volatility, scarcity, and market panic.

For companies, the prize may be great, but the challenges are daunting. It is not surprising that few companies have been successful in both China *and* India.

Companies that have tried and failed have misunderstood the very different business environments in the two countries. Success will not come from tweaking goods and services designed for Western consumers. Success will not come from adapting go-to-market strategies developed for the United States and Europe. Success will not come from duplicating the business models designed to work in New York, London, and Frankfurt.

So what are the secrets to success? It requires an enormous amount of executive time. You cannot delegate the understanding of these consumers' needs. It requires building alliances with local business partners and government institutions—provincial, central, tax, judicial. It also requires enormous amounts of energy. It is physically and emotionally challenging work. "Blood, sweat, and tears" is not an exaggeration. But the changes in rank, influence, and power of the next decade are unfolding now, and you cannot afford to miss out on this opportunity.

As we were finishing this book, *Women's Wear Daily*, a New York–based fashion newspaper, published an article about the celebration of Chinese New Year at the Empire State Building in New York.[1] According to the article, one night in January 2012, the top of this giant office tower's lights changed color to bright red and gold: the colors of the Chinese flag. Some three hundred of the most affluent Chinese were privately celebrating Chinese New Year on the eightieth floor. It was an affair organized by Affinity China, a start-up that offers invitation-only events to rich and curious Chinese. Later in the week, many of these Chinese had private shows at Montblanc, Piaget, Bergdorf Goodman, Ralph Lauren, Coach, and Estée Lauder.

The event provided a glimpse of the newly affluent Chinese consumer. To earn your share of the prize, we recommend that you embark on five tasks:

1. Meet consumers "up close and personal." Understand how they make decisions about goods and how their hopes for the future translate into astounding market growth. Get into your innovation bones the truth about local and regional Chinese and Indian consumer needs.

2. Understand the shape, size, and timing of the opportunity. Segment the market according to income and geography (especially the urban and rural divide). Get deep and original in your thinking.

3. Build the *paisa vasool* approach into your global tool kit. Engineer every product and service with this approach. Make it the standard for benefits and pricing in Chinese, Indian, *and* Western markets.

4. Understand the differences and similarities between China and India: one child versus five children; autocracy versus democracy; speed and authority versus choice; massive investment with few market

safeguards versus returns guarded by capital markets; state capitalists versus private entrepreneurs.

5. Ask—and answer—the ten questions in the sidebar "The BCG Playbook" to unlock spectacular growth and organizational resolve in China and India.

China and India provide a once-in-a-lifetime growth opportunity. Over the next decade, these two countries hold the prospect of the largest unfolding of consumer purchasing ever. But the prize will not be handed to you on a plate. These are battlegrounds—and the spoils of victory will go to those who figure out how to captivate the newly affluent consumers in brutally competitive markets. There will be volatility, risks, and obstacles, and there will be many powerful, local new competitors arising to fight for markets. But the force of demand is happening before our eyes, and it is the opportunity of a career.

We believe this presents an opportunity for the bold, the wise, and the strong-willed. It is a chance to create new engines of growth and to bring the lessons and the competitive mind-set home.

Are you ready? Do you have what it takes? To find out, answer the questions that follow.

THE BCG PLAYBOOK: TEN QUESTIONS FOR CAPTIVATING THE NEWLY AFFLUENT CONSUMER IN CHINA AND INDIA

This book is intended to serve not only as a manifesto, setting out the once-in-a-lifetime opportunity in China and India, but also as a manual, providing a practical how-to guide to winning in these two countries and the rest of the world. We would like to leave you with a set of ten questions that should be in your head as you take on the challenge of winning a share of the biggest prize in history.

The $10 Trillion Prize calculates what we believe is almost certain growth in the world's most populous nations over the next ten years. But to seize the opportunity, you must act now. There is no time to lose. As you prepare, ask yourself these questions:

1. Do you have your best and brightest deployed in China and India?
2. Have you set a bold enough aspiration for yourself—and are you spending in proportion to future market size?

3. Have you created a profitable business model that delivers sustainable growth now?

4. Are you innovative enough to reach many different markets with strong and distinct value propositions?

5. Are you developing an operating model that can deliver at the right cost?

6. Do you, your top decision-makers, and your board members spend enough personal on-the-ground time to be able to sort fact from fiction, belief from reality?

7. Can you paint a detailed picture of the hopes and dreams of the newly affluent consumers and their evolving needs—and communicate this to your employees?

8. Is your set of investments (size, scale, timing) sufficient so that in 2020, you will have no regrets, no hesitations, no "should have, would have" conversations around the boardroom?

9. Are you taking the lessons home—and to other markets around the world?

10. Are you certain that you will earn your fair share of the $10 trillion prize?

---

1. Do you have your best and brightest deployed in China and India?

We recommend: Raise the percentage of your top two hundred executives in China and India so that it approaches the percentage of the growth that you expect to come from India and China—*and* put 10 percent of your potential leaders in these markets through executive development programs. Give tomorrow's leaders a deep primary experience in the markets—an experience that will dominate in the peak of their careers.

2. Have you set a bold enough aspiration for yourself—and are you spending in proportion to future market size?

We recommend: Understand your product category's consumption curve in these two markets (don't rely on historical curves from advanced economies), and time your investments accordingly. Allocate spending according to your company's anticipated share of the market. Set a target of growing at least twice as fast as the market.

3. Have you created a profitable business model that delivers sustainable growth now?

We recommend: Adopt a scorecard that measures what you are "building" in China and India. This should track financial performance, brand equity, distribution channels, and the recruitment and retention of talent. You need a formula that delivers attractive gross margins within a three-year time frame and that builds out a sustainable profitable business plan.

4. Are you innovative enough to reach many different markets with strong and distinct value propositions?

We recommend: Segment the markets—regions, cities, rural districts— so that you can develop innovative products appropriately designed for specific consumers.

5. Are you developing an operating model that can deliver at the right cost?

We recommend: Keep the *paisa vasool* attitude of these consumers at the forefront of your mind while you are developing business models to serve them. Analyze your competitors, and catch their innovations while they are in the testing phase. In these fast-moving markets, it is often necessary to imitate to ultimately dominate.

6. Do you, your top decision-makers, and your board members spend enough personal on-the-ground time to be able to sort fact from fiction, belief from reality?

We recommend: Pursue a fly-the-skies strategy—spending time with consumers in their local markets and, better still, relocating for an extended period. To be successful, companies need experience, informed hypotheses, and a quantitative method for separating truth from misunderstanding—and so the rule is to talk, listen, and engage, and to do so face-to-face. You need to engage with the state—the central government, local government, and regulators. Partnerships with the state can translate into competitive advantage, fast regulatory approvals, and lucrative deals.

7. Can you paint a detailed picture of the hopes and dreams of the newly affluent consumers and their evolving needs—and communicate this to your employees?

We recommend: Develop a proprietary set of data so that you properly understand the pattern of consumer behavior across these markets. Learn to speak with authority about the segments in the market— their hopes and dreams. Have a vision of how these consumers live, what they want, where they hope to go. Provide them with avenues to achieve that dream.

8. Is your set of investments (size, scale, timing) sufficient so that in 2020, you will have no regrets, no hesitations, no "should have, would have" conversations around the boardroom?

We recommend: Do the math to calculate what your company will require to gain a leadership position—in particular, how much it will cost in management time and resources. It's not just about not investing enough; it's about being smart in managing and overcoming the risks.

9. Are you taking the lessons home—and to other markets around the world?

We recommend: Rethink the way you do business everywhere—and reapply the lessons learned in China and India across your entire organization. Your next two global conferences should be field visits in China and India with exposure to tier 2 and 3 markets.

10. Are you certain that you will earn your fair share of the $10 trillion prize?

We recommend: Estimate how big your market will be over the next ten years, how much share will be required for leadership, how strong your competitors are, and how many risks and hazards you must deal with to succeed. Then build a plan, resource it adequately, and frequently monitor and engage its progress. Give the on-the-ground team a blank check with a framework. Use metrics to gauge success: calculate market share, and go for leadership; measure the most inventive products; measure competitive points of distribution; benchmark low-cost operations; count up cumulative relative experience; and add capacity in the submarkets.

A Letter to the Next Generation

Renewal and the American Dream

JENNIFER WU IS A REMARKABLE music teacher. She is a graduate of China's Central Conservatory of Music in Beijing (China's equivalent to the Juilliard in New York) and a master pianist. If you make your way to her studio, you will meet many children, all of whom yearn to play at a concert hall like their idol, Lang Lang.

Lang Lang, of course, is the twenty-nine-year-old China-born master pianist. He began playing at the age of three and won the Shenyang piano competition. By the age of thirteen, he had played the complete twenty-four Chopin études in the Beijing Concert Hall. At seventeen, he became a star when he played Tchaikovsky with the Chicago Symphony. In China, he is a musical celebrity and worshiped by children in Wu's studio.[1]

"I help children like music," Wu says in her crowded facility. It is located in a Beijing suburb. The building is frigid in January and hot and humid in July. But the children come. She sees one hundred students, seven days a week, and her studio is generally open from 6 a.m. to 11 p.m. every day. The students start at the age of three.

"Some of the children come for five hours a day," she says. "They want to drill, drill, drill. They want to be like Lang Lang."

A pianist in China can make a handsome living. Lessons range in price from $15 to $100 per hour. It takes ten thousand hours of practice to become a master. Wu says only 2 percent of her students have the potential to make it as a concert pianist. But this does not stop them from trying to be the best.

"The parents have the money," she says. "They want their children to experience the competition. They want the son or daughter to know music, to develop their left and right brain, to be cultured and creative. The mothers can be tough on their children. Sometimes I have to tell them not to be ugly with their children. We want them to play out of joy, not out of obligation or to satisfy their parents' ambition." Wu works closely with each student.

As we are sitting in her studio, we ask her to play a small piece. She is a modest woman and declines, but she asks one of her eight-year-old students, a girl named Flora, to put on a demonstration. Flora bows mightily and then sits on the piano bench. With drama and flair, she nods her head and begins to play. The music, a Bach concerto, is mesmerizing. She plays for about five minutes without looking at a sheet of music, in perfect rhythm and with perfect grace. Wu smiles broadly as her pupil finishes. She is justly proud of the unrehearsed performance. Flora, who weighs in at about sixty pounds and stands about four feet four, bows deeply with her hands behind her back and smiles.

"Flora could be one of the 2 percent," Wu says. As she ushers us out of the studio, she adds, "In Atlanta, nobody cares about music—they play football. In China, piano and music are taken very seriously. Winning a competition can mean acceptance to university, and the road to wealth."

The Flora model is a call to action for the next generation in the West. You need to compete to win. And to compete, you need to become a domain expert—you need to apply yourself to your chosen task with energy and commitment.

We ask that you tell your children and grandchildren a story. Once upon a time, there were demands and dreams for life beyond subsistence. There was a critical mass of poor who became economically able, foreign domestic investment to prime the pump, high-pressure academic screening to sort the best and brightest, role models for the journey from rags to riches, technology to copy and industrialize, a labor cost advantage, and a global supply chain for low-cost raw materials. For three decades, the two most populous countries on the planet engaged in a sustained period of economic growth.

The result is the creation of the $10 trillion prize: a chance to win in China, win in India, and bring the lessons home.

If they are older and still interested, read the following with them: there is an emerging global contest for water, energy, building and agricultural commodities, and technology. So far, the West has been winning. Americans and most Europeans enjoy standards of living four times that of the average Chinese and twelve times that of the average Indian. For the average citizen, life in China and India is brutally challenging—there is no free health care or access to social security networks; only minimal amounts of education are available to all; and infrastructure is comparatively primitive. First-generation migrants from the farm live hard lives in crowded cities—poor housing, end-of-supply-curve employment, and occasional, harsh, periodic intervention by the government in their shantytowns. Family and friends provide a kind of safety network, but it is uneven and accidental.

In the next ten years, the world will be reordered. China's and India's overall economies will grow dramatically in real terms; much of the West, which is stuck today in a deep malaise, will be lucky to retrack to a low-single-digit real growth rate.

But in this scenario, the potential for individual progression remains high in every corner of the world. The growth in China and India is a magnet for entrepreneurs, wannabes, and innovators. Inventors will devise new business models that will break the compromises of today's offerings. People will create brilliant new products using innovative materials technology, cutting-edge science, and applications of existing raw materials to new purposes. Entrepreneurs will provide solutions optimal to individual consumers by customizing for the local market. These business leaders will distinguish themselves with the respect and honor that they offer their new customers.

There will be a need for new solutions to the problems of the new world. The relentless demand for growth—which is causing what we have called a boomerang effect—will require sustainable, nonpolluting solutions. Billions of dollars will be made providing higher-quality, safer, sustainable food; completely recyclable packaging; and end-to-end distribution systems that require 80 percent less energy and have total system loss ratios of 50 percent of the current model. Billions of dollars will be made providing appropriately priced health care, occupational training, and elite education for the masses. Billions of dollars will be made in the water market—providing solutions that save water and deliver safe water to the people of these two water-stricken markets. Billions of dollars will be made solving some of the day-to-day problems of living in the modern world: the time it takes to build a house or office building, the transport of commuters living sixty miles from the office, or the provision of day care so that women can go to work without prejudice, emotional trauma, or fear.

Because of the sheer size of the opportunity, this gold rush of value creation will be available to the many and not the few. No one need be a Terry Malloy from *On the Waterfront*. No brother need betray his sibling. But this is not to say that the prize is an easy one to win. The new world will not be inherited by the lazy, the uneducated, the fearful, or the weak.

To the next generation, we have this to say: you live in a world being radically reshaped by global forces that you cannot see and that your parents have had only limited exposure to—but they are epic in scale. These forces will shape your career prospects and fortunes. For the first time, your competitors for a job or your most important customers may be in other parts of the world, speaking different languages. The best of them carry an ambition, drive, and work ethic like nothing you have seen in your own experience.

You also live in a world of friction among groups, nations, and civilizations, and in a political climate where there is a great incentive to demonize. Inevitably, some leaders whom you are familiar with and respect will demonize the civilizations that you read about in this book. But don't be drawn into demonization. This comes from ignorance, and it is an irony of this highly connected, information-always-available world that people have the opportunity now to be ignorant about so many things.

Don't envy, either. The ambitious kids of China and India live in cutthroat and uncertain environments, lacking many things (even clean air and fresh water) that people in the West take for granted. In each of these markets, there are tens of thousands of people, literally, who would happily change places with you.

And don't begrudge the success of others. The rise of China and India are driving growth and creating opportunity for all. Just as mechanization freed your own ancestors from a life tied to the farm, the rise of these markets is creating new possibilities while forcing painful change.

You live in a world where extrapolating from your immediate surroundings, and from your parents' career journeys, is not a sure way to navigate. Today, the world is much more diverse, and the demographics and economic forces of your parents' generation are all moving in very different directions. The future is being driven by very different patterns.

To succeed in the future, you will need to build lasting skills. You will need to find your own specific balance of skills based upon your own interests and capabilities. But there is a combination of skills that will be especially key for everyone, which we describe with the long acronym LASTING: leadership, attitude, science/technology, interpersonal, numeric, and global (including language) skills. Picking up skills in each of these areas, and in combination, will position you for the tumultuous but exciting times ahead.

You can apply the principles of LASTING skills to your education, your ambition, your use of time. You have the benefit of knowing that there will be tremendous growth and intensified competition.

The $10 Trillion Prize is full of advice for companies and executives. But here's a piece of advice for you: go live in China or India, learn Mandarin or Hindi, spend a semester or year in Beijing or Kolkata. Also, consider how important choosing the right major in college will be. We live in a world where invention makes the difference; where consumer understanding breaks competitors; where science, math, engineering, and business drive investment and wealth accumulation.

The fastest-growing sectors in the U.S. job market require higher education. The biggest call will be for biomedical engineers, network analysts, financial examiners, medical scientists, physicians' assistants, biochemists, and computer software engineers. More than one million workers will be needed in these high-paying categories, according to the U.S. Bureau of Labor Statistics Occupational Employment Statistics survey.[2] An aging population will also drive the health-care sector. Top wages will be earned in management, law, architecture, engineering, business operations, and life sciences.

This new world will be inherited by the energetic, the inventive, and the curious. We still live in a world of haves and have-nots. But hundreds of millions of young people in China and India are intent on moving from have-not to have. Born into relative poverty, Mr. Number 19 worked ninety hours a week for years preparing for his entrance test to the Indian Institutes of Technology. Harvard Girl lost some of her childhood playtime to serious study, memorization, and skill development. The farmer WX Liu decided that her family needed to live in a safer home with more modern amenities, and she put her mind to building the dream brick by brick.

Everyone must reframe his or her future around a set of personal choices. Education, ambition, hard work, entrepreneurial energy, collaboration, and true innovation are the values that will come to dominate the world.

Those who do not rise to the challenge risk suffering a relative decline in their standard of living—those who take too much for granted, who dissipate wealth and power, who fail to invest in technology, who idle away their time on Twitter and Facebook.

But there is no threat, per se, from Mr. Number 19 and his ninety-hour work regime. He is a role model for those who seek to perform to their full potential. He and millions like him are living the Eastern version of the great American dream—which has long held out the hope of prosperity and success for those willing and able to strive for them.

The world is at a turning point in history, where relative wealth will shift but absolute wealth should increase. It is not a zero-sum proposition. But to take your share, you need to act now. The choice is yours. Do you want to be a contender? It's time to remake the great American dream for the modern era. It's time to write your own next chapter. Make your story one of diligence, imagination, and a refusal to fall into the malaise of affluence.

Worlds of Difference
The Regions of China and India

C HINA AND INDIA ARE CONTINENT-SIZED COUNTRIES. They are rich, vast, heterogeneous countries. To be fully successful, you will need to get your hands dirty and your shoe leather worn out with travel, visits, and understanding local customs and tastes. In this appendix, we offer a snapshot of the regional differences—covering the variety of religions, languages, and dietary preferences as well as the contrasting wealth and poverty of neighboring provinces.

A Cornucopia of Chinese Consumers

"China is not one country," one corporate leader told us. "It is a collection as vast and different as Europe."

On the face of it, China is a single nation, dominated by a single race—the Han people—who speak one official language, Mandarin, and operate in one time zone. By contrast, the European Union has twenty-seven member countries, with a multitude of peoples, who speak twenty-three official languages and who operate across three time zones.

In fact, China has many more languages. Although it has one official language, it has eighty spoken languages, compared with the sixty such languages in Europe. About 70 percent of Chinese actually speak Mandarin, the language of Beijing and the north.[1] In the south, particularly in Guangdong province, the dominant tongue is Cantonese, otherwise known as Yue, which is the popular Sinitic language in Hong Kong. Shanghaians tend to speak Wu, which is sufficiently different to make the language next to impossible for Yue speakers to understand without translation.

In all, there are seven Sinitic dialects, and many more subdialects. In addition, there are many more languages spoken by people from the fifty-six officially recognized ethnic minority groups, such as the Mongolians, the Uighurs, and the Manchus. Only a few people still speak Manchu, the mother tongue of the country's last emperors, and it is on the brink of extinction, but it points to the extraordinary breadth of China's linguistic heritage.

It is precisely because of this geographical and cultural diversity that we divide China into seven regions.

The east region is the richest. It has seven provinces: Anhui, Fujian, Jiangsu, Jiangxi, Shandong, Zhejiang, and Shanghai. Together, they generate GDP of $2.5 trillion—more than double the next-richest region.[2] The number of middle-class and upper-class consumers is high: 60 million, or 29 percent of the population. This is expected to more than double to 144 million by 2020, meaning that 56 percent of the population will be from the middle or affluent classes. It is not altogether homogeneous: in Jiangsu and Shandong, the people tend to speak the northern dialect of Mandarin, while in Zhejiang, the main language is Wu, and the people of Fujian speak Min.

The next-wealthiest region is the north, including Inner Mongolia, Hebei, Tianjin, and Beijing. It generates GDP of $997 billion. Some 20 million people are middle class or affluent. We calculate that this number will triple over the next ten years—rising to 62 million, or 54 percent, by 2020.

The south, with Guangdong, Guangxi, and Hainan, is the third-wealthiest region, generating GDP of $891 billion. Guangdong, which benefits from its proximity to Hong Kong, has an economy that is broadly equivalent to Indonesia's. Its middle- and upper-class population numbers 24 million, or 26 percent. By 2020, this is expected to rise to 56 million, or 50 percent.

Close behind the south, in terms of wealth, is the central region, with Henan, Hubei, and Hunan. Its GDP is $854 billion, and while its middle- and upper-class population numbers only 13 million, or 14 percent, these new consumers are expected to grow fourfold to 53 million, or 44 percent, by 2020.

The southwest, which includes Chongqing, has an economy the size of Qatar's, generating $580 billion. This is about the same as the northeast region, where Liaoning has an economy the size of another Arab state: the United Arab Emirates.

The poorest region is the northwest, where there are five provinces: Gangsu, Ningxia, Qinghai, Shaanxi, and Xinjiang. It boasts Xi'an, the fabled start of the old Silk Road that connected China and Europe, but now the region generates only $352 billion in GDP. Yet it is expecting to see the biggest growth in middle- and upper-class consumers: from 4 million, or 11 percent, in 2010, to 19 million, or 37 percent, in 2020.

One way we gauge the differences is by looking at the consumers of specific cities—and the cluster of villages around them—within these regions. The people of Xi'an, for example, are traditional, hardworking, and risk-averse, and they prefer "classic" products rather than the latest newfangled model. Our research shows that 41 percent of consumers are intent on trading up, and 73 percent on spending more money.

By contrast, the people of Nanjing, 650 miles away in Jiangsu province in the east region, are altogether more optimistic. This proud city, which was once known as Nanking and has served as China's capital at different times throughout history, is fiercely patriotic. Yet its people welcome new ideas and new products. Our research shows that 45 percent are ready to trade up, and 79 percent plan to increase their spending on consumer goods. We found that what drove their optimism was a strong sense of financial security.

Another optimistic cluster is around Chengdu, in the southwest region. The capital of Sichuan province, which is one of the last redoubts of wild giant pandas, it is dubbed "the land of abundance" because of its position on a fertile plain with rich natural resources. Its people are laid-back and family oriented, and they know how to enjoy life. They are impulsive buyers and are not especially loyal to any one particular brand. Our research found that some 43 percent expressed their intention to trade up, with 80 percent saying they were going to increase their spending on goods and services. But a different factor drove their optimism: the sense of being relatively insulated from the global downturn. Located far from the eastern seaboard, which has seen much of the stellar growth over the past few years, Chengdu has been able to develop its industry in a more measured way than some of the coastal cities. Also, as a center for food production, it has prospered from China's growing appetite for a wide variety of meat, dairy products, and vegetables.

This leads to another important regional difference—diet. There are many different food tastes and styles, with major implications for companies developing food and drink for the Chinese market. Around Shanghai, where the mighty Yangtze River flows into the Yellow Sea, there is a preference for nutritional, sweet-tasting, fresh food such as steamed crab. Further up the river, there are subtle differences, with people in Hunan preferring spicy food and those in neighboring Jiangxi favoring a sweet-and-sour taste.

Understanding China's regional variations is an important first step toward the development of a commercial strategy. But it is essential to go even deeper and get to grips with its fast-growing cities.

China publishes a thousand-plus-page book called the *China Statistical Yearbook*, which is compiled by the National Bureau of Statistics. It is a dense tome with a range of data from family incomes to government spending, input-output tables, sex ratios, and household composition by region. There are incredible time-series data marking the development of the world's most populous country. It is also a "did you know?" fact book. For example, China's largest direct investment partner is Latin America at $7.3 billion, compared with the United States at $0.9 billion and Africa at $1.4 billion. The number of full-time higher-education teachers increased from 463,000 in 2000 to 1.3 million in 2009. The number of mobile phone subscribers grew from 180,000 in 2000 to 747 million in 2009. The divorce rate is now 8.2 percent in China, and one-fifth of marriages end in divorce, up from one in twenty-four in 1978. In 1990, only 48 percent of the population had access to drinkable tap water. Today, 96 percent do. Remarkably, 63 percent of visits to China from overseas are from Asia (dominated by Japan and Korea), and the number of Europeans visiting China is double the number of Americans.

A Kaleidoscope of Contrasts in India

If China is varied, India is a veritable kaleidoscope of regions, cultures, religions, and languages.

Manmohan Singh, the prime minister as of this writing, is a Sikh who was born in what is today Pakistan and who was educated at Oxford and Cambridge. Sonia Gandhi, the leader of the Congress Party, the country's largest political party, was born in Italy and married into the Nehru-Gandhi family. Pratibha Patil, India's first woman president, is a lawyer and a member of the Maratha caste, a group known for its high political participation in the state of Maharashtra. Mayawati, the former chief minister of Uttar Pradesh, the biggest state, is a Dalit by birth, a caste traditionally referred to as "untouchable," although there have been reports that she may convert to Buddhism.

The diversity of the leadership indicates the diversity of the country. India is a country with twenty-eight states, seven union territories run directly by the federal government, and an extraordinarily varied geography: the wettest place on earth (Mawsynram, which is regularly deluged by the monsoon rains); one of the hottest places (Thar Desert in Rajasthan, where temperatures rise to 50 degrees Celsius [122 degrees Fahrenheit]); one of the coldest (Siachen glacier, where the temperature can drop to minus 50 degrees Celsius [minus 58 degrees Fahrenheit]); and some forty-five hundred miles of coastline.

There are twenty-two official languages and hundreds of dialects, and new ones are being discovered even today: in October 2010, linguists announced that they had traced a new tongue—called Koro—spoken by about eight hundred people among the hill tribes of Arunachal Pradesh in the far northeast of the country. Some of these languages are so established that users of Google's Indian Web site, the country's most popular Internet destination, are offered a choice of ten languages: English, Hindi, Bengali, Tamil, Telugu, Kannada, Gujarati, Malayalam, Marathi, and Punjabi.

This diversity means that like China, India should not be treated as one country. So, when advising companies, we start by segmenting this vast nation into four distinct regions: north, south, east, and west.

The north, which includes Delhi but is dominated by rural communities, is an agricultural hub and accounts for 30 percent of India's population. The main language is Hindi, along with Punjabi and Pahadi. The region has a significant population of Sikhs and Muslims. It is not a wealthy area, as a whole, and the GDP per capita is $900.[3]

The south, which includes Bangalore, is richer, and GDP per capita is $1,100. A technology hub, it has India's biggest community of Christians. The region's people, who constitute 21 percent of the total population, speak Tamil, Malayalam, Telugu, and Kannada.

The west, which is centered around Mumbai, is the richest region, with GDP per capita of $1,200. As India's business hub, its people account for 23 percent of the population and speak not only Hindi but also Gujarati and Marathi. Besides Hindus and Muslims, there are Parsis, whose ancestors came from Persia.

The poorest region is the east, centered around Kolkata, where Mother Teresa, the renowned Roman Catholic nun, worked in the rat-infested slums. It possesses great natural resources, with large coal and iron ore deposits, but the local population, speaking mainly Hindi and Bengali and accounting for 26 percent of the population, generates only $850 of GDP per person.

If a regional breakdown is a good starting point, it is necessary to take the segmentation even further, as there are great variations within regions, too. Take the south, which comprises four states. At one end of the spectrum is Andhra Pradesh, which is the largest territory, with the biggest population: its 84 million people mainly speak Telugu, a language heavily influenced by Sanskrit. Life expectancy is sixty-four years, and the literacy rate is low—just 68 percent. Run by India's ruling Congress Party, Andhra Pradesh has a GDP per capita of $1,180.

This GDP statistic is not as low as Karnataka's, which averages $1,160 per person. But it is significantly lower than Kerala's, which is nearly $1,500. Kerala, India's southernmost state, is small geographically, around seven times smaller than Andhra Pradesh, with a population of 33 million. But its wealth is reflected in a number of statistics: life expectancy is seventy-four years—a decade longer than for people in Andhra Pradesh—and the literacy rate is 94 percent.

Another way to see India's extraordinary variety is to look at the big cities in each region. Mahatma Gandhi, who viewed the major metropolises as centers of foreign influence, preferred to promote the villages as the best sign of "authentic India." Today, however, the capitals of the north, south, east, and west are strikingly different—with contrasting cultures and communities.

In the north, Delhi, as the country's political capital, is akin to Washington, D.C. People are socially competitive—it matters where you live and which car you drive—and they are hugely proud of their city as a kind of showcase for the whole country. The Delhi Metro subway, which spreads over 110 miles, is one of the largest metro networks in the world. It is one of the most ambitious projects and was built on time and within budget—proof that India can deliver if and when it has to do so. Users today say it is already at capacity.

In the west, Mumbai is rich, cosmopolitan, and business and finance oriented. The city has a buzz and energy—it is a city on the move. It is the home of the country's film industry—known as Bollywood, which merges Hollywood and the city's former name, Bombay. But also, as discussed in chapter 4, it is home to some of the biggest slums in the world. Driving in

Mumbai is a kaleidoscope of blaring horns, food vendors, dire poverty, and luxury high-rises.

In the south, Bangalore is India's answer to Silicon Valley. Traditionally known as "the garden city" because of its green and temperate setting, Bangalore was once the place where the well-to-do went to retire. Over the past twenty years, it has lost this sleepiness and now serves as the base for major technology companies, including Infosys and Wipro. However, the development of its roads and rail networks has not always matched the growth of its businesses. For example, visitors to Infosys's plush, green, college-style campus struggle to move anywhere when they step out into the city.

In the east, Kolkata, formerly called Calcutta, was India's capital during the halcyon days of the British Raj. In an echo of the past, the people affected a certain laid-back approach to life, and the city was not known as a center for business and industry. But things are changing—not least because of China's influence. In 2008, China established a consulate in the city, having been invited by the then-ruling Communist Party of West Bengal. There are now strong trade links between the city and some of China's major centers, such as Yunnan province and Shenzhen. In another sign of change, Mamata Banerjee, the female leader of a regional party, ousted the Communists in 2011.

The diet also reflects such variations. In the north, which is the country's wheat belt, *roti* accompanied by vegetable sauces and dairy-based products is a standard meal. In the Punjab's urban centers, people eat four times as much wheat as they do rice, and five times as many dairy products as meat and fish products. In the south and west, rice is central to the diet, along with vegetables, chutneys, and *papadums*—large, flat wafers made of rice. The south also consumes coconut, while fish is prominent all around the country's extensive coastline. In Andhra Pradesh's urban centers, people consume ten times as much rice as they do wheat, while in West Bengal, people eat twice as much fish and meat as do people in the other regions.

APPENDIX B

Risks and the Hit-the-Wall Scenario
How to Manage Volatility

C HINA AND INDIA ARE NOT SURE bets. They are fraught with risks and dangers. The leaders of these countries must confront massive challenges in the decade ahead, and success is not guaranteed. Corruption, asset bubbles, political and social disharmony, pollution, natural disasters, and political and economic conflict—these pose serious threats to growth and prosperity (figure B-1). Companies must navigate these markets with their eyes open. Successful companies will work to mitigate risks while remaining committed to winning and not retreating. They will also actively engage governments and stakeholders to influence events and reduce risks.

China's and India's growth projections are, of course, quite extraordinary. But in any growth cycle, there will be ups and downs, particularly for an economy that is not yet fully mature. In the late nineteenth and early twentieth centuries, U.S. industrial growth was marked by periods of decline and financial agony. In 1893, U.S. industrial production declined by 17.3 percent, measured on a peak-to-trough basis, and it similarly declined by 20.1 percent in 1907 and 32.5 percent in 1920.[1] Extraordinary declines were followed by periods of rapid recovery.

We have developed what we call a hit-the-wall scenario. It is modeled on the experience of South Korea, which saw real GDP growth decline by half between 1985 and 1995 and between 1995 and 2005. Such a decline would

Potential threats to growth and prosperity

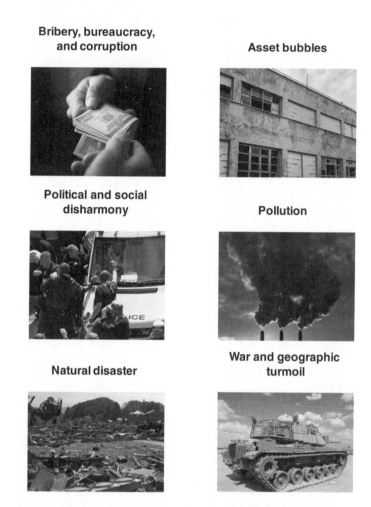

Bribery, bureaucracy, and corruption

Asset bubbles

Political and social disharmony

Pollution

Natural disaster

War and geographic turmoil

Source: Image for "Bribery, bureaucracy, and corruption": www.nomad4ever.com/wp-content/uploads/2008/04/corruption-a-paralyzing-pest.jpg. Image for "Pollution": photo by Owen Byrne, from "Smoke One," www.flickr.com/photos/ojbyrne/2167696800.

yield a real GDP growth rate of 5 percent for China and 4 percent for India between 2010 and 2020. In this downside case, China's consumer economy would grow from $2 trillion in 2010 to $4.2 trillion in 2020, while India's consumer economy would grow from $1 trillion to $2.4 trillion—and the size of the prize would be $6.6 trillion, not $10 trillion (figure B-2).

Hit-the-wall scenario: Effect on GDP and consumption

A reduction in combined GDP of up to $7 trillion lowers total consumption by $3.2 trillion.

	2010	Billions of nominal dollars		
		2020 base case	2020 downside case	Decrease from base case
China				
Total GDP	5,923	17,186	12,287	4,899
Total consumption	2,036	6,187	4,227	1,960
India				
Total GDP	1,653	5,981	3,940	2,041
Total consumption	991	3,584	2,362	1,224
Combined GDP	7,576	23,167	16,227	**6,940**
Combined consumption	3,027	9,771	6,589	**3,184**

Source: Based on consensus of Euromonitor, Countries and Consumers; International Monetary Fund; Economist Intelligence Unit, Market Indicators and Forecasts; World Bank, World Development Indicators; Goldman Sachs; Oxford Economics; BCG analysis.

Bureaucracy, Bribery, and Corruption

Corruption—particularly at local and regional levels—remains a day-to-day challenge for multinational companies in both China and India. The World Bank ranks India a lowly 134 out of 183 countries for "ease of doing business." It takes up to ten years to get a high-rise built in Mumbai—a long, drawn-out process requiring more than sixty approvals.[2] China, meanwhile, is ranked 79—below Rwanda, Namibia, and neighboring Mongolia. In the 2010 Transparency International Corruption Perception Index, the world's most credible measure of domestic public-sector corruption, India languishes in 87th place out of 183, with China ranked 78th.[3]

Corruption can take many forms. At one level, it is the handing out of contracts on the basis of political and private connections. At another level, it is backhanders and petty bribes to overcome red tape and other bureaucratic obstacles. For example, Chinese luxury producers tell us that up to half of their sales of $5,000-plus watches and $200-plus bottles of imported French wine are purchased in Hong Kong in bulk as "gifts" for government officials and businesspeople.

If you look at the conviction records of Chinese politicians and businesspeople convicted of corruption, there is a focus on payoffs, tax evasion, and embezzlement. It involves procurement, loan approvals, misuse of funds, infrastructure projects, real estate and land use rights, and preference in regulated industries. A Carnegie Policy Brief notes, "The bill for bailing out China's state-owned banks, prime victims of corruption in the financial sector, is close to $500 billion. Corruption at the local level sparks tens of thousands of riots and protests, undermining social stability. Corruption has also contributed to China's massive environmental degradation, deterioration in social services, and the rising costs of housing, health care and education."[4]

The consequences—for both China and India—are dire. "Corruption is a large tax on Indian growth," says Ravi Ramamurti, a professor at Northeastern University's College of Business Administration. "It delays execution, raises costs (for both Indians and multinationals), and destroys the moral fiber."[5] Also, according to some, it is the single largest deterrent to foreign domestic investment.[6]

India's bureaucracy-ridden democratic system and China's autocratic system exacerbate the effects of corruption. Government officials have enormous influence over major government contracts, appointments, and project approvals—and the ability to delay a project after ground is broken. Periodically, the countries launch high-publicity exposés. China is the world leader in executions of corrupt officials, with twenty-four violent crimes and thirty-one nonviolent crimes subject to the death penalty. Wen Qiang, Chongqing's police chief, was executed after his conviction for bribery, rape, and protecting organized crime.[7] In 2011, Liu Zhijun, China's railway minister, was removed from his top post and charged with corruption. Meanwhile, his brother, Liu Zhixiang, who was the head of the railway bureau in the city of Wuhan, was convicted of taking bribes and embezzling more than $5 million in public funds over a nine-year period.[8]

Corruption and crippling bureaucracy are a corrosive and defeating combination. If they are not addressed, then the governments' efforts to transform their economies will be undermined. But on balance, we believe corruption will fade over time. It helps that the Internet has given anticorruption activists a public platform.

Bubble Troubles, Fiscal Fears

In Shanghai in April 2011, hundreds of truck drivers staged a protest against the rising cost of fuel, forcing concessions from a government that had tried to limit their ability to pass along price increases. In Mumbai in November 2010, hundreds of people lined up in the streets to protest against the rise in the price of onions—a staple in the Indian diet. In July 2011, the global price of copper suddenly collapsed from nearly $10,000 per ton to below $7,000 per ton. At first the reasons were unclear, but later it was revealed that one major factor was the collapse of a syndicate of copper speculators in Wenzhou, China. The syndicate had been enjoying a one-way bet for several years, hoarding copper amid ever-rising prices—indeed, global copper prices had more than tripled from $3,000 per ton in January 2008 to a peak of $10,000 in mid-2011—while also using copper imports as a way to access capital. But the speculators fell victim to a Chinese government crackdown on informal lending.

What is the connection between these scattered events? After two decades of rapid growth—founded on seemingly limitless supplies of land, labor, and resources—China and India are having to face up to the consequences of inflation. Wen Jiabao, China's premier, has gone on record to say that inflation can be kept in check. "There is concern as to whether China can rein in inflation and sustain its rapid development," he wrote in the *Financial Times*. "My answer is an emphatic yes."[9]

In our base case, we have assumed some high inflation rates: 5.9 percent per year in China and 8.4 percent per year in India. But even so, the effect on food prices, wage rates, and house prices is likely to have an impact on the countries' competitiveness and productivity. A housing bubble is especially worrying.

It is the housing boom and, more broadly, the infrastructure revolution that are fueling the race for resources, which in turn is driving inflation rates ever higher. Take iron ore, for example. As we explained in chapter 13, we frame iron ore as a consumer business—driven by the demand for better housing, cars, appliances, dependable utilities, transportation, hospitals, and schools. It is a core component of a middle-class life.

But it is not just inflation that is a problem—it is also the volatility of demand and prices and, as a result, the unpredictability. Take another commodity: cement. In 2010, China accounted for more than 50 percent of the world's consumption of cement—up from 19 percent in 1990—as a result of a remarkable number of new and significant infrastructure and housing projects.[10] On average, China's annual demand for cement amounted to more than 1,000 kilograms per person—versus 300 kilograms in the United States.[11] But we calculate that this will peak soon—it is already doing so in the coastal regions—and it will leave a gray wave of 250 million tons of unwanted cement, which could force prices down again.

Political and Social Disharmony

China and India, for all their extraordinary growth over the past thirty years, are strikingly poor and divided countries. There is also an entrenched divide between urban and rural communities. In India, according to our analysis, 81.8 percent of people in the "deprived" category—those with approximately $2,000 per year, who account for about 50 percent of the population—live in rural areas. In China, the *hukou* system of residency—which has historically regulated the status of rural and urban dwellers—continues to pigeonhole people and limit their freedom of movement.

Many of the efforts of the Indian and Chinese governments have been to alleviate the plight of the poor—and the stellar growth that each country has enjoyed has helped with this. But a slowdown in growth—particularly with rising food prices—could trigger a wave of social unrest. In China, security police already contend with riots almost daily, and there is great concern that radical protesters could find encouragement in the transformation of North Africa—known as the Arab Spring—which was sparked by ordinary people angry at rising food prices in Tunisia. The memory of the Tiananmen Square protest in 1989 weighs heavily on the minds of China's leaders.

In India, where the population is young and vibrant, there is concern that young people's energy could be directed toward protests if they are not given jobs and opportunities. Here, also, the Maoist Naxalite movement poses a risk to the country's stability. This group traces its origin to a West Bengal village called Naxalbari. Its members, who number more than twenty thousand armed revolutionaries and another fifty thousand regular cadres, advocate the militant, violent overthrow of the ruling class—and a redistribution of wealth.[12] They have carried out bombings and police assassinations.

But arguably the biggest social and political risk is the collapse of the so-called grand bargain between the ruling classes and the middle classes. This could happen if the governments fail to meet the needs and expectations of the property-owning, Internet-surfing, and increasingly well-informed urban middle classes—on issues such as safety, the quality of key public services (health care, education, environment), corruption, an overall sense of fairness, and inflation control. And it is inevitable that some kind of collapse will take place over the next few years. For example, in order to maintain fast growth, China will have to persuade its urban middle classes to agree to have sixty nuclear power plants built near its major cities—or persuade these urbanites to accept much more air pollution from new coal-fired power plants as an alternative.

Pollution and the Poisoned Populace

The polluted environments of China and India may really begin to take a significant, measurable toll on the population's health and productivity. Many of the world's most polluted cities are in these countries. Poisoning could result from various heavy metals, pesticides, hazardous chemicals, airborne particulates from coal, and indoor air pollutants.

The dash for growth has devastated much of the landscape and led to many health problems, including pollution-related cancers. China is the world's biggest producer of carbon dioxide emissions as a result of its reliance on cheap coal, and according to BCG analysis, its emissions are expected to increase by 6.5 percent annually through the year 2020. India, the world's third-largest producer of carbon dioxide, behind the United States, is expected to see an annual increase of 4.4 percent over the decade. In Beijing, the U.S. embassy posts hourly pollution reports. It caused quite a media frenzy when a Tweet described the air quality in Beijing as "crazy bad," with a measurement of PM2.5 (tiny particulate matter) at the meter's maximum of 500, twenty times the World Health Organization level for unhealthy.

Besides the damage caused by factories spewing out black smoke, there are the harmful side effects that will result from the growing number of farm animals needed to feed a growing population with a new taste for meat. In China, our calculation is that the extra pigs and chickens will cause a spike in greenhouse gas production: in particular, 34 percent more nitrous oxide and 18 percent more methane.

Moreover, in both countries, the sheer number of people living near one another is also causing problems. For instance, in India, more than four hundred million people live along the Ganges, Hinduism's sacred river. As it enters the holy city of Varanasi, the river contains sixty thousand fecal coliform bacteria per hundred milliliters of water, 120 times more than is considered safe for bathing. It is not surprising that one thousand children die of diarrheal sickness in India every day.[13]

Indeed, large-scale unhealthy workforces are a very real scenario. The World Bank says that chronic tobacco and alcohol use, poor diet, high consumption of fast food, and physical inactivity are risk factors in China. The country has the world's largest number of smokers—an estimated 300 million—and suffers from high rates of lung cancer and heart disease.[14] Added to this is the growing number of elderly people. The number of people aged sixty-five and over will grow from 130 million in 2010 to 180 million in 2020.[15] This is up from 63 million in 2000. Imagine walking the streets of the United Kingdom, France, and Germany and seeing entire populations over sixty-five years old. This aging of the population will slow growth and increase the national health-care bill—which, in turn, will siphon off public funds from the capital investments needed to spur growth. The World Bank forecasts a doubling of heart disease, diabetes, and lung cancer. This epidemic of elderly and smokers poses a $1 trillion health-care spending diversion. It is a tax that surely would lead to crisis.

The Original China Study: Diet Impact on Health

T. Colin Campbell has written a remarkable book, *The China Study*. It is primarily a health and nutrition book aimed at helping Westerners avoid heart disease, diabetes, and cancer. Its source is a little-known study conducted in the 1970s by China premier Zhou Enlai, who was then dying of cancer. According to Campbell, the study is the most ambitious medical survey ever, with 650,000 surveyors touching 880 million of China's population (96 percent of the population of the time). The survey correlates diet and disease, and it demonstrates cancer incidence as a function of environmental and lifestyle factors.

At the time, according to Campbell, cancer rates in China ranged from 35 per 100,000 to 721 per 100,000. Campbell concludes that the rural Chinese diet, with only 9 to 10 percent of calories from protein, 14.5 percent from fat, and thirty-three grams of dietary fiber, correlated with low blood cholesterol. He points out that in the southwestern Chinese provinces of Sichuan and Guizhou during the 1973–1975 period, not a single individual among the population of more than 400,000 died from coronary heart disease under the age of sixty-five.

In some ways, Campbell's book forecast the now looming epidemic of diseases of affluence in China. He says nutritional extravagance is tied to cancer (colon, lung, breast, leukemia, stomach, liver), diabetes, and coronary heart disease. Nutritional inadequacy and poor sanitation drive diseases of poverty. These include pneumonia, ulcers, gastrointestinal diseases, tuberculosis, parasites, endocrine diseases, and infant and mother mortality. As the Chinese diet becomes rich and higher in calories—more like the Western diet—epidemics of disease are possible. Treatment has the potential to swamp health-care spending in China.[16]

Meanwhile, in India, chronic diseases, as the leading cause of death in the country, pose a major threat to steady economic growth. The World Health Organization says that 24.3 percent of Indian men are smokers.[17] Small, hand-rolled cigarettes called *bidis* and smokeless tobacco are popular. The concentration of smoking and drinking is highest among low-income consumers, and smoking is twice as popular among rural consumers as among urban consumers.

Natural Disaster

Of the ten deadliest natural disasters in history, five were earthquakes, floods, or famines in China. The earthquake at Shaanxi in 1556 killed an estimated 830,000. The Yellow River flood in 1887 in China may have killed as many as 2 million.[18] More recently, the Sichuan earthquake, which took place in 2008, was the twentieth-most-deadly earthquake of all time. It killed some 69,000. The economic loss was estimated at $150 billion.[19]

India also faces floods, droughts, earthquakes, heat waves, cyclones, and landslides. It accounts for 24 percent of the disaster deaths in Asia and loses 2 percent of GDP to disaster every year, according to the country's home secretary.[20] In each year from 2004 to 2010, floods, storms, and landslides damaged more than ten million homes.

Beyond this, the close proximity of millions of people means that devastating pandemics can strike at any time. In 2003, severe acute respiratory syndrome—better known as SARS—effectively shut down Greater China and Southeast Asia for three months. And such a pandemic could happen again: strains of bird flu appear regularly. It is clear that were a pandemic to hit not only China but also India and South Asia (including Pakistan and Bangladesh, for example), it could overwhelm public health systems.

War and Economic Conflict

Every day, India and China are confronted by the risk of military conflict in their regions. India is bordered by some of the most volatile countries on earth. China, meanwhile, faces the threat of collapse or dramatic change in North Korea, which in certain scenarios could bring China and the United States into a greater degree of conflict. For instance, it is not clear that China would tolerate absorption of North Korea into South Korea. There is also significant regional tension over territorial disputes with regard to areas of the South China Sea, which has created confrontation between China and several Southeast Asian nations. Could these boil over into more direct confrontation in the region? Would the confrontation escalate rapidly?

One likely flashpoint is over water—in particular, the water provided by the Himalayas, which supply the Ganges, Yangtze, and Yellow Rivers. China and India face acute water shortages—not least because of changing patterns of consumption. China's available water per capita is just a quarter of the world average—the lowest of any large economy.[21] Nearly half of China's population lives in the north, which has only 8 percent of China's water resources.[22] Complicating this usage pattern, the typical middle- or upper-class Chinese family has piped water, a private bathroom, a washing machine, and often a car that needs washing.

In India, the water problem is even worse. The country has 17 percent of the world's population, but it has only 4 percent of the world's water, so its local supplies are being depleted at a rapid rate.[23] Already, scientists are talking about "peak water" in the same way that they are talking about peak oil: the moment when sustainable sources of fresh water finally run out. Farmers are the biggest consumers of water, accounting for 86.5 percent of consumption, but the rising middle class wants a growing share of the scarce resource.

It does not help that there is great inefficiency: in New Delhi, for example, water runs through fifty-six miles of pipes and suffers a loss rate of up to 40 percent.[24] Nor is climate change helping. The Himalayan glaciers are shrinking, and global warming is also increasing the incidence of extreme weather patterns. As it is, 50 percent of India's annual rainfall occurs over fifteen days during the monsoon season, which runs from June to September.[25]

The two countries require urgent action—including massive investment in infrastructure. In China, there has been talk of moving the parched capital, Beijing, although a costly and ambitious project to reroute the nation's water supply from the flood plains of southern China and the snow-capped mountains of the west may prevent the need for this drastic option. Known as the South-North Water Diversion, the proposed project will, if built, cost up to $62 billion, twice as much as the famous Three Gorges Dam. Separately, the Chinese government says it is investing $600 billion in water reservoir improvements.[26]

India, meanwhile, has only half of what The World Bank estimates is needed to ensure a stable supply.[27] Given that the Ganges supplies one-third of Indians with their water, this is a frightening situation. No water equals no growth in rural incomes, and if there is no growth in rural incomes, then GDP growth slows dramatically. And no growth in GDP spells disaster: Indian rural life freezes at a low level of consumption and a low level of literacy—and the left-behinds become locked in time.

Any of these factors, if they were to slow growth, could have cataclysmic consequences for China, India, and the companies that are pinning their hopes on the new and dynamic generation of consumers. We fully expect that there will be volatility and unforeseen tragic events ahead. We are, however, encouraged by the resilient spirit of both countries. We believe that China and India will overcome their challenges over the next ten years.

NOTES

Chapter 1

1. The Boston Consulting Group (hereafter cited as BCG), Center for Consumer and Customer Insight: China & India Consumer Reports 2011.

2. Euromonitor: Countries and Consumers, Income and Expenditure; BCG consumer research; BCG analysis.

3. Karen Ward, "The World in 2050: Quantifying the Shift in the Global Economy," HSBC Bank, January 4, 2011, www.research.hsbc.com/midas/Res/RDV?ao=20&key=ej73gSSJVj&n=282364.PDF.

4. International Monetary Fund, World Economic Outlook database, October 2010; World Bank, World Development Indicators.

5. The Mahatma Gandhi National Rural Employment Guarantee Act (MGNREGA), homepage, www.nrega.net/.

6. Euromonitor: Countries and Consumers, Consumer Expenditure and Prices, 2010.

Chapter 2

1. Euromonitor, Countries and Consumers; Indian Ministry of Statistics and Programme Implementation, "Annual Report 2010–2011," http://mospi.nic.in/Mospi_New/upload/mospi_annual_report_2010-11.pdf; Indian Revenue Service, http://www.irsofficersonline.gov.in/; BCG proprietary consumer research; BCG analysis.

2. Ibid.

3. BCG proprietary consumer research; BCG analysis.

4. Ted Conover, "Capitalist Roaders," *New York Times*, July 2, 2006, www.nytimes.com/2006/07/02/magazine/02china.html?pagewanted=all.

5. Much of the data in this paragraph and the next can be found in "Taking Off: Travel and Tourism in China and Beyond," BCG report, March 2011, https://www.bcgperspectives.com/content/articles/retail_transportation_travel_tourism_taking_off_china_beyond/.

Chapter 3

1. Kerry A. Dolan and Luisa Kroll, eds., "Billionaires 2001," table in "The World's Richest People," *Forbes*, June 21, 2001, http://www.forbes.com/2001/06/21/billionairesindex.html.

2. HCL total revenue was about $6.2 billion in 2011, including both hardware and software business; Tata Consultancy Services revenue was about $8.4 billion in 2011, which ranked first in India's IT industry (HCL annual report, 2011; Tata Consultancy Services, annual report 2011).

3. *Forbes*, March 9, 2011, http://www.forbes.com/lists/2011/10/billionaires_2011.html. (Note that there were three billionaires from Hong Kong ranked ahead of Li.)

4. Russell Flannery, "A New No. 1 on the Forbes China Rich List," *Forbes*, September 7, 2011, /www.forbes.com/sites/russellflannery/2011/09/07/a-new-no-1-on-the-forbes-china-rich-list/.

5. James Fallows, "Mr. Zhang Builds His Dream Town," *Atlantic Magazine*, March 2007, www.thetlantic.com/magazine/archive/2007/03/mr-zhang-builds-his-dream-town/5616/; "The 400 Richest Chinese: #210 Zhang Yue," *Forbes* Web page, (www.forbes.com/lists/2011/74/china-billionaires-11_Zhang-Yue_ZM52.html).

6. "Ark Hotel Construction Time Lapse Building 15 Storeys in 2 Days (48 Hrs)," August 13, 2010, www.youtube.com/watch?v=Ps0DSihggio.

7. "Global Wealth 2011: Shaping a New Tomorrow," BCG report, May 2011, www.bcgperspectives. com/content/articles/financial_institutions_pricing_global_wealth_2011_shaping_new_tomorrow/.

8. Ibid.

9. World Federation of Exchanges, "Annual Report," 2005 and 2010, http://www.world-exchanges. org/statistics/annual/.

10. Hurun.net, http://www.hurun.net/usen/HRRL.aspx; "The 400 Richest Chinese," *Forbes* Web page (www.forbes.com/lists/2011/74/china-billionaires-11_land.html), "The Forbes 400: The Richest People in America," Forbes Staff, September 21, 2011, http://www.forbes.com/forbes-400/; BCG proprietary research; BCG exit interviews in Shanghai, Beijing, Hong Kong, and Nanjing, October and November 2008.

11. "The Billionaire Factory: Roaring Markets, Sudden Fortunes," *Forbes Asia Magazine*, March 28, 2011, www.forbes.com/global/2011/0328/billionaires-11-balwa-bangur-gaur-goenka-billionaire-factory. html.

12. BCG Wealth Management database, 2009.

Chapter 4

1. Euromonitor, Countries and Consumers, www.euromonitor.com; BCG analysis.

2. Neil Munshi, "Advice for India's Real-Life Slumdog: Funds and Guns," *Financial Times*, November 3, 2011, http://blogs.ft.com/beyond-brics/2011/11/03/indias-real-life-slumdog-funds-and-guns/#axzz1hBSJ96eI.

3. "KBC's Winner Wants to Prepare for the Civil Service Exams," *Times of India*, October 28, 2011, http://articles.timesofindia.indiatimes.com/2011-10-28/tv/30332188_1_civil-services-sushil-kumar-hot-seat.

4. Euromonitor, Countries and Consumers; Indian Ministry of Statistics and Programme Implementation, "Annual Report 2010-2011," http://mospi.nic.in/Mospi_New/upload/mospi_annual_report_2010-11.pdf; BCG proprietary consumer research; BCG analysis.

5. Little Swan, "LittleSwan Won Reader's Digest Trusted Brands Gold," press release, November 30, 2006, www.littleswan.com/english/News/content.aspx?id=569.

6. *Last Train Home*, directed by Lixin Fan, DVD (2009, Zeitgeist Video).

7. Victor Mallet, "A Tour of Mumbai's Slums," *Financial Times*, February 6, 2009, www.ft.com/intl/cms/s/0/d588517e-f3db-11dd-9c4b-0000779fd2ac.html#axzz1mOF1Pgpy.

8. Jennifer Reingold, "Can P&G Make Money in Places Where People Earn $2 a Day?" *Fortune*, January 6, 2011, http://features.blogs.fortune.cnn.com/2011/01/06/can-pg-make-money-in-places-where-people-earn-2-a-day/.

9. Hindustan Unilever, "Shakti: Economic Development Through Micro Enterprise," Hindustan Web page, n.d., www.hul.co.in/sustainability/casestudies/enhancing-livelihoods/Shakti.aspx.

Chapter 5

1. Euromonitor, Countries and Consumers, www.euromonitor.com; BCG analysis.

2. Euromonitor, Countries and Consumers, www.euromonitor.com; National Council of Applied Economic Research, "The Next Urban Frontier: Twenty Cities to Watch," *Macrotrack*, August 12, 2008, www.ncaer.org/downloads/journals/macrotrack_august2008.pdf.

3. *China Economic Quarterly* 15, no. 4 (December 2011).

4. Michael Geraghty, "Urbanization: Big Cities Getting Bigger," *Citi Research*, February 9, 2011, p. 5, Publisher: Citi Group.

5. National Bureau of Statistics of China, "China's Total Population and Structural Changes 2011," National Bureau of Statistics of China, January 20, 2012, www.stats.gov.cn/was40/gjtjj_en_detail.jsp?searchword=rural+populations&channelid=9528&record=3; Jamil Anderlini, "China's City Population Outstrips Countryside," *Financial Times*, January 17, 2012, www.ft.com/cms/s/0/7b9a25ba-410e-11e1-8c33-00144feab49a.html.

6. Euromonitor, Countries and Cousumers Annual Data, Population and Homes.

7. Tushar Poddar and Eva Yi, "India's Rising Growth Potential," Goldman Sachs Global Economics Paper No. 152, January 22, 2007; Euromonitor, Countries and Consumers, www.euromonitor.com; BCG analysis.

8. Josh Noble, "Shanghainese: Living Longer than Canadians?" *Financial Times*, March 3, 2011, http://blogs.ft.com/beyond-brics/2011/03/03/shanghainese-living-longer-than-canadians/#axzz1kygugbZG.

9. "Big Prizes in Small Places: China's Rapidly Multiplying Pockets of Growth," BCG report, November 2010, www.bcgperspectives.com/content/articles/consumer_products_globalization_big_prizes_in_small_places/. Much of the material that follows draws from this report.

10. "Winning in Emerging-Market Cities," BCG report, September 2010, www.bcgperspectives.com/content/articles/globalization_growth_winning_in_emerging_market_cities/.

11. Lydia Polgreen, "India's Smaller Cities Show Off Growing Wealth," *New York Times*, October 23, 2010, www.nytimes.com/2010/10/24/world/asia/24india.html.

12. City population data are from the India Census 2011, http://censusindia.gov.in; Indicus Analytics City Skyline database 2010, www.indicus.net; BCG's Emerging Cities database 2010; BCG analysis.

13. Robert Malone and Tom Van Riper, "The World's Densest Cities," *Forbes*, December 14, 2007, www.forbes.com/2007/12/14/cities-pollution-asia-biz-logistics-cx_tvr_1214densecities.html.

14. Indicus, India Census 2011, BCG analysis.

15. National Highway Authority of India, www.nhai.org.

16. BCG, "Winning in Emerging-Market Cities."

17. Abheek Singhi and Amitabh Mall, eds., *Building a New India: The Role of Organized Retail in Driving Inclusive Growth* (Mumbai: Boston Consulting Group; New Delhi: Confederation of Indian Industry, February 2011).

18. "US$ 448 Million IPO for Chinese Dairy Farming Company," *China Law & Practice*, December 2010, www.chinalawandpractice.com/Article/2736368/Channel/9947/US-448-million-IPO-for-Chinese-dairy-farming-company.html.

19. "E-commerce Injects Vitality into Rural Development in China," Xinhua News Agency (China), May 6, 2011, http://news.xinhuanet.com/english2010/china/2011-05/06/c_13862044.htm.

20. BCG, "Winning in Emerging-Market Cities."

21. David Michael, Harold Sirkin, and David Jin, "The 'Many City' Growth Strategy," *Bloomberg Businessweek*, October 20, 2010, www.businessweek.com/globalbiz/content/oct2010/gb20101019_397376.htm.

Chapter 6

1. United Nations Development Programme, "Human Development Reports 2002–2010," http://hdr.undp.org/en/reports/global/hdr2002/; International Labour Organization, LABORSTA database, http://laborsta.ilo.org; Euromonitor, Countries and Consumers, www.euromonitor.com; BCG analysis.

2. Mao Tse-Tung, *Quotations from Chairman Mao Tse-Tung*, edited and with an introductory essay and notes by Stuart R. Schram (New York: Frederick A. Praeger, 1968), ch. 31.

3. BCG consumer interviews of more than 22,000 women in 25 countries, including representation from all income levels.

4. Jenna Johnson, "Chinese Students Enroll in Record Numbers at U.S. Colleges," *Washington Post*, November 14, 2011.

5. Meghan Casserly, "The World's Richest Women: The Most Elite Women's Club," *Forbes*, March 10, 2011, www.forbes.com/sites/meghancasserly/2011/03/10/the-worlds-richest-women-billionaires/.

6. Didi Kirsten Tatlow, "Setting the Pace with Toughness," *New York Times*, January 26, 2011, www.nytimes.com/2011/01/27/world/asia/27iht-dong27.html?ref=thefemalefactor.

7. Ricardo Hausmann, Laura D. Tyson, and Saadia Zahidi, *The Global Gender Gap Report 2011* (Geneva, Switzerland: World Economic Forum, 2011), www3.weforum.org/docs/WEF_GenderGap_Report_2011.pdf.

8. Jon Huntsman, "China's Attempts to Address Gender Imbalance Problem," leaked cable from Embassy Beijing, January 10, 2010, WikiLeaks document 10BEIJING35, www.cablegatesearch.net/cable.php?id=10BEIJING35.

9. Michael J. Silverstein and Kate Sayre, *Women Want More: How to Capture Your Share of the World's Largest, Fastest-Growing Market* (New York: HarperBusiness, 2009); 2011 BCG Consumer Sentiment Barometer, published in "Navigating the New Consumer Realities: Consumer Sentiment 2011," https://www.bcgperspectives.com/content/articles/consumer_products_retail_navigating_new_consumer_realities/, an annual international survey of more than 24,000 people to explore general sentiment and spending plans.

10. Most of our conversations were in urban markets where we met with women a generation ahead of their rural counterparts. Our survey methodology was unable to capture many lower-class participants in India, who accounted for only 0.4 percent of the sample compared with 7 percent globally.

11. Hausmann, Tyson, and Zahidi, *Global Gender Gap Report 2011.*

12. Tripti Lahiri, "Which Has More Female CEOs: India Inc. or Fortune 500?" *Wall Street Journal Blogs*, November 18, 2010, http://blogs.wsj.com/indiarealtime/2010/11/18/which-has-more-female-ceos-india-inc-or-fortune-500/.

13. Indian School of Business, "Placement Report," 2011, www.isb.edu; Harvard Business School Class of 2013 MBA Class Profile, http://www.hbs.edu/mba/admissions/class-statistics/; INSEAD, "2010 Employment Statistics," http://mba.insead.edu/documents/MBA_EMPLOYMENT_STATISTICS.pdf.

14. Chaya Babu, "Indian Girls Shed Names Meaning 'Unwanted' to Rise Above Gender Discrimination," thestar.com, October 22, 2011, www.thestar.com/news/world/article/1074446–indian-girls-shed-names-meaning-unwanted-to-rise-above-gender-discrimination.

Chapter 7

1. National Bureau of Statistics of China, Agriculture, http://www.stats.gov.cn/tjsj/ndsj/2011/indexeh.htm; United States Department of Agriculture Research Services datasets, http://www.ers.usda.gov/Data/; Economist Intelligence Unit Market Indicators and Forecasts; Euromonitor, Industries, Food related; Economist Intelligence Unit; Srikanta Chatterjee, Allan Rae, and Ranjan Ray, "Food Consumption and Calorie Intake in Contemporary India," Paper 07.05, Massey University, Palmerston, North New Zealand, August 2007.

2. Euromonitor, Industries, All food related.

3. Xianping Lang, *Why Is Our Life So Difficult?* (Shanghai: Oriental Publishing Center, 2010). Only available in Chinese.

4. Reuters, "Update 2—China's Tingyi Q4 Net Profit Down on Sluggish Beverage Sector," March 21, 2012, www.reuters.com/article/2012/03/21/tingyi-earnings-idUSL3E8EK0O920120321; Tingyi (Cayman Islands) Holding Corp., *2009 Annual Report*, www.masterkong.com.cn/InvestorInformationen/financial/2009/index.shtml.

5. BCG, "Kangshifu—Three Stages of Distribution," November 2, 2010, https://www.bcgperspectives.com/content/articles/consumer_products_retail_tingyi_three_stages_distribution/.

6. "Amul Ranked No. 1 Indian Brand," *Economic Times*, July 4, 2011, http://articles.economictimes.indiatimes.com/2011-07-04/news/29735993_1_amul-dairy-brand-indian-brand.

7. Amul, "Amul Sponsors Sauber F1 Team in India," press release, *Business Wire India*, September 29, 2011, www.businesswireindia.com/PressRelease.asp?b2mid=28415.

8. P. G. Bhatol, "Chairman's Speech," 37th Annual General Body Meeting (Amul), June 21, 2011, www.amul.com/m/chairman-speech-37th-annual-general-body-meeting-held-on-21st-june-2011.

9. Yum! China Investor Conference, Slide 98, September 8, 2011, http://phx.corporate-ir.net/External.File?item=UGFyZW50SUQ9MTA2ODk5fENoaWxkSUQ9LTF8VHlwZT0z&t=1.

10. Victoria Moore, "Let's Raise a Glass to China's Wine," *Telegraph* (London), September 8, 2011, www.telegraph.co.uk/foodanddrink/wine/8747202/Lets-raise-a-glass-to-Chinas-wine.html.

11. Patti Waldemeir, "Chinese Acquire Taste for French Wine, " *Financial Times*, September 16, 2010, www.ft.com/cms/s/0/057979bc-c1c6-11df-9d90-00144feab49a.html#axzz1mrJfGtBJ.

12. Deutsche Bank, "Luxury Goods Quarterly: The World in Charts," August 2010; Ipsos 2010 Market Research (Chinese sample size: N=802); Altagamma, *Luxury Consumer Insight 2009*, December 2009, www.altagamma.it/temp/060333224412288.pdf; European Luxury Goods, China Consumer Survey, Credit Suisse, 2008; International Monetary Fund, Data and Statistics, http://www.imf.org/external/pubs/ft/weo/2012/01/weodata/index.aspx; BCG estimates and analysis.

13. Kepler Capital Markets research; Bernstein Research.

14. Stanley Pignal, "Vine Life for Moët As It Branches into China," *Financial Times*, May 12, 2011, www.ft.com/intl/cms/s/0/ec1230fa-7cb3-11e0-994d-00144feabdc0.html#axzz1mOF1Pgpy.

15. Mitch Frank, "Château Lafite Rothschild Owners Launch Chinese Wine Project," *Wine Spectator*, April 3, 2009, www.winespectator.com/webfeature/show/id/Chateau-Lafite-Rothschild-Owners-Launch-Chinese-Wine-Project_4699.

16. Cofco website: http://cofcomag.cofco.com/en/product/p_food.aspx?con_id=3395.

17. Alan Rappeport, "Pernod Taps Asian Thirst for Top Spirits," *Financial Times*, May 30, 2011: http://www.ft.com/cms/s/0/fe6a417c-8b07-11e0-b2f1-00144feab49a.html#axzz1sU2eYV6B.

18. Mure Dickie, "LVMH Soaks Up Wenjun Stake," *Financial Times*, May 17, 2007, www.ft.com/intl/cms/s/0/933addac-0407-11dc-a931-000b5df10621.html#axzz1mOF1Pgpy.

19. Patti Waldemeir and Leslie Hook, "Diageo Deal Shows China Thirst for Investment," *Financial Times*, June 28, 2011, www.ft.com/cms/s/0/31a00704-a1b8-11e0-b9f9-00144feabdc0.html#axzz1mrJfGtBJ.

20. BCG, "Irene Rosenfeld on Transforming Kraft Foods," October 3, 2011, www.bcgperspectives. com/content/videos/leadership_transformation_irene_rosenfeld_an_appetite_for_growth_and_risk.

Chapter 8

1. Indian Ministry of Statistics and Programme Implementation, http://mospi.nic.in/mospi_new/Site/India_Statistics.aspx?; Euromonitor, Global Market Information Database, Countries and Consumers.

2. National Housing Bank, "Report on Trend and Progress of Housing in India," company report, National Housing Bank, India, June 2002, www.nhb.org.in/Publications/T__P_2002_FINAL.pdf; Renus S. Karnad, "Housing Finance and the Economy: Regional Trends; South Asia—Perspectives," presented for Housing Development Finance Corporation, to 25th World Congress, International Union for Housing Finance, Brussels, June 23, 2004, www.hdfc.com/pdf/hdfc-iuhf04.pdf.

3. TechSci Research, "India Loans Market Opportunities & Forecast 2016," TechSci Research Web page, September 9, 2011, www.techsciresearch.com/indialoansnews.

4. Rob Minto and Steven Bernard, "China Property Prices Map," *Financial Times*, May 31, 2011, www.ft.com/cms/s/0/70bdcad6-8ba4-11e0-a725-00144feab49a.html#axzz1kycbGLbE.

5. Dutch Trader [screen name], "China's Property Tightening Measures and Xinyuan Real Estate," *Seeking Alpha*, January 30, 2011, http://seekingalpha.com/article/249572-china-s-property-tightening-measures-and-xinyuan-real-estate.

6. Euromonitor, Countries and Consumers; Indian Ministry of Statistics and Programme Implementation, "Annual Report 2010–2011," http://mospi.nic.in/Mospi_New/upload/mospi_annual_report_2010-11.pdf; BCG proprietary consumer research; BCG analysis.

7. Lodha Group, "Lodha Presents World's Tallest Residential Tower in Mumbai, India," press release, June 8, 2010, www.lodhagroup.com/backoffice/data_content/pdf_files/WorldOnePressreleasefinal.pdf.

8. BCG, "Deepak S. Parekh on Weathering the Crisis in Mortgage Lending," BCG Perspectives, April 7, 2010, https://www.bcgperspectives.com/content/interviews/leadership_organization_weathering_crisis_mortgage_markets_deepak_parekh/.

9. HDFC investor presentation, Summer 2011, http://www.hdfcbank.com/assets/pdf/Investor_Presentation.pdf.

10. Anjli Raval, "Care for Some Poppadoms with That McAloo Tikki Burger?" *Financial Times*, October 14, 2010, http://blogs.ft.com/beyond-brics/2010/10/14/care-for-some-papadums-with-that-mcaloo-tikki-burger/#axzz1kD1AlJwx.

Chapter 9

1. Laurie Burkitt, "Coach Hitches Its Wagon to China," *Wall Street Journal*, November 18, 2011, http://online.wsj.com/article/SB10001424052970204517204577043701556706074.html.

2. Deutsche Bank, "Luxury Goods Quarterly: The World in Charts," February 25, 2011; Aaron Fischer and Mariana Kou, *Dipped in Gold: Luxury Lifestyles in China/HK* (CLSA Asia-Pacific Markets, January 2010), http://www.iberglobal.com/Archivos/china_luxury_clsa.pdf.

3. Flouquet, Melanie, et al., J.P. Morgan, "Luxury Goods: PPR (OW) Ranks on Risk/Reward," December 15, 2011.

4. Fisher and Kou, *Dipped in Gold*.

5. Liza Lin, "Rich Chinese Women Open Throttle on 'Man's World' with $400,000 Maseratis," *Bloomberg News*, January 13, 2011, www.bloomberg.com/news/2011-01-13/chinese-women-millionaires-enter-man-s-world-with-400-000-maseratis.html.

6. Eyder Peralta, "About $22 Billion in Gold, Diamonds, Jewels Found in Indian Temple," *NPR Online*, July 5, 2011, www.npr.org/blogs/thetwo-way/2011/07/06/137627235/some-22-billion-in-gold-diamonds-jewels-found-in-indian-temple.

7. Fisher and Kou, *Dipped in Gold*.

8. Euromonitor, Apparel.

9. Jui Chakravorty, "Luxury Retail Not Part of India's Success Story," Reuters, August 24, 2011, www.reuters.com/article/2011/08/24/india-luxury-idUSL4E7JM1E920110824.

10. BCG Global Wealth Market Sizing Database, 2011.

11. Ibid.

12. Wang Wen, "Ads Promoting Wealth Goods, Lifestyles Banned," *China Daily*, March 21, 2011, www.chinadaily.com.cn/cndy/2011-03/21/content_12199764.htm.

13. Clare McAndrew, "The Global Art Market in 2010: Crisis and Recovery," TEFAF, 2011.

14. Sheila Gibson Stoodley, "A Tiger Market," *Robb Report*, August 1, 2011, http://robbreport.com/Art-Collectibles/A-Tiger-Market.

15. Ipsos 2009 market research on mature countries (7,496 consumers surveyed); Ipsos 2010 market research on emerging countries (4,810 consumers surveyed).

16. Based on company Web sites and reports.

17. BCG, "Chinese Travelers, Ready for Take-off," July 2011, www.bcgperspectives.com/content/commentary/transportation_travel_tourism_retail_chinese_travelers_ready_for_takeoff/.

18. Andrea Felsted, "Burberry Targets Chinese Consumers," *Financial Times*, September 19, 2010, www.ft.com/cms/s/0/332ddae6-c40b-11df-b827-00144feab49a.html#axzz1mrJfGtBJ.

19. Flouquet, Melanie, et al., J.P. Morgan, "Luxury Goods: PPR (OW) Ranks on Risk/Reward," December 15, 2011.

20. Kepler Research; Bernstein Research.

21. BCG analysis.

22. Jennifer Thompson, "LVMH Profits Jump 25% As Sector Defies Woes," *Financial Times*, July 26, 2011, www.ft.com/cms/s/0/82bddb3c-b7ae-11e0-8523-00144feabdc0.html#axzz1mrJfGtBJ.

Chapter 10

1. Loretta Chao and Josh Chin, "A Billionaire's Breakup Becomes China's Social-Media Event of Year," *Wall Street Journal*, June 17, 2011, http://online.wsj.com/article/SB10001424052702304563104576357271321894898.html.

2. Paul de Bendern, "Analysis: India Risks Facing Its Own Arab Spring," Reuters, August 17, 2011, www.reuters.com/article/2011/08/17/us-india-protests-idUSTRE77G2E220110817.

3. "Anna Goes Tech Savvy, to Start Blog, Twitter, FB Accounts," *One India News*, September 29, 2011, http://news.oneindia.in/2011/09/29/anna-hazare-start-blog-open-facebook-twitter-accounts.html).

4. International Telecommunication Union, "The World in 2011: ICT 2011 Facts and Figures," www.itu.int/ITU-D/ict/facts/2011/material/ICTFactsFigures2011.pdf.

5. Telecom Regulatory Authority of India, "Highlights of Telecom Subscription Data as on 31st December, 2011," press release no. 14/2012, January 30, 2012, http://www.nftemaharashtra.org/PR-Dec-11.pdf (these are numbers of mobile subscriptions; the number of actual users is likely to be smaller, because of multiple connections).

6. David Barboza, "In China, Apple Finds a Sweet Spot," *New York Times*, July 24, 2011, www.nytimes.com/2011/07/25/technology/apple-sales-in-china-zoom-ahead-of-competitors.html?_r=4.

7. James Fontanella-Khan and Neil Munshi, "India Unveils Cheapest Tablet Computer," *Financial Times*, October 5, 2011, www.ft.com/cms/s/2/9e714b34-ef53-11e0-918b-00144feab49a.html#axzz1mrJfGtBJ. See also Thomas L. Friedman, "The Last Person," *New York Times*, November 12, 2011, www.nytimes.com/2011/11/13/opinion/sunday/friedman-the-last-person.html?scp=3&sq=fthomas%20friedman%20india&st=cse.

8. BCG, "BCG e-Intensity Index," October 11, 2011, https://www.bcgperspectives.com/content/interactive/telecommunications_media_entertainment_bcg_e_intensity_index/.

9. BCG, "The World's Next E-Commerce Superpower," November 22, 2011, www.bcgperspectives.com/content/articles/retail_consumer_products_worlds_next_ecommerce_superpower/.

10. China Internet Network Information Center, www.cnnic.net.cn/; Japan Ministry of Internal Affairs and Communications, www.soumu.go.jp; iResearch Consulting Group, www.iresearch.com.cn; Economist Intelligence Unit; J.P. Morgan, "Nothing But Net: 2011 Internet Investment Guide," J.P. Morgan (Goldman Sachs), January 12, 2011; International Telecommunication Union, www.itu.int; BCG report, "The World's Next E-Commerce Superpower," November 2011, www.bcgperspectives.com/content/articles/retail_consumer_products_worlds_next_ecommerce_superpower/; BCG analysis.

11. "Digital India: The $100 Billion Prize," January 4, 2011, www.bcgperspectives.com/content/articles/media_entertainment_telecommunications_digital_india_100_billion_dollar_prize/.

12. "Sunil Mittal Speaking: I Started with a Dream," *Times of India*, December 22, 2002, http://timesofindia.indiatimes.com/city/delhi-times/Sunil-Mittal-speaking-I-started-with-a-dream/articleshow/32019056.cms.

13. "Sunil Mittal & Family," *Forbes*, March 2011, www.forbes.com/profile/sunil-mittal/.

14. Neeraj Aggarwal, Nimisha Jain, and Arvind Subramanian, "Capitalizing on Technological Innovations," *Communications Today*, August 5, 2011, www.communicationstoday.co.in/index. php?option=com_content&task=view&id=4117&Itemid=41; BCG analysis.

15. "SBI and Airtel Join Hands to Usher in a New Era of Financial Inclusion for Unbanked India," Bharti Airtel press release, January 21, 2011, www.airtel.in/wps/wcm/connect/About%20 Bharti%20Airtel/bharti+airtel/media+centre/bharti+airtel+news/mobile/pg-sbi_and_airtel_join_ hands_to_usher_in_a_new.

Chapter 11

1. Itishree Samal, "Hyderabad Boy Tops IIT-JEE," *Business Standard*, May 26, 2011, http://business-standard.com/india/news/hyderabad-boy-tops-iit-jee/436789/.

2. Seven original, eight new, and one currently operating under Banaras Hindu University, according to the IIT Web sites.

3. The data in this chapter draw from the following sources: UNESCO; World Bank; International Monetary Fund, World Economic Outlook; United Nations Development Programme; National Bureau of Statistics of China; Oppenheimer & Co., "Stay in School: A Secular Growth Story for China Education," December 17, 2009, http://wenku.baidu.com/view/7392d35f312b3169a451a440.html; Edelweiss Research, "Indian Education: A Leap Forward," October 7, 2009; Economist Intelligence Unit; Institute of International Enrollment; Gary Gereffi and Vivek Wadhwa, "Framing the Engineering Outsourcing Debate," Duke University, December 2005, www.soc.duke.edu/resources/public_sociology/duke_out-sourcing.pdf; Gary Gereffi, Vivek Wadhwa, Ben Rissing, and Ryan Ong, "Getting the Numbers Right," *Journal of Engineering Education*, January 2008, www.cse.msu.edu/~stockman/CV/engineersSSRN-id1081923.pdf; Klaus Schwab, ed., *The Global Competitiveness Report 2010–2011* (Geneva, Switzerland: World Economic Forum, 2010), www3.weforum.org/docs/WEF_GlobalCompetitivenessReport_2010-11.pdf; Cowen and Company research; U.S. Census Bureau; National Center for Education Statistics; Datamonitor; *Higher Education in India*, August 2009.

4. The global literacy rate is from the UNESCO Institute for Statistics, September 2011, http://www.uis.unesco.org/FactSheets/Documents/FS16-2011-Literacy-EN.pdf.

5. *U.S.News & World Report*, http://www.usnews.com/education/worlds-best-universities-rankings.

6. U.S. Embassy, New Delhi, India, "U.S. Welcomes Indian Students, Prepares for PM Singh," press release, November 18, 2009, http://newdelhi.usembassy.gov/pr112509a.html; Jenna Johnson, "Chinese Students Enroll in Record Numbers at U.S. Colleges," *Washington Post*, November 14, 2011, www.washingtonpost.com/blogs/campus-overload/post/chinese-students-enroll-in-record-numbers-at-us-colleges/2011/11/14/gIQAyYlKLN_blog.html.

7. Martin Beckford, "Big Rise in Number of Chinese Students in UK," *Telegraph* (London), September 10, 2008, www.telegraph.co.uk/news/2779681/Big-rise-in-number-of-Chinese-students-in-UK.html; "Why Students Prefer to Study in UK Colleges or Universities," *Sunday Times* (Sri Lanka), May 30, 2010, http://sundaytimes.lk/100530/Education/ed12.html.

8. Norman R. Augustine, *Is America Falling Off the Flat Earth?* (New York: National Academies Press, 2007) 49, http://www.nap.edu/openbook.php?record_id=12021&page=49.

9. Peking University Web site, http://english.pku.edu.cn/.

10. Zhou Zhong, "Beijing Banks on C9 to Break into Higher Education's Elite," *Showcase Asia*, 2012, www.qsshowcase.com/asia/mainfeature2.php; Wang Wei, "China's Ivy League May Lift Higher Education," *China Daily*, November 24, 2009, www.chinadaily.com.cn/metro/2009-11/24/content_9031116.htm.

11. China Education Center Ltd., Homepage, www.chinaeducenter.com/en/; China Education and Research Network, Homepage, www.edu.cn/; "Over 10 Billion Yuan to Be Invested in '211 Project,'" *People's Daily*, March 26, 2008, http://english.people.com.cn/90001/6381319.html; "What Is Project 985 in China," China Service Mall, n.d., http://news.at0086.com/China-University-Guide/What-is-Project-985-in-China.html.

12. "Grads Leaving Big Cities for Lower Living Costs," *China Daily*, June 10, 2011, www.china.org.cn/china/2011-06/10/content_22750587.htm.

13. People's Republic of China, "The 11th Five-Year Plan," Gov.cn, Chinese government's official Web portal, 2012, www.gov.cn/english/special/115y_index.htm.

14. "China's 'Sea Turtles,'" ABC News, video, December 2, 2010, http://abcnews.go.com/WNT/video/chinas-sea-turtles-pfizer-vice-president-chinese-home-opportunity-12299240; Jaime FlorCruz, "'Sea Turtles' Reverse China's Brain Drain," CNN World, October 28, 2010, http://articles.cnn.com/2010-10-28/world/florcruz.china.sea.turtles.overseas_1_china-chinese-experts-overseas-chinese-students?_s=PM:WORLD; Wanfeng Zhou, "China Goes on the Road to Lure 'Sea Turtles' Home," Reuters, December 17, 2008, www.reuters.com/article/idUSTRE4BH02220081218; Melinda Liu, "Steal This Scientist," *Newsweek Magazine*, November 13, 2009, www.newsweek.com/2009/11/13/steal-this-scientist.html; Maureen Fan, "In China, Pulled by Opposing Tides," *Washington Post*, February 5, 2008, www.washingtonpost.com/wp-dyn/content/article/2008/02/04/AR2008020403219_2.html.

15. *U.S.News & World Report*, http://www.usnews.com/education/worlds-best-universities-rankings/best-universities-civil-engineering.

16. Sandipan Deb, *The IITians: The Story of a Remarkable Indian Institution and How Its Alumni Are Reshaping the World* (New Delhi: Viking, 2004).

17. India Planning Commission, "Drop-out Rates in Classes I-V, I-VIII and I-X in States (2009–2010)," www.planningcommission.nic.in/data/datatable/index.php?data=datatab.

18. Calculated on the basis of the literacy rate of 74 percent reported in the 2011 census.

19. Harvard University, *Harvard University Fact Book, 2009–10* (Cambridge, MA: Office of Institutional Research, 2010).

20. Phil Baty, "Rankings Update: Reputations on the Line as Survey Nears Closing Date," *Times Higher Education*, May 5, 2011, www.timeshighereducation.co.uk/story.asp?storycode=416029.

Chapter 12

1. Damian Whitworth, "Ratan Tata: The Mumbai Tycoon Collecting British Brands," *Times*, (London) May 21, 2011, www.thetimes.co.uk/tto/magazine/article3021187.ece.

2. "Ark Hotel Construction Time Lapse Building 15 Storeys in 2 Days (48 Hrs)," YouTube, August 13, 2010, www.youtube.com/watch?v=Ps0DSihggio.

3. BCG, "The 2011 BCG Global Challengers: Companies on the Move," BCG report, January 18, 2011, www.bcgperspectives.com/content/articles/globalization_companies_on_the_move_2011_global_challengers/.

4. BCG, "The African Challengers: Global Competitors Emerge from the Overlooked Continent," June 2010, www.bcgperspectives.com/content/articles/globalization_mergers_acquisitions_african_challengers/#chapter1.

5. Leslie Hook, "Zambia: Striking the Dragon," *Financial Times*, October 24, 2011, http://blogs.ft.com/beyond-brics/2011/10/24/zambia-striking-the-dragon/#axzz1l4Y2pXdp.

Chapter 13

1. George Stalk and David Michael, "What the West Doesn't Get About China," *Harvard Business Review*, June 2011, http://hbr.org/2011/06/what-the-west-doesnt-get-about-china/ar/1.

2. "China Can Use More Copper Than World Has Now with Yang's Stove," *Bloomberg News*, November 2, 2010, http://www.bloomberg.com/news/2010-11-02/china-seen-using-more-copper-than-world-produces-now-with-yang-s-new-stove.html.

3. GaveKal Research, referenced in Frank Holmes, "China Fears Much Ado About Nothing," *Business Insider*, September 15, 2011, http://articles.businessinsider.com/2011-09-15/markets/30158884_1_global-economy-moon-festival-china/2.

4. Mineral Information Institute, http://www.mii.org/; Platts.

5. BHP Billiton, "BHP Billiton Iron Ore—Growth and Outlook," March 20, 2012, http://www.bhpbilliton.com/home/investors/reports/Documents/2012/120320_AJMConference.pdf.

6. UN Conference on Trade and Development (UNCTAD) Trust Fund Project on Iron Ore Information, *The Iron Ore Market 2009–2011* (Geneva, Switzerland: UNCTAD).

7. Ibid.; Simandou Project Overview, http://www.riotintosimandou.com/ENG/index_projectoverview.asp; Vale and BHP Billiton company Web sites.

8. National Bureau of Statistics of China, Agriculture, http://www.stats.gov.cn/tjsj/ndsj/2011/indexeh.htm; United States Department of Agriculture Research Services datasets, http://www.ers.usda.gov/Data/; Economist Intelligence Unit Market Indicators and Forecasts; BCG analysis.

9. Michael Silverstein, "China's Food for Thought," *Financial Times*, April 22, 2011, http://blogs.ft.com/beyond-brics/2011/04/22/guest-post-chinas-food-for-thought/#axzz1ks7MPLSb.

10. Dan Basse, interview with authors, January 23, 2012.

11. Gabe Collins and Andrew Erickson, "U.S. Pecan Growers Crack into Chinese Market," *China SignPost*, December 9, 2010, www.chinasignpost.com/wp-content/uploads/2010/12/China-Signpost_9_US-Pecan-growers-crack-into-the-Chinese-market_2010-12-09.pdf; David Wessel, "Shell Shock: Chinese Demand Reshapes U.S. Pecan Business," *Wall Street Journal*, April 18, 2011, http://online.wsj.com/article/SB10001424052748704076804576180774248237738.html.

12. Silverstein, "China's Food for Thought."

13. As of year-end 2011.

Chapter 14

1. "Adi Godrej & family," *Forbes*, March 2011, www.forbes.com/profile/adi-godrej/.

2. Dhirubhai Ambani, quoted in "Spirit of Shri Dhirubhai H. Ambani: Quotes at Various Forums," Reliance Industries Web site, n.d., www.ril.com/html/aboutus/quotes.html.

3. Damian Whitworth, "Ratan Tata: The Mumbai Tycoon Collecting British Brands," *Times* (London), May 21, 2011, www.thetimes.co.uk/tto/magazine/article3021187.ece.

4. BCG, "The 2011 BCG Global Challengers: Companies on the Move," BCG report, January 18, 2011, www.bcgperspectives.com/content/articles/globalization_companies_on_the_move_2011_global_challengers/.

5. "Out of India: The Tata Group," *Economist*, March 3, 2011, www.economist.com/node/18285497.

6. Georgina Enzer, "Huawei Relinquishes 3Leaf Assets," *ITP.net*, March 1, 2011, http://www.itp.net/584043-huawei-relinquishes-3leaf-assets.

7. Tarun Khanna, *Billions of Entrepreneurs: How China and India Are Reshaping Their Futures—and Yours* (Boston: Harvard Business Review Press, 2011), 11–12.

Chapter 15

1. Lara Farrar, "Dragon Week Caters to China's Rich," *Women's Wear Daily*, January 26, 2012, www.wwd.com/eye/lifestyle/bergdorf-goodman-designers-court-chinese-5572400?full=true.

Epilogue

1. "Biography," Lang Lang Web site, n.d., www.langlang.com/us/biography.2.

2. Bureau of Labor Statistics, U.S. Department of Labor, *Occupational Outlook Handbook, 2012–13 Edition*, Projections Overview, March 29, 2012, http://www.bls.gov/ooh/about/projections-overview.htm.

Appendix A

1. M. Paul Lewis, ed., "Statistical Summaries: Summary by Country," table in *Ethnologue: Languages of the World*, 16th ed. (Dallas, TX: SIL International Publications, 2009), table available at www.ethnologue.com/ethno_docs/distribution.asp?by=country.

2. GDP figures for China's regions as of 2010, National Bureau of Statistics of China and BCG analysis.

3. GDP figures for India's regions as of 2010, Indian Ministry of Statistics and Programme Implementation (2010), National Council of Applied Economic Research, India Census 2011; BCG analysis.

Appendix B

1. Christina D. Romer, "Business Cycles," in *The Concise Encyclopedia of Economics*, 2nd. edition, Library of Economics and Liberty, 2008, http://www.econlib.org/library/Enc/BusinessCycles.html.

2. KPMG, "Survey on Bribery and Corruption," December 15, 2011, www.kpmg.com/IN/en/IssuesAndInsights/ArticlesPublications/Documents/KPMG_Bribery_Survey_Report_new.pdf.

3. Transparency International, "Corruption Perceptions Index 2010 Results," 2010, http://www.transparency.org/policy_research/surveys_indices/cpi/2010/results.

4. Minxin Pei, "Corruption Threatens China's Future," policy brief 55, Carnegie Endowment for International Peace, Washington, DC, October 2007, www.carnegieendowment.org/files/pb55_pei_china_corruption_final.pdf.

5. Ravi Ramamurti, quoted in "In India, Will Corruption Slow Growth or Will Growth Slow Corruption?," *Arabic Knowledge@Wharton*, February 1, 2010, http://knowledge.wharton.upenn.edu/arabic/article.cfm?articleid=1177.

6. Geoff Colvin, "Corruption: The Biggest Threat to Developing Economies," *CNNMoney*, April 20, 2011, http://money.cnn.com/2011/04/19/news/international/corruption_developing_economies.fortune/index.htm.

7. Jane Macartney, "Chongqing Police Chief Wen Qiang Sentenced to Death in Triad Crackdown," *Sunday Times* (London), April 14, 2010.

8. Edward Wong, "China's Railway Minister Loses Post in Corruption Inquiry," *New York Times*, February 12, 2011, www.nytimes.com/2011/02/13/world/asia/13china.html.

9. Wen Jiabao, "How China Plans to Reinforce the Global Recovery," *Financial Times*, June 23, 2011, www.ft.com/cms/s/0/e3fe038a-9dc9-11e0-b30c-00144feabdc0.html#axzz1l8SlhfAh.

10. International Cement Review, *Global Cement Report 1990–2008* (Dorking, Surrey, United Kingdom: Tradeship Publications, 2009).

11. U.S. Geological Survey, *Minerals Yearbooks 1932–1989* (Washington, DC: U.S. Government Printing Office, 1932–1989); International Cement Review, *Global Cement Report 1990–2008*.

12. Philip Bowring, "Maoists Who Menace India," *New York Times*, April 17, 2006, www.nytimes.com/2006/04/17/opinion/17iht-edbowring.html.

13. "Up to Their Necks in It," *The Economist*, July 17, 2008, www.economist.com/node/11751397.

14. "Toward a Healthy and Harmonious Life in China," The World Bank, 2011, http://www.worldbank.org/content/dam/Worldbank/document/NCD_report_en.pdf.

15. United Nations, Department of Economic and Social Affairs, Population Division, Population Estimates and Projections, 2010.

16. T. Colin Campbell, *The China Study: Startling Implications for Diet, Weight Loss and Long-Term Health* (Dallas, TX: BenBella Books, 2004).

17. WHO Report on the Global Tobacco Epidemic, 2011, Country profile: India. World Health Organization, http://www.who.int/tobacco/surveillance/policy/country_profile/ind.pdf.

18. "The World's Worst Natural Disasters: Calamities of the 20th and 21st Centuries," *CBC News*, August 30, 2010, http://www.cbc.ca/news/world/story/2008/05/08/f-natural-disasters-history.html; Kate Hudec, "Dealing with the Deluge," NOVA, March 26, 1996; Dan Fletcher, "Top 10 Deadliest Earthquakes," *Time Magazine*, January 13, 2010, http://www.time.com/time/specials/packages/article/0,28804,1953425_1953424,00.html.

19. Jonathan Watts, "Sichuan Quake: China's Earthquake Reconstruction to Cost $150bn," *Guardian*, August 14, 2008, www.guardian.co.uk/world/2008/aug/15/chinaearthquake.china.

20. "Public Policy Towards Natural Disasters in India: Disconnect Between Resolutions and Reality," Centre for Budget and Governance Accountability, 2005, http://www.indiagovernance.gov.in/.

21. Leslie Hook, "China Faces Worst Drought in 50 Years," *Financial Times*, May 25, 2011, www.ft.com/intl/cms/s/0/7d6e4db8-861e-11e0-9e2c-00144feabdc0.html#axzz1mg9iAjM7.

22. Steven Mufson, "As Economy Booms, China Faces Major Water Shortage," *Washington Post*, March 16, 2010, www.washingtonpost.com/wp-dyn/content/article/2010/03/15/AR2010031503564.html.

23. Kurt Achin, "India Warns of Water Scarcity," *Voice of America*, April 10, 2012, http://www.voanews.com/english/news/asia/India-Warns-of-Water-Scarcity-146809245.html.

24. Somini Sengupta, "In Teeming India, Water Crisis Means Dry Pipes and Foul Sludge," *New York Times*, September 29, 2006, www.nytimes.com/2006/09/29/world/asia/29water.html?pagewanted=all.

25. Nina Brooks, "Imminent Water Crisis in India," Arlington Institute, August 2007, www.arlingtoninstitute.org/wbp/global-water-crisis/606.

26. Ibid.; Peter Foster, "China to Invest £400bn to Overcome Water Shortage," *Telegraph* (London), October 12, 2011, www.telegraph.co.uk/news/worldnews/asia/china/8822609/China-to-invest-400bn-to-overcome-water-shortage.html.

27. "India's Water Economy: Bracing for a Turbulent Future," The World Bank, http://go.worldbank.org/QPUTPV5530.

SELECTED BIBLIOGRAPHY

Boot, Max, *War Made New: Technology, Warfare and the Course of History.* Gotham, 2006.

Campbell, T. Colin. *The China Study: Startling Implications for Diet, Weight Loss and Long-Term Health.* Dallas: BenBella Books (2004).

Dikötter, Frank. *Mao's Great Famine: The History of China's Most Devastating Catastrophe 1958–1962.* London: Bloomsbury, 2010.

Ferguson, Niall. *Civilization: The West and the Rest.* London: Allen Lane, 2011.

Ghemawat, Pankaj. *World 3.0: Global Prosperity and How to Achieve It.* Boston: Harvard Business School Press, 2011.

Khanna, Tarun. *Billions of Entrepreneurs: How China and India Are Reshaping Their Futures and Yours.* London: Penguin, 2008.

Khanna, Tarun and Krishna Palepu. *Winning in Emerging Markets: A Road Map for Strategy and Execution.* Boston: Harvard Business School Press, 2010.

Kissinger, Henry. *On China.* London: Penguin, 2011.

Meredith, Robyn. *The Elephant and the Dragon: The Rise of India and China and What It Means for All of Us.* New York: W. W. Norton & Company, 2008.

Morris, Ian. *Why the West Rules—For Now: The Patterns of History, and What They Reveal about the Future.* New York: Farrar, Straus and Giroux, 2010.

Nilekani, Nandan. *Imagining India: Ideas for the New Century.* New York: Penguin Group, 2009.

Spence, Michael. *The Next Convergence: The Future of Economic Growth in a Multispeed World.* New York: Farrar, Straus and Giroux, 2011.

INDEX

Dom Perignon brand, 134, 170
Dong Mingzhu, 107–108
Donna Karan brand, 170
driving clubs, 44
Dubai, 35, 45, 58, 59
Dudhsagar Dairy, 90
Dunhill brand, 167

e-Choupal project, 100
economic growth of China, 4–7
    economic reforms in, 49–50
    factors in, 4–6
    female employment and, 104–105, 113–114
    iron ore consumption and, 228
    left-behinds and, 61
    potential threats to, 271, 272f
    productivity gains and, 5, 7
    urbanization and, 85
    as world's largest economy, 7, 8f
economic growth of India
    female employment and, 104–105, 113–114
    iron ore consumption and, 228
    left-behinds and, 61
    License Raj system and, 6
    potential threats to, 271, 272f
    productivity gains and, 7
    reforms and, 6–7
    as world's third-largest economy, 7, 8f
    urbanization and, 85
educated professionals, in India, 41–42, 43
educated rich, in India, 58–59
education, 193–210
    aspirational products in, 47
    BCG E4 Index on, 196–197, 197f, 199, 201, 210
    in China, 5–6, 21, 68, 69, 196, 197, 198, 199, 199f,
        200f, 202, 202f, 204–205
    decisions on, 16, 32, 35, 42, 59
    economic development and, 5–6
    enrollment in, 196, 197–198, 198f, 199f, 202,
        202f, 204
    expenditures on, 21, 105, 196–197, 198f, 199f,
        204, 208, 209
    high schools and, 106, 204–205
    in India, 21, 42, 43, 65, 193, 196, 197, 198, 199f,
        200f, 202, 202f, 208
    left-behinds and, 63, 65, 67, 68, 71
    middle-class consumers and, 42, 43, 46
    middle-class spending on, 42, 43
    migrant workers and, 69
    mothers' support in, 103, 104, 105, 167, 204,
        205, 258
    new consumers and, 16, 30, 32, 54, 58, 78, 91,
        103–106, 167, 168, 193–195, 203–204, 238–239
    population and investment by country (2010)
        in, 198, 199f
    postsecondary degree graduates (2011–2020)
        and, 198–200, 200f
    primary schools and, 196, 204–205
    studying abroad in, 106, 107

women's access to, 104, 105
    See also colleges and universities
Educomp, 208
E4 Index (BCG), 196–197, 197f, 199, 201, 210
Egypt, 23, 222
e-Intensity Index (BCG), 181
Ellison, Larry, 50
emerging markets, 221–223, 224
emerging rich, in India, 59
engineers, 47, 152, 196, 197f, 199–201, 216, 237, 240,
    248, 261
entrance exams, 30, 47, 106, 193, 194, 201, 205,
    206–207, 261
entrepreneurs
    accelerator mind-set of, 236, 237, 241
    in China, 16–18, 201
    emerging rich and, 59
    examples of new consumers among, 16–18,
        22–23
    License Raj system as barrier to, 6
    studying abroad by, 201
Ericsson, 190, 242, 244
Ermenegildo Zegna brand, 167
Escorts Group, 248
e-shopping, 184–187
Esprit brand, 18
Estée Lauder brand, 18, 167, 251
eTao, 187
Everonn, 209

Facebook, 179, 183, 188, 242, 262
factories
    air quality and, 277
    in China, 5, 17, 48, 52, 67, 69, 70, 78, 79, 84, 100,
        107, 231, 238, 244, 277
    in India, 40, 153, 154, 190, 248
    rural migration to, 48, 69, 84, 94
families
    foods enjoyed by, 117–118
    gender-selective abortions and, 108, 113
    migrant workers in China and return to,
        68–69
    one-child policy in China and, 16, 20, 105, 109, 205
    size of, in China, 20–21, 20f
farmers and farming
    agricultural reforms in, 93–101
    in China, 77, 78–81, 80f, 93, 94–97
    corn farming, 78–81, 80f
    cotton farming, 64–65, 95
    crop choice and, 94–95
    dairy industry improvements and, 96–97
    examples of, 78–81
    in India, 64–65, 93, 95, 97–99
    infrastructure problems and, 95–96
    irrigation systems and, 97–99, 100
    left-behinds and, 64–65
    mobile phones for price data in, 99–101
    pollution and, 277–278
    wages of, 78

multinational companies
   competition among, 214, 241
   consumption forecast of $10 trillion a year by
      2020 and, 7, 9f, 250
   corruption as challenge for, 273–274
   global leadership by, 233
   LASTING skills needed by, 261
   leadership teams of, 141
Mumbai, xiv, 44, 58, 72, 89, 92, 93, 145, 151–152, 155,
   160, 161, 214, 216, 235, 267, 268–269, 273, 275
Muslims, 70–71
music classes, 257–258
Mycos Institute, 204

Nadar, Shiv, 49
Nagouri, Sachin, 89
NASDAQ, 53, 54
National Bureau of Statistics of China, 85,
   146, 266
National Health System (U.K.), 220
National Institute of Technology (India), 209
National Museum of China, 172
natural disasters, 279–280
Naxalite movement, 276
Nehru, Jawaharlal, 27
Nestlé, 22, 47
Neusoft Corporation, 238, 239, 240
Neusoft University, 239
New Delhi, xii, 54, 281
New York Stock Exchange, 56, 127
New York Times, 108
Nigeria, 223
Nihar brand hair oil, 23
NIIT, 209
Nike, 40, 164, 216
Nilekani, Nandan, 53–55, 195
Ning, Frank, xiii, 133, 134, 201
Ningxia Nongken, 134
Nokia, 40, 42, 100, 110, 111, 183, 188,
   189, 191
Nokia Life Tools, 100, 191
Nongxintong farming information service, 99
Northeastern University of China, 238, 239
Novak, David, 127–130
NTT Docomo, 182

Obama, Barack, 245
Occupational Employment Statistics survey, 261
Olympic Games (2008), 134, 157
Omega watches, 167, 168
one-child policy in China, 16, 20, 105, 109, 205
100 Global Challengers report (BCG), 241
operating models, 253, 254
optimism about future, 249
   female consumers and, 107, 110, 111–112
   left-behinds and, 65, 68
   middle class and, 36, 43
Oreo brand cookies, 136–141, 142

paisa vasool
   checklist for companies wanting to use, 217,
      218–219
   in China, 215–216, 217, 224, 251
   emerging markets and, 221–223, 224
   example of, 219–220
   in India, 213, 215–217, 215f, 219–220, 223–224,
      249–250
   markets and bazaars and, 90, 216–217, 224
   meaning of, 215–216, 215f
   pricing with, 217
   Western consumers and, 217, 221
Paisa Vasool Checklist (BCG), 217, 218–219
Pakistan, 247, 280
pandemics, 280
Pan Shiyi, 179
Pant, Pradeep, 141–142
Parachute brand, 22, 23, 73
Paranjape, Nitin, 74
Parekh, Deepak, 152–153
Paris, 135, 161, 167, 168
Patel, Bharat Kumar, 64–65
Patil, Pratibha, 266
pecan industry, 230–231
Peking University, 202–203, 209
Pepsi brand, 123
PepsiCo, 118, 130–131
Pernod Ricard, 118, 135–136
PetroChina, x
Philips, 150
Pinault, François-Henri, 161–162, 163–165
Pinault-Printemps-Redoute (PPR), 161–162
Pizza Hut, 123, 129
politics
   protests involving, 276
   women's involvement in, 108, 113, 266
pollution, 39, 52, 271, 277–278
poor. *See* left-behinds; lower class
pork consumption, 117, 118, 122f, 129, 230
poverty. *See* left-behinds
PPR, 161–165
Prada brand, 167
Prakash, Shantanu, 208
Premji, Azim, 49
price
   aspirational products and, 47, 48
   boomerang effect and, xviii, 225, 226,
      227, 231
   fit-to-constraint products and, 73
   home appliances market and, 154
   market forces and, 5
   online shopping and, 186
   paisa vasool and, 217, 218–219
privatization, in India, 7
Procter & Gamble, 73, 128, 137
protectionist measures, India, 6, 241
Pucci brand, 169
Puma brand, 162, 163, 164, 216

Wu, Jennifer, 257–258
WX Liu, 15f, 78–81, 94, 95, 117–118, 261–262

Xinhua News Agency, 100
Xue Ping, 88

Yahoo!, 178, 183
Yao Ming, 140
Yeltsin, Boris, 245
Yonghui, 67
YouTube, video of 15-story hotel construction, 52, 214
Yum! Brands, 101, 123, 127–129
Yves Saint Laurent, 163

Zain, 222
Zambia, 223
Zenith watch brand, 169
Zhang Chi, 84
Zhang Jing, 132
Zhang Wei, 88
Zhang Yue, 52
Zhou Enlai, 278
Zhou Zhanghong, 16–18,
Zhu Rongji, 5

ACKNOWLEDGMENTS

Behind a book like this one is a team of colleagues who have offered insights, practical lessons, and advice. We would like to particularly thank the tireless and talented associates who worked on our research effort over the past eighteen months. Nine in particular were instrumental in uncovering facts, assisting with the research, and participating in the fieldwork. They include two associates from our Chicago office, Sarah Minkus and Craig Minoff. Sarah worked without complaint for nearly a year on the booming consumption demand and education investments in China and India. Craig took over when Sarah left for business school. He shepherded the book through multiple iterations and helped synthesize the lessons learned from comparing and contrasting China and India. Youchi Kuo was our on-the-ground go-to person for all elements of research in China. She is our trusted expert on the hopes and dreams of Chinese consumers, leveraging The Boston Consulting Group's Center for Consumer and Customer Insight. Akshay Sehgal is one of our voices of India. He also carefully ran our model of demand, scenarios, and global comparisons. Kanika Sanghi led the consumer insight work and provided critical perspective to much of the consumer work in India. Payal Agarwal helped provide the company insights. Lydia Qiao and Stella Ji were our fantastic on-the-ground team in China during the research phase. Lydia rejoined the team after she transferred to our Chicago office and helped with all the final details. Special thanks also to Matt Coleman for company insights.

Our three most important sponsors of the research investment in Chinese and India consumers are Hans-Paul Bürkner, CEO of BCG; Janme Sinha, chairman of BCG's Asia business; and Patrick Ducasse, global consumer practice area leader for BCG. We are grateful for their advice, direct input on elements of the book, and support. They each provided guidance on messages, experience, and examples. We also need to thank all of our Asian partners who participated in workshops and discussion groups and provided detailed client vignettes. Eight in particular are actively engaged partners in our Asia-Pacific offices: Hubert Hsu, John Wong, Miki Tsusaka, Arindam Bhattacharya, Arvind Subramanian, Christoph Nettesheim, Sharad Verma, and Amitabh Mall. In addition, we acknowledge the support and advice of other BCG partners, including Sharon Marcil, the incoming consumer practice area leader; Gerry Hansell, an expert in corporate development; Russell Stokes, a leading BCG expert on emerging economies; Takashi Mitachi, head of BCG's Japan business with an active China policy view; and Rich Lesser, our Americas regional chair and CEO-elect, and Bjørn Matre, our Europe/Middle East regional chair. Special thanks go to René Abate, Jean-Marc Bellaïche, Christy Carlson, Jim Jewell, Ivan Bascle, Jeff Gell, Marin Gjaja, Matt Krentz, Andrew Tratz, Tom Hout, George Stalk, Hal Sirkin, and Cliff Grevler for encouragement and support.

This book would not have been possible without the advice of our agent, Todd Shuster, and our publisher, Melinda Merino. We are indebted to both for edits, message points, and encouragement. Melinda and Todd have helped in countless ways. Todd encouraged us to bring out the business messages. He went beyond the role of agent to thought partner on all the elements of bringing the book to market. Melinda patiently encouraged us to find ways to be concise, direct, and provocative. We cannot thank Melinda and Todd enough.

Michael's long-term executive assistant, Kristin Claire, managed many elements of the editorial process. We thank her for many extra late-night hours as well as her continuous support and encouragement. Meghan Perez helped direct us to many sources within BCG. Special thanks to David Cahill for help in creating the video that captured the story of the book in a four-minute online movie and for his help with the exhibits. Special thanks are also due to Janice Willett, who served as chief copyeditor on the book. Alexis Lefort and Katharine Halstead also helped with copyediting and fact checking. We thank Ted Riordan and Chris Weiss for their work on the exhibits, Amanda Vrany for tracking down extensive practice area materials, and Gary Callahan for advice on exhibits and the book cover. We also thank Eric Gregoire and Beth Gillett for their help with the book's promotional efforts. The BCG knowledge management staff provided fast, directed facts.

We also thank our families for support and encouragement. Without their blessing, this book would not be possible.

Perhaps the most important single contributor to the book's creation was Simon Targett. Simon is BCG's editor in chief and a former *Financial Times* editor. He grasped the power of *The $10 Trillion Prize* from the beginning. He operated as our thought partner and editor. We gratefully acknowledge his advice, insights, and very hard work to translate the rough manuscript into a book we hope you enjoy.

ABOUT THE AUTHORS

MICHAEL J. SILVERSTEIN joined The Boston Consulting Group in 1980, after completing his MBA with honors at Harvard University and AB degree in economics and history at Brown University. Based in Chicago, he has been head of the firm's global consumer practice, served on BCG's Executive Committee, and led engagements for consumer companies on innovation, brand development, global growth, and consumer understanding. His clients include some of the world's largest and most prominent packaged-goods companies and retailers. He has written three previous books, including the *Businessweek* bestseller and Berry AMA Prize winner *Trading Up: The New American Luxury* (2003), *Treasure Hunt: Inside the Mind of the New Consumer* (2006), and *Women Want More: How to Capture Your Share of the World's Largest, Fastest-Growing Market* (2009). His work in China and India has included category development, consumer innovation, and acquisitions and partnerships. He is BCG's worldwide expert in consumer understanding and innovation.

ABHEEK SINGHI is the leader of BCG's India consumer practice. He is based in Mumbai and joined BCG in 1998 after completing an MBA at the Indian Institute of Management in Ahmedabad, the country's foremost business school. He is an honors graduate of Indian Institute of Technology Delhi. He has been invited to be a member of both the National FMCG and Retail Committees of the Confederation of Indian Industry.

CAROL LIAO is the leader of BCG's Asia consumer practice. Based in Hong Kong, she joined BCG in 1995 after earning a BA in commercial law at Peking University and an MBA at Harvard University. She coleads BCG's Center for Consumer and Customer Insight in Asia.

DAVID MICHAEL is the leader of BCG's global advantage practice. Based in Beijing, he joined BCG in 1992 after completing a BA in economics at Harvard

University, an MBA at Stanford University, and a Rotary Scholarship at the Chinese University of Hong Kong. He is coauthor of *Asia's Digital Dividends: How Asia-Pacific's Corporations Can Create Value from E-Business* (2000), and has written articles published in *Harvard Business Review* and *Bloomberg Businessweek*. He is a member of the World Economic Forum's Global Agenda Council on Emerging Multinationals. From 2004 to 2009, he served on the Strategy Advisory Board of China Mobile Corporation, one of China's five largest companies and the world's largest telecom operator.

SIMON TARGETT is BCG's editor in chief. Based in London, he joined BCG in 2008 and is responsible for the firm's editorial activities and global media relations. Previously, he worked at the *Financial Times,* where he was the features editor, ft.com editor, and associate editor in charge of supplements and special reports. He has a BA degree in history from Sussex University, a PhD in history from Cambridge University, and a postgraduate diploma from City University's Graduate School of Journalism in London.